Nicole's Diary

Nicole's Diary

Running the World . . . Losing Our Marbles

Nicole Roetheli
with Serge Roetheli

DUNHAM
books

First published as *La Terre à en perdre la boule* 2005 by Editions La Sarine, Fribourg, Switzerland. Text by Nicole Roetheli. Adapted by Jean-Bernard Repond. *Concept and realization by Saint-Paul SA, Fribourg, Suisse.* English translation © 2007 by Agnes Roetheli Gaertner and Josiane Karlsson.

Published in Nashville, Tennessee by Dunham Books in cooperation with The Roetheli Lil' Red Foundation, North Kansas City, Missouri. For information regarding sales, marketing or licensing, contact the publisher:

Dunham Books
63 Music Square East
Nashville, Tennessee 37203
www.dunhamgroupinc.com

Book design by River House Media Inc. and Price & Associates.

Translators' Note: All information in parentheses is part of the original text. Brackets have been used for metric conversions and other clarifications that have been added by the translators. All monetary exchange rates are base on 2005 rates, the original French publication date. The translators made every effort to retain the beautiful imagery of the original manuscript.

For other books about Serge and Nicole's adventures around the world, please see their memoir, *The 25,000 Mile Love Story* (Dunham Books, 2013) and a coffee-table book of their journeys, *Keep on Running* (Dunham Books, 2013). A documentary film, *The 25,000 Mile Love Story*, will also be released in 2013.

Trade Paperback Edition ISBN: 978-0-9851359-9-7
Ebook ISBN: 978-0-9855328-1-9

Printed in the United States of America

Contents

A Note from the Translators vii

Foreword by Jean-Bernard Repond ix

Chapter One: *The Departure* 1

Chapter Two: *West Africa* 6

Chapter Three: *South Africa and Madagascar* 70

Chapter Four: *The Middle East* 104

Chapter Five: *Asia* 123

Chapter Six: *Oceania* 168

Chapter Seven: *South America* 204

Chapter Eight: *North America* 232

Chapter Nine: *Europe* 249

Epilogue 270

About the Authors 272

About the Translators 273

. . . A Note from the Translators

You are about to embark on the adventure of a lifetime, accompanying Serge and Nicole Roetheli on their epic run around the world, traversing six continents over the span of 63 months. The first leg of their journey across France with its familiar customs and language seems like a warm-up exercise compared to their later forays into countries (and continents) with vast cultural differences, languages bearing no similarity to their own, weather conditions beyond the scope of human endurance, and trials and tribulations as well as joys and discoveries beyond the imagination.

All of this became apparent, not as I and other distant American relatives awaited their crossing of the finish line at Saillon, Switzerland on May 7, 2005, but rather months later when Josiane and I undertook an adventure of our own—the translation of Nicole's diary. We often discussed the conditions under which they pursued their dream and by the end of their trek through Morocco (just over three months on the road), we were certain that we would have been heading home even though we consider ourselves rather adventuresome. So what motivated this Swiss couple to give up the security of their homeland and the fellowship of their loved ones to run 25,422 miles—roughly the circumference of the world—through some of the poorest, most disease-infested, war-riddled countries of the world and across the most arid deserts and humid jungles of this planet?

As we were translating, we marveled at the amount and detail of world culture and geography they experienced at the rate of 7.4 miles per hour. What would it have been like to be in their shoes, to be virtually alone and only have each other to rely upon for over five years? After traveling on foot for over a thousand days, how do you motivate yourself to run another 25-30 miles on a seemingly endless trail? How do you even find a doctor, and then communicate effectively, in the middle of nowhere when struck by a life-threatening disease? Or, for that matter, how do you find adequate nourishment and water in the middle of the desert when you need 5,000 calories a day to sustain yourself on marathon runs? How do you survive civil unrest and coming face-to-face with wild animals? How do you handle the loss of financial support from the foundation you were working through and then still forge ahead in order to achieve your aim of raising the awareness of the plight of children in third world countries?

These and many other issues are addressed in *Nicole's Diary*, a chronicle of Nicole's impressions, her joys, her sadness on a tremendously fascinating, enterprising, and adventurous trek around the world. Enjoy the awesome imagery as well as the great adventure as you read and understand what this couple endured on this 63-month trek through thirty-five countries, wearing out [can you guess how many?] pairs of shoes, and drinking [can you guess how much?] of Serge's specially selected drink!

As translators, we devoted ourselves to maintaining both the message and its spirit as conveyed in the original French version by Nicole Roetheli, entitled *Running the World . . . Losing Our Marbles*. It was indeed a challenge (but also great fun) to preserve the vivid imagery and poetic language that Nicole utilized in her diary. Enjoy!

-*Agnes Roetheli Gaertner* and *Josiane Karlsson*

...*Foreword*

Two years after having crossed the finish line of an unbelievable "American Challenge" at Fairbanks, after having traveled more than 24,000 kilometers [14,880 miles] between Tierra del Fuego and Alaska, Serge and Nicole returned on February 13, 2000, to the roads of the world, he running, and she at the handlebars of her motorcycle. Five years, two months, and twenty-five days later, they arrived at Saillon (Valais, Switzerland), welcomed by many, many friends, journalists, and strangers. On their odometer: 40,912 kilometers [25,422 miles]!

You may wonder, what is it that can possibly motivate a human being to run the world? Glory? Money? The allure of performance? Serge's speech leaves no doubt whatsoever: "Fundamentally, in all that I have undertaken these past ten years with Nicole, one type of motivation stronger than all the others guided our decisions. It is called freedom, emotion, and feelings. These values, which I have cherished since my youth, and which permeate all my actions, inspire me to surpass my previous expectations. The roads of the world allowed me to make the most of the very strong energy potential that I possess. And along the way, I had the good fortune of crossing paths with Nicole. We found ourselves having identical huge aspirations at the same moment. Thus, we were able to forge an authentic human adventure as a couple."

Serge belongs to that exceptional group of people who pursue their dreams to their very end. As a Swiss boxing champion numerous times and as a mountain guide, for more than thirty years he has been exploring worlds that leave scarcely any place for the faint of heart. Strong in mind, strong in body, he is, nonetheless, a vulnerable person who suffers the grief of others. He can testify to these misfortunes from thousands of encounters, including those Nicole experienced, which stand as markers on their journey, during more than six years on foot, in more than sixty lands, over six continents.

From their tour across the world, the Roethelis did not return rich... in money. Serge defines wealth in this manner: "It is the capability to make free choices. For this, it is necessary to have received a little love in the first years of your existence, a minimum of instruction and education, and the availability of health care. Now, I have the feeling that if you do not receive one of these three 'gifts,' you are condemned to mere survival for your entire life. In Switzerland, only the first item might possibly be lacking. But in the vast majority of the countries of the world, education and access to health care are the missing elements."

From this reflection, the idea was born during the running of the "American Challenge" to associate a humanitarian cause with this desire to run the world. To this end, all the various races allowed for the collection of more than 300,000 Swiss francs [about US$240,000, which grew to over $400,000 by 2012] thus far for the benefit of children who are victims of a "wounded childhood." Serge and Nicole financed their projects entirely from their own resources (75 percent of the total budget) and from the financial support of a loyal fan club.

The humanitarian adventure continues. All of the collected donations are earmarked to support the missions led by Dr. Ron Zamber. This eminent American ophthalmologic surgeon from Alaska gives the gift of sight back to the poorest, free of charge. He operates directly in third-world countries.

Step by step: it is thus that Serge has attained his slightly crazy objective. With Nicole, he solemnly wills that you, dear readers, be receptive to the altruistic work carried out by their friend Ron. Penny by penny, there are ten, a hundred, a thousand individuals among the most deprived on the planet who will regain their sight. It's now up to you and to us.

-Jean-Bernard Repond

A starting line is an arrival, a victory,
and we have won this one.
Because we are there, and nothing is missing.
-*Nicolas Vanier,* L'Odyssée Blanche

The steps uncoil, and the world tour
Has started
Every torment

We disregard,
One step after another
Relishing the view of the world
Living our motto:
Doing one kilometer for each child's smile

To find my eyes fixed
One knows not where; already behind
Us, our footprints,
Realizing anew the world is ours

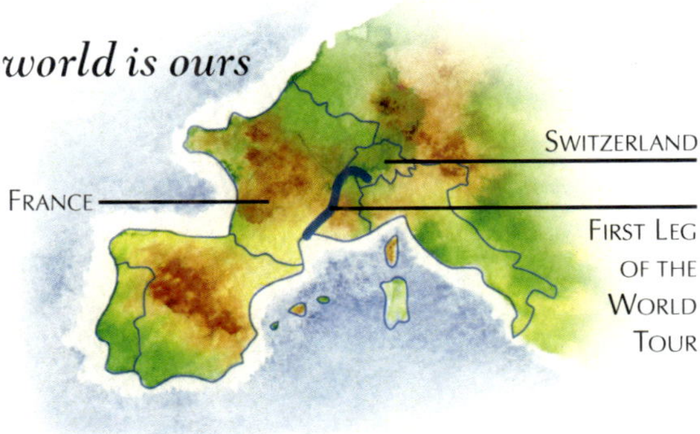

the Departure

...February 13, 2000: the first kilometer has begun!

In less than two hours, the road is going to open up like a rose after the storm. This road will be ours for a long, long time.... Intense emotion on this Sunday, February 13, 2000.

People come from all directions; an exchange of looks and smiles. Tears of joy, tears of infinite sadness, all entwined. A sudden desire overwhelms me: to hold time still in my arms. If only time would stop and whisper in my ear: "Go for it, my dear!"

Suddenly, a little girl is standing there, looking at me with a mischievous smile on her lips: "You are the strongest woman in the world!" One more time, I fall apart. Does this come from being modest or just weak?

It is impossible to turn back. The moment has already come for taking the first step. One more fleeting glance toward my parents, toward Clara and Steve, and toward my brother. Vexing moments. A certain guilt washes over me and pulls at my heart.

Do I have the right to impose such a departure on others?

I think so, because it is so beautiful to live for a purpose, for a dream, for the simple reason that we exist.

...The road

So long, our beautiful Valais! Forgive us this new disloyalty!

Here we are again on the world's road, for the conquest of ourselves. It is quickly understood that the road belongs to us. This line, infinitely long, represents our source of energy and of inspiration; this line is our only mistress.

We quickly rediscover our emotions, our desires, our markers and our benchmarks. We're back on track.

... *Thirst for freedom*

As far back as I can remember, adventure and escape have always been a part of me. In school, whenever possible, I chose the place closest to the window. A call, a need...truly I had this "beyond the horizon" desire, like an escaped prisoner on a quest for his own freedom. "Nicole, you must follow along a little bit...." I was very quickly put in my place. I was certainly unaware of the manner in which my life would integrate this urge for new horizons. I did not know that one day I would cross paths with a man impassioned by the same feelings. Serge, this man of such strong passions, has helped me thrive. For more than fifteen years, we have shared this same thirst for life. We are in love, quite simply, perhaps a little more than the average.... In order to live our choices so intensely, we have made the decision to tear ourselves away from our families, our friends, and our comfort. Our life is a whirlwind of dizziness, of acceleration...of acceleration at the rate of 12 km/h [7.4 mph].

... *The tree that travels*

A smile, a horn, a wave of a hand. Much human warmth. Switzerland is flooded with rain on the roads, but there is so much sun in our hearts!

In Geneva, we are welcomed into the home of our friends, Samuel and Sylvia. They lead us to their garden. Four days earlier, at the time of our departure from Massongex, they had planted a cherry tree, a symbol of life, a gesture of great authenticity. This tree will grow in this ground; it will shoot forth, weather willing, as will we who are going to travel, the years willing.

One day, this tree will be the most beautiful tree in our secret garden, in our hearts.

...February 19, 2000: Crossing the border

Some friends, relatives, Clara and Steve, are there to greet us. It's an extremely cold day, but nothing stops us, not even the customs officials who wish us a good journey. Without a noise, without any fanfare, the first page of our five-year good-bye has been turned. A twinge of the heart...

We will return, to be sure, but in what physical condition and in what state of mind?

...A bend in the road

My glance oscillates between rearview mirrors and a straight line as far as the eye can see. Serge, my runner on the soles of the wind, I listen to the pounding of each of your steps upon the asphalt.

Suddenly, at a bend in the road, in the curve of life, here comes a horn, a wave, a face. My vision is blurred. Papa! Mama! What a surprise! A burst of feeling outside of time. Five hundred kilometers [311 miles] in a car to bring us all their parental love.

...Difficult vision

I love to soak up every moment that this style of travel offers me. I allow the road to guide me, and I listen to the wind sing and dance, twisting my hair. Unbeknownst to Serge, I observe him with an uneasy glance. I tell myself: "What a strange destiny! He, alone, facing his trials, his desire to conquer the obstacles and I, alone, facing the Eternal."

An imposing fortress appears before us: a prison. A feeling of guilt seizes me. We are on the road, in the plentitude of our freedom; they are smack in a place of no return. There, in this prison of gray concrete, men are confined, alone, facing their own destiny. What did they do to be incarcerated?

Suddenly, a difficult vision. Far off, a woman gestures lovingly toward a man who traipses around a courtyard encircled by bars. Our glances meet on the path of life....

She sends a message of hope with infinite tenderness. As for me, I continue on my way, my throat constricted, my eyes watery....

...France

In a known land, the emotions are rich, but they have already been experienced. For Serge and me, France is a transitional stage, permanently adjusting our luggage, finding an ideal balance, breaking in the kilometers, preparing emotionally.

For some days, we have been experiencing the authentic charm of fishing villages and narrow back streets, all typically Mediterranean. The sun, the sea, the vast lagoons. Here, nature is queen. She reveals herself only to those who know how to love her. She preserves her world and its secrets. Fauna and flora live side by side in daily harmony. Wild horses and pink flamingos meet, yet are seemingly unaware of one another. This untamed and jealous nature gently takes us away from the heartlands of France.

This crossing of France endows us with human resources—serenity and confidence—for the continuation of a long string of new experiences. Running still is, and will always remain, a world of its own.

Managing one's life for
Others
Restarting
Overlooking our
Current steps
Concluding that running is
One's life

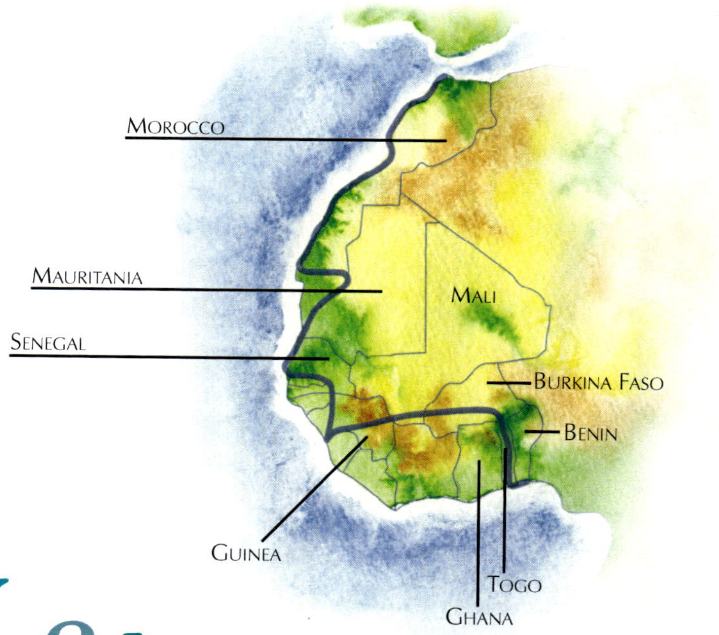

West Africa

...March 9, 2000: Tangier

Morocco is there, on the horizon, where the barren sky and the earth meet. Already our World Tour takes on a quasi-indescribable dimension. We disembark, uncertain what lies ahead of us, but this uncertainty is transformed into a sublime wisdom.

Straightaway, the most bizarre street scenes abound. A mix of new and ancient, of tradition and modernity. The women, with or without a veil, brush past one another. The comparison between them and me begins—a game that permits me to understand a country, its habits, and its customs.

However, there is nothing shocking about this mixture; it is part of a life that we have already experienced. We very quickly regain our confidence, despite the imposing stares directed at me, the foreign woman that I am. But an atmosphere of serenity is established between us, the French language having facilitated our communication. The people are receptive to foreigners. We are like a newborn baby; we open our eyes to the outside world.

On the streets of Tangier, life is teeming; it is colorful, motley. Our nostrils are attacked by the most diverse smells. Before our eyes, the carousel of life is unwinding. Here with the sharing of mint tea, all is ritual and communion. The first night bespeaks a land full of promises.

...Muslim prayers

Five o'clock! This morning, our awakening took place in an unexpected manner: the Muslim prayer resounded over the nascent day. I want to know a little more; my curiosity grows. Five times per day, the faithful participate in meditation and adoration. Always facing Mecca, barefoot, heads bowed toward a mat, they perform this daily ritual.

...Leaving Tangier

It is time to launch out onto the Moroccan roads, time to brush up against new realities. With knotted stomachs and parched throats, we embark on the

"Run for Kids" journey through a landscape that dissipates under our feet. The traffic is dense and dangerous. Our first contact is unsettling. Already, I curse the truck and taxi drivers. They speed along, pass, honk...they are the masters of the road. Unbearable! Far off, a cloud of dust appears, and already we witness an accident. The collision is horrifying. Three dead! Helpers and the curious swarm all around. Powerless in the face of death, we take to the road again.

Serge looks at me, tears in his eyes. The adventure has just started. Fatalist that I am, I believe in an inner force that protects us and allows us to move ahead with assurance through this jungle littered with obstacles.

...Asilah

One more day passes under the pressure of danger and 45 additional kilometers [28 miles] of running. Engulfed in the warm cheering of its inhabitants, we make a stop in Asilah. Its white houses and narrow streets remind us of a Greek island. A true marvel!

...Confrontation

While sitting facing the sea, my gaze lost in the blue of the waves, a man approaches me. His age is indeterminate, his face scorched by the sun. He is a beggar who asks for money. Without contempt, I give him the signal for no. He does not insist but goes away.

I suddenly become aware of the good fortune that is ours. I am filled with remorse and doubt, but I must indeed accept that I cannot relieve all the misery of the world. A hard realization!

...Running through the countryside

From the right and from the left, from everywhere, both children and the elderly stream forth. These scenes of life have a captivating richness of soul. Each time we are welcomed by generous smiles, contagious gestures—a special way of communicating with a stranger. But very quickly, the spontaneous smiles and gestures are accompanied by a request for money. A girl with stern features bends down and pelts us with stones.

It is difficult to protect yourself in the face of so much misery. However, I must learn to endure by adopting an authoritarian demeanor, which is something I do not like to do. To help a child here is to help a whole village, and that is quite simply not possible.

Step by step, day after day, year after year...

...Rabat

Facing the blinding sunlight, we arrive in the capital of Morocco without any problems. Our first impression is that the city is asleep, as if living on the margins of time. But this image does not correspond at all to that of a great capital. On the streets, there is a bit of disenchantment.

Evening falls, and still we have not found anywhere to sleep. It is our tight budget that scarcely permits us any extravagance....

Being too choosy is out of the question. We are engulfed by a dark corridor. The silence is deafening. There is no great enthusiasm. As for the comfort of the room...surprise! Hot water runs from the rusted faucet. We can only be grateful for the present moment.

It seems to us that Rabat is difficult to tame. There are animated conversations and lusty embraces in the popular restaurants, but the real show is on the street. Rabat is the apprenticeship of the sublime with the sordid, between ecstasy and sorrow.

...Casablanca

Casablanca shelters 3.5 million inhabitants, which makes it the largest city of the Maghreb. It is a young and dynamic city, a city with a hundred expressive faces. This city is the epitome of life! The mosques enjoy the gazes of passers-by. The plazas are large.

We stroll down the streets. We love to explore, to probe the sometimes sordid and dark parts of a city, the nooks of a building. I love these unique moments. I love to tell myself that behind every window a face is hidden, a story is unfolding.

Morocco is a holy and religious land, but also a place where the poverty of the congested streets, the human misery, and indifference are all shamelessly displayed. The unbearable reality runs like a river that cannot find its course.

...A center for outcast unwed mothers in Casablanca

Today, we impatiently await the arrival of friends who work for humanitarian causes, as well as the arrival of some journalists. Together, we make our way to a center for outcast unwed mothers. For us, it's a matter of visualizing a concrete plan of action, of giving human distress a face. Then we will be able to bear witness to all of this. Ever since our first journey, Serge has been crisscrossing this planet with his sole luggage being his experience and his will to overcome obstacles in order to come to the aid of unfortunate children. As for me, I keenly focus on the sights I see; I observe the scenes where the humanity and the inhumanity of mankind—poverty, tenderness, respect, and dignity—are displayed side by side.

With great sensibility, Soadia, the project coordinator, shares with us her approach to, and her love for, these women in distress whose destiny is so fragile. All of the women welcomed into the center are single, divorced, or repudiated. They're all mothers who have been rejected by their relatives and by society. They have been banished forever. Often, in order to avoid total rejection, they abandon their children in the street. Even worse, in their great helpless desperation, many murder their babies. Left to themselves, they have but two options: to beg or to become prostitutes.

In this center, they regain a bit of their dignity: some love, some reassurance. It's here that the task of communication, of encounters, of exchanges, and of training begins. The staff works in the shadow of the problem. One has the feeling that without the energy, will, and motivation of the whole team, things would not move forward. All of these mothers in distress have absolutely no education and do not know how to read or write. At the young age of five, these kids were already slaves of labor, servants for landlords who rent out rooms and exploit and create ghettos of women. Hardly are they born and already they are broken by life; the burden of destiny weighs very heavily on their shoulders.

We are well aware that we are not going to change the world with this run, but I can assure you that when closing the door of the center, you cannot remain insensitive when confronted by so much misery. This is why we have to move forward without ever giving up.

After spending the morning with those in charge, we go to a meeting with single mothers and their children. We ascend a dark stairwell. A door opens, and a charming smile greets us. I must control myself in order not to burst into tears at the sight of the absent stares of the babies. I have only one desire: to take them in my arms, to cherish them, to impart all my love to them. In bending down toward the face of a two-month-old boy, something irresistible occurs. Through vigorous gestures, he asks me to take him in my arms. I cannot resist. I adopt him in a fraction of a second for five minutes of his life. I have the feeling of being his mother for a brief moment. How good and, at the same time, how painful it is to experience this feeling!

...*Children of the streets in Bayti*

We stop by another center in Casablanca, in the Bayti neighborhood. Our being here is part of an action taken on behalf of street children. We plunge anew into a labyrinth of suffering. It's a difficult step to take, because one touches upon the core and the intimate life of children. I feel somewhat ill at ease: Are we not a little like voyeurs? On the other hand, it will subsequently be easier to bear witness and to attempt to change things.

In order to understand the path of these traumatized children, their destiny, their disappointments, and their hopes, we enter into a discussion with them. Their perception of reality surprises us. In this center, they seem to have found a feeling of belonging again. Their faces are marked by suffering, but in the depth of their eyes, you can detect a glimmer of hope. They need for us to consider them as human beings in their own right.

Everything is a symbol.

Serge questions them: "How do you envisage your future in the world of men?" Without beating around the bush and without equivocation, all respond with composure: to have an occupation and to return to their family. The complete absence of love and an enormous lack of parental identification certainly cause their greatest pain. At the end of the discussion, Serge and the children run a symbolic kilometer together.

...Southern bound

We leave Casablanca, which strongly resembles the great Western metropolises in contrast to the other, quainter Moroccan cities.

Our adventure unfolds as time allows. Like a pebble that slowly sinks into silence, we lose ourselves in our solitude and our routines. There are contrasted days, varied sentiments, and the joy of progressing through this land marked by liberty.

...Starting yet again

Alone, in the aftermath of the storm that gripped the whole country for a few days, Serge runs with rigor and willing determination, starting yet again, only to see nothing dawning on the horizon.... Nothing stops him, even if our progress is quite chaotic. Our means of transport, as difficult as it is, tells us that we must never lose faith, that we must forge ahead in spite of the difficulties, and that the desire to fight to the finish is stronger.

The sky turns dark; the clouds rumble. We have to pitch our tent on a landscape that belongs to another time. Serge smokes his pipe while contemplating the crackling of the fire; the flames dance for him. He speaks to them in a secret language. Looking at him, I know that he is thinking about Clara and Steve, and that he is wishing them goodnight at the other end of a dream.

...One more leg of the journey

This leg of the journey was a bit highly charged for Serge. He ran 64 kilometers [40 miles] to escape an additional night of rain. For him, it is a moment of intoxication, because it is important in his runner's mind to cross the goal of fifty kilometers [31 miles] that he often sets for himself. We arrive in the industrial city of Safi, an important sardine boat port. Safi houses some Portuguese monuments, but most interesting is the potters' district, with a very cultural marketplace animated by casual traveling merchants, shoe shiners, pastry bakers, and fishmongers displaying their catches.

...Essaouira, city of a thousand faces

Essaouira welcomes us and opens its doors, its vestiges, and its past to us. What a charming city with such a unique character! It has inherited an architecture that strongly recalls the Greek islands with its houses of molded walls with white paint and blue motifs. The great diversity of the houses astonishes us, yet they all have their quite particular style of a narrow and unobtrusive house on two levels in a gorgeous setting. All have a terrace. It feels like people here are married to the ocean, as we are to the road.

...A distinctive face

Here everything reminds us of Patagonia, that lost and forgotten land. How strange it is to recollect those past years, to mull over those distant memories. Yet, this allows us to evaluate our maladies. I look at Serge; his face is entrenched with pain. His eyes, reddened by the sand, reflect his discouragement. I stop the run, forcing him to eat a little and to regain a semblance of strength.

At the same time, in the distance, a hunched-down silhouette, as though left behind by the ages, wearily attempts to cross the road, which is encumbered by traffic. The old lady draws near us. Her face is worn down by existence, by the ravages of time. She extends a shaking hand to us; we give her three dirhams. She takes my hand and delicately places it on her cheek. All of the art of charm is at work. She leaves us without making a sound. This grandmother has succeeded in her attempt to charm us, leaving us only with her distinctive face, her pert smile.

Remaining a woman in every situation.

...A ruined evening

We pitch our tent on a bluff that offers a panoramic view refined by the beauty of the place. The scents and the spray of the sea beat upon our faces. We love this type of camping above all. Three liters of water for each of us for the ritual of a shower...a luxury after five days! Naked, Serge dances and leaps, facing the churning sea. My turn comes. I am a little more modest, because indiscreet eyes may be hiding behind every tree....

It is now time to kindle the fire. We scan the horizon: the waves dance over this immensely huge ocean. Suddenly, lo and behold, we are questioned by the police, who have been looking for us for two hours. A trying discussion ensues, and we are required to leave this place right away. Just four months ago, right here, some tourists were attacked and savagely raped. A few hours later, we are sleeping at the royal police station. For security reasons, it is difficult to do better!

"Having already run 1,069 miles, we are now at the gateway to the Sahara."

The Sahara, the largest desert in the world.

...*Agadir*

Arriving in Agadir means rejoining Clara and Steve, who have come to spend a few days with us...to play, to laugh like children...simply to renew contact, to create an ever-stronger bond between us. It has been two months since we last saw one another, already an eternity! I am not their mother by blood, but in heart. I love them to the depth of the vastness of our World Tour.

They are here, in great shape, in front of us. I do not want to describe the intimate family moments in my road journal, because these moments are jealously guarded in a box, which we may perhaps open one day. To us belongs the freedom of sharing what is exceptional.

Having already run 1,720 kilometers [1,069 miles], we are now at the gateway of the Sahara. We depart into the infinite vastness, thinking of you.

Surveying the route
Across wind and sand
Height of the dunes which extend beyond; in
Advance of crossing them
Richness of emotion
As we pause, before our encounter with the Sahara

…May 2000: At the gateway of the desert

We are very quickly taken with the tantalizing scent…the Sahara! The motorcycle and loaded-down trailer have the look of a true camel. Logistics become a serious business. A new leg of the journey begins with our entrance into the desert. Our stomachs are knotted like braids of bread that rise in the oven. We feel quite humble in the face of such vastness, in this land of austerity. Already we meet our first sandstorms. In a universal language, this means: "Welcome to this desert land."

At this moment, Serge is in great pain with the aches that make him suffer terribly, because the heat and the wind desiccate him like a bean that shrivels up. When you run a long distance, the greatest difficulty is to manage to divorce yourself mentally from the run, to break away from your own thoughts. You must be capable of listening to your body without thinking of the pain; without this, even for Serge, it's impossible to continue. He needs to think about many different things: about his childhood, about Clara and Steve, but never about the kilometers that lie before him, which would drive him crazy. Serge is endowed with a great sensitivity; that is why I love him so much. When the runner is transformed into a child in need of protection, he lets tears flow down the length of his gaunt cheeks, true pearls…of love.

At a bend in the road, on the curve of life, there is always something to discover—a grain of red sand and a grain of golden sand, racing relentlessly in the Saharan storm....

...A helluva birthday party

It is Serge's birthday. On the edge of time, a sleepy village of fishermen appears, on the threshold of the surreal. Opulent misery runs along the gray walls. People are filthy and distrustful. Nauseating odors mingle with our fatigue. We stop at the first roadside shack to have some green tea and work out a plan for the night, because we have no desire to pitch our "four walls" in this village.

A fisherman turned into a restaurant owner offers us a place behind his dilapidated establishment. He opens the door. It is a sordid cave with an option for cockroaches that already creep on the damp walls.... We do not have a choice. As for the meal, it is no better: a disgusting fish, rotten potatoes, dry bread, and a salad into which the ants have invited themselves. Have a great party, Serge, and bon appétit!

When the sun has barely risen, we decide to flee this village as quickly as possible. We only need to settle the bill. And even with that, the swindling continues. This wretched fisherman understood that in one evening he could make a month's salary off of white tourists. He asks us for the equivalent of a hundred Swiss francs. A fortune! To keep your composure in these situations is not an easy thing. With gentleness, Serge tells him that he must be mistaken, but this headstrong fisherman remains firm, to the point that Serge requests the intervention of a police officer.

We readily sense that the policemen do not want to get embroiled. Eventually, the end result of the litigation is a payment of twenty francs. In any circumstance such as this, it is best to remain stoic....

...*Magical moments*

With disheveled hair and a face marked by a night of camping, Serge prepares the wake-up coffee. But at that moment, a single idea crosses my mind. Serge reads my thoughts like an open book and hands me the satellite telephone. As if by magic, it still works. I punch in the number of my mother, Jeanine. Happy birthday, dear mother, whom I love so much! It is a moment of great pleasure, of magic extending to the other end of the world, from some point in the middle of the Saharan sand.

...*Initiation*

We have the feeling of enduring an initiation. Our senses are blurred by the enormous barrenness of this misunderstood wasteland. The unceasing wind adds another dimension to our adventure. The relentless solitude takes hold of us a little more every day. The straight lines are endless. There is no point at the end of them other than the infinite horizon. The black tar melts like snow in the sun.

You must find a way, sometimes a long and painful way, a mental equilibrium in order to have the strength and the conviction to keep moving forward without falling back. Here we are pursuing an unknown vision. We are renewed by the minutest detail, something infinitely small: a cloud that passes by, a grain of red sand rather than one of yellow. Each gesture, each movement, each gaze remains crucial to our nervous mental equilibrium. Our encampment will be here and not elsewhere. A touch of nostalgia overcomes me while beholding the starry sky. I am famished and cold.

...*Tarfaya, city lost in the infinite desert*

A city of a thousand inhabitants, Tarfaya permits us to replenish our food supplies. We endure persistent stares. The readers of *Courrier Sud* and *Vol de Nuit* by Antoine de Saint-Exupéry will recognize Tarfaya as the former airmail stopover between the old continent and the *cordillera* [mountain range] of the Andes.

We leave Tarfaya in a sandstorm.

...The magic of the place

This evening we deviate from our "magic line" by 5 kilometers [3 miles] to go look for an official campsite. We place all our heart, all our hope in this campsite, because Serge has aged a few months in a few days. The desert swallows us whole. Our run has been idling for some days. Mentally, it is difficult to accept the harshness of this landscape. Nothing parades before our eyes, except for dozens of crushed snakes each day. The hostile nature of the place can be magical in a car, but not while running. The fight is unfair. We have the impression that our run, at this moment, resembles an old man who is fighting not to fall asleep. His pulse must not falter....

We arrive at the "King Bedouin" campsite. The place hides magical faces that attract our attention. It evokes in us the wealth of human diversity. We go to sleep under a Berber tent. The chestnut-brown tent (*khaima*) made of the wool of sheep or goats is decorated with geometrical motifs. The ground is carpeted with braided mats.

A good meal will help us to rekindle the sparkle in our eyes, which has had the tendency of going out.... Like a game, our shadows stretch playfully on this Saharan desert. My heart is softened in the face of so much beauty.

...Kilometer after kilometer

Oh, the kilometric markers! At every kilometer of the desert, as far as the eye can see, there is a stone decorated with a number. This marker either gives us energy to tell ourselves "today we're progressing well," or else it kills us without warning, without consideration. Here, it is necessary to find our own balance. We get the feeling of becoming vulnerable; everything in our heads can still topple over. Then we hold on to one idea, to a white speck that appears on the horizon, and we tell ourselves: "And what if that were a restaurant?" And when we reach that spot, there's nothing!

We curse the trucks that pass us by, with "cool drinks" or "Danone" inscribed in large letters. At this moment, on our route around the world, we dream of fresh products.... Then we become bluntly intolerant of these drivers, who do not even lift their little fingers to greet us good day. In such a desolate place, that would do so much good!

But the most unbelievable thing is the phenomenon of mirages. Unbelievable visions! We swear to have seen great trees, water at will, and when we reach the spot, nothing exists. It's only the fruit of our imagination.

...A cheerful star is shining

Gazing at the starry sky, this evening I choose the most beautiful star. It shines in the heavenly sky of the Sahara. I speak to it, imagining that up there, it is she, my grandmother Louisa, whom I lost during the "American Challenge," which is now already three years ago. She responds to me; she cheers me up. She whispers in my ear about her long journey into the beyond. I tell her about my day full of emotion.... With a tear in the corner of my eye, it is time to tell you good-bye, luminous star, but it is so good to have spoken with you this evening in the midst of nowhere, in the middle of the world.

Finding shade...
a matter of survival.

...The intoxication of savory stops

There is only one good subject of conversation that makes us advance in the slowness of our pace and the heat of our steps, in the vastness of the desert: the flavors of Moroccan cuisine, from olive oil to fish, from fruits to vegetables. And herbs, such as kamour, an aromatic plant related to cumin. All the colors and aromas parade across the table. But first and foremost, Morocco is defined by the fruits of the sea, a sea that nurtures, like a mother who generously nourishes her children.

...May 30, 2000: The end of a long leg of the journey

This is the end of Moroccan land, the end of the desert of the Western Sahara. We have discovered a world that is not ours. We have lived through truly stormy times, but we have also spent delightful moments contemplating the stars while pursuing our journey in the essence of the beauty of the world. The difficult endeavor during this entire crossing is rewarded a hundredfold by the natural joy of exerting ourselves in a place that moves the human soul. Our looks betray our fatigue, but above all, an amazement to have already finished a bit of the course. Each day, the greatness of the myth of the desert adds to the satisfaction of having gone beyond ourselves. Here, more than elsewhere, the spectacle of nature is both upsetting and marvelous.

If we have succeeded in crossing this desert, it is because we overcame the monotony that would have undoubtedly led to failure. Knowing how to live in the present, how to savor all the little things and all the changes—therein resides the key to success, the road to happiness, the path that leads to others.

Dakhla, May 30, 2000: 2,659 kilometers [1,652 miles]. Tomorrow is the departure for Mauritania in a mandatory convoy, because of the danger elicited by the presence of mines; 440 kilometers [273 miles] in a convoy under army surveillance.

...Robbery at the Doumss Hotel

A terrible surprise upon jumping out of bed after our last night spent on Moroccan soil: robbed, we have been robbed! Our trailer has disappeared, with all its contents. Our morale is at its lowest. Our anger is enormous, because we had pulled into the hotel that was supposed to be the best watched in Dakhla. A night guard had been hired, but in vain. We alert the police, who firmly interrogate the guard. We fear that he has been beaten up. The interrogation is trying. We were robbed, but we feel guilty seeing so much aggression.

For this poverty-stricken old man, this theft represents an entire year's salary. For us, it is the loss of a tent, sleeping bags, pillows, sleeping mats, running shoes, and a mountain backpack. In other words, this means a definite lack of basic comforts for the continuation of the "Run for Kids" and the next legs of the journey in the Mauritanian desert. Oh well, let us not dramatize more than necessary. We must keep a cool head, no matter what happens. We leave Doumss with the assurance that the guard will not suffer any negative consequences.

Make the choice: to die or to run
Across the great void
Universe of the misunderstood
Really nothing can
Illustrate the
Traversing of Black
Africa
Nothing at all
Imminent continent
Always locked away in our silence

...A train like no other in the world

The train between Nouadhibou and Choum may well be the longest and, without a doubt, one of the most dangerous in the world. It has no less than three hundred cars and four locomotives. We are told that it can derail once a day...encouraging!

The loading will last eighteen hours in the dust, with the choking heat and the biting flies. To protect them against wind and dust, the vehicles and our motorcycle are tied down with old pieces of wire. What we witness is beyond comprehension. Turbaned men and their disheveled goats take advantage of the bargain of traveling cheaply on the roof of the coaches. All that is left to do is to believe in our lucky star.... We occupy our minds by admiring the splendors of the Saharan desert.

...Paris—Dakar

Our adventure is far from being finished. Exhausted, we arrive in Choum, and the train drops us off in an isolated place. Our motorcycle and new trailer are unloaded. Here we have arrived in the heart of Africa. The desert is like a gate that opens. Fortunately, we can count on the company of Christophe and Michel, two men we had met while traveling in a mandatory convoy in Morocco. Without them, it would have been very difficult for us to continue over the African roads. They facilitated all the "red tape," dealing with our logistics and our equipment. And they helped us by taking us in their bus for a journey on a track similar to a mini "Paris—Dakar" race.

Gusts of wind brush across our path, wrinkling the sandy crests of the dunes. We begin the crossing of a vast mineral plateau, whose rock is a dark brown color—a striking contrast. We come into the valley of Adrar, situated in eastern Mauritania. The crests scrape the sky. We juggle between dust and the heat of hell. We have to expend much cooperative energy in order to free our sand-imprisoned vehicles. But here, at the end of the world, a beautiful friendship was born, thanks to the kings of the desert road.

...Atar

Atar was founded in the seventeenth century. The city became a necessary stop on the trans-Saharan trail. This capital of Adrar is hedged by palm groves. A motley crowd is hurrying along the alleys: numerous children, women clothed in green, yellow, azure, and pink, and men with a dignified stature, draped in lavender-blue.

It is a window into another world, into a new land. The poverty is indescribable. You have the feeling of being hurled back into the Middle Ages. The pride of noble warriors is branded on their faces. A complex mosaic of crossbreeding makes up the human landscape of Mauritania. It is necessary to arm yourself with courage to brave this new country that breathes incandescent poverty.

You may lose yourself in the infinitely large, which sometimes becomes infinitely small. You let yourself be guided by the incomprehensible appearance of this savage land. Between desert and ocean, Mauritania stretches majestically to the borders of Black Africa and the Maghreb. A vast territory, where discovery is queen and the desert king.

...The tenderness of a gesture

Here, the scenes of life represent a gamut of colors and aromas sprinkled with levity. The children play with any object found, regardless what it may be. Their favorite game: car wheels. These children captivate and charm you with their big dark eyes full of warmth. For me, a new journey begins through their glances and smiles. In South America, I learned everything by reading their eyes, but here I still have everything to learn.

While crossing a village, the mothers, surrounded by their toddlers, chitchat in front of their dilapidated huts. These impromptu reunions are their only amusement before going to cook the midday soup. Filled with curiosity, the children watch us while waving their small hands, hoping like all the children of the world for a gift from a stranger. All run toward us, while watching us. One grabs me by the sleeve, another takes my hand. I already love them and I fall apart. Their eyes are mesmerizing. Serge watches me. I interpret his look: I must be careful not to let their tenderness get to me, or else they will "eat me alive." The magic of children works like a frenzy in this place, rocked by the tenderness of a gesture, of a look....

...The shock of images

An infinite array of shocking images. During our "American Challenge" journey, we had already brushed up against poverty quite often, yet Mauritania still surpasses the inconceivable. We had been warned: in Africa, to be poor is to be truly poor, to possess nothing. But what is most amazing is that these people never complain. With a generous smile, they say: "Such is life." What a beautiful lesson in humility and in courage!

...Serge falls apart

Today is a day unlike the others. Stride after stride, the heat increases very quickly. The desert is drying up right before my eyes. The thermometer reaches 48°C [118°F]! The limit of physical and mental endurance has been reached. At this time of the year, this place is considered the hottest in the world.

Serge fell apart. I saw him weeping, while fully exerting himself. He was inconsolable. For me, it is a sign I must take into consideration from now on. Although he possesses exceptional endurance, Serge also has his limits. I had never seen him like this. Despite all that, he succeeded in running his marathon.

While writing these lines, I fear that we may have to give up on continuing the run. We simply cannot jeopardize our health for the sake of completing a world tour. We drink up to twenty liters of liquid per day. And despite that, Serge suffers from severe dehydration; he has blood in his urine.

48°C [118°F] in the shade...
but there isn't any shade.

...Expensive cost of living

In Mauritania, consumer goods are expensive for us, so just imagine how it is for the people who live here! Yet this country lives in poverty. Inflation is unbelievably high. Prices are constantly increasing. Nevertheless, it is a well-known fact that Mauritania itself is considered very rich (in natural resources). Its coast, at the confluence of several warm and cold currents, boasts the most plentiful supply of fish in the world. Fishing has become the leading national resource.

Copper, iron, gypsum, and phosphate can be found, and prospecting efforts are under way to find gas and oil. But the population seems indifferent to so many natural resources. Fatalism reigns supreme.

While I write these lines, a caravan of camels is drinking from a fountain of life—a spellbinding image!

...Passing the 3,000-kilometer mark

Three thousand kilometers [1,864 miles]! We dedicate them to all the children already encountered on our run around the world. Three thousand kilometers of love and colorful encounters!

Mauritania brands us with a red-hot iron. Our faces bear the scars of the sun's bites. These may have been the most difficult moments of our existence. Nothing, nothing, nothing is on the horizon. We've been alone for more than 1,500 kilometers [932 miles], alone in the silence of the desert. The harshness of the place has profoundly altered our morale. Focused on ourselves as never before, we have even lost a bit of our beautiful complicity. We've simply had enough.

...Nouakchott

Upon our arrival in the capital of Mauritania, we are welcomed by a delegation. Several people run with Serge to show their enthusiastic support for our run. There's a lot of emotion. We feel as though we've crossed our first finish line.

Nouakchott bears witness to the terrible droughts that have hit Mauritania these past years. A quarter of the population has settled here. For more than two months, we have not seen trees, nor flowers, nor heard the songs of birds. Life has returned....

...Pédro, eight years old

I wind my way across the abject streets, flea-ridden and crowded; there are people running in all directions. You must hang on tight and force yourself to look in order to confront this reality that hides wounds and insurmountable suffering. Here neither smile nor affectionate glance reigns. The majority of the people carry out a daily fight for survival.

My gaze softens when I catch sight of a boy crouching underneath a table to avoid the terrible heat. I timidly approach him and hand him a bottle of water. He is dirty and emits a strong odor; his eyes are reddened by the sand. He squints them, as if to thank me. I ask his name and his age, but the question that preoccupies me is how long it has been since he bathed. He responds that it must be well over two months. How I would have loved to take him in my arms and stick him under the shower! But this belongs to the realm of the impossible. I cannot just come here and push for what is not expected. I leave, giving him my most beautiful smile, and he, with a tender gesture, waves good-bye with a very telling look.

In one moment, I captured a bit of the life of a child submerged in the frailty of existence...Pédro, eight years old, met on a curve in the road on June 17, 2000.

...Shantytowns

The shantytowns of Nouakchott resonate like a permanent alarm. Everyone hides his wounds. Opening our eyes up to the wounded childhood here moves us to vow to never close them again, to open our hearts, our arms, to try to give a bit of human warmth during the time of our short stay. It is not the manifestation of a sudden rush of generosity, but rather a responsibility.

Don't all children have the right to grow, to cry, to laugh, to play, and to love? But here, hardly have they come into the world, and they already know that they are destined to poverty.

I am very impressed by the work that so many charitable organizations accomplish in such trying conditions. Their representatives must continually face crisis situations. Every day, they organize a "commando" to come to the aid of the most unfortunate children of the shantytowns. What an awesome commitment!

...Le Cren Nutrition Center

When entering the buildings of Le Cren Nutrition Center, you feel quite humble in the face of so much misery. Today, the institution shelters thirty-five babies and their mothers. A dozen are in critical condition. They no longer have the strength to fight. Their eyes are lifeless; their heads sway back and forth. Their mothers are there, powerless. You get the impression that their children represent the burden of their life. Can you blame them! Not a single one of these mothers has received any schooling. Since the age of fourteen, they have been married, without any other choice for themselves.

In this center, the mothers learn how to feed their children properly. The problem resides not so much in the lack of food, but rather in the lack of education and hygiene, which must be taught. This is why prevention is so very important. Malnutrition is a hunger, invisible to the naked eye, which impedes growth and the mental and physical development of a child.

...July 2000

Mauritania has been a country from another time, from another world, from another generation. We have moved around constantly in a universe that is not ours, that does not belong to us. But from Mauritania, we will retain the memory of the welcoming faces of desert nomads, and also the memory of bivouacs around a fire, quite modest, yet so luminous that it seems to chase away the twilight.

But like the Little Prince, we are already dreaming of our next encounter with the stars. We are eager to discover new treasures, new aromas, new faces.

Smiles everywhere: For sure, it is an African village!

Steps and tracks toward the discovery of another
Ethnicity
No doubt it is
Exhilarating and
Grand to journey to an
Amicable encounter with the Senegalese people
Light upon the river

...Mauritania-Senegal

A new country emerges on the horizon. But first we must cross the Senegal River by ferry. On the Mauritanian side, we are jostled and almost panic-stricken, because we are pressured by the ferrymen who seek to earn their living by claiming strangers as "their own" (territorial fashion). Tempers flare with some of them. Serge loses his. His attitude offends. We hear someone say: "The white man has his nerve; someone will get him." It is better to play it cool....

Serge hired a guide to facilitate going through customs, because we were told to expect many complications. This evening we are anxiety ridden, as we are slowly getting over food poisoning, after having eaten fish in the Mauritanian capital. Serge was the most affected (fever, diarrhea, violent stomach pains, blood in the urine). A checkup at the doctor's, a stool analysis, and finally, a good week of antibiotics. Tomorrow, we will resume our trip.

...The sun rises on Senegal

The sun rises; the morning haze slowly dissipates. We are impatient to discover new horizons. The crossing only takes four minutes, and here we are on the other side of the river. Then the three-ring circus of formalities begins. The guide and Serge start the tedious procedure. As for me, I keep watch over our luggage, because here the least bit of inattention...and their disappearance is assured. Suddenly, I see Serge leaving, furious, his hair disheveled, damp from the humid heat. He shouts to me, "They are insane; one must pay a fortune for motorcycle insurance." Corruption, you have us in your grip. I caution him to watch out "because the insurers are swindlers." I should have refrained from commenting. A furious madman attacks me. He wants to beat me up, because he believed that I had called him a swindler. He insults me: "White whore, stay in your country and don't come here to say that the Blacks are swindlers and thieves!" A crowd forms instantly. Some people come to my aid, but the other man does not calm down and tells me: "I'm going to kill you; I'm going to cut your throat." Enraged, I am about to respond, but I am advised not to add anything. I have just learned that in Africa it is better to bite your tongue and to swallow your pride rather than to confront the other person.... After three hours of cold sweats, we finally cross the border; the incident is behind us.

...Rediscovered smiles

The arrival in Senegal revives our spirits, because here everything inspires life and respect for rediscovered nature; there's an explosion of colors. Magical hidden faces attract our attention. This wild beauty makes up the wealth of human diversity. We rediscover, little by little, the charms of life and our lost smiles, which had been buried in the depths of the sand.

We arrive in the city of Saint-Louis, the former colonial capital of Senegal, which is the center of one of the most beautiful regions of West Africa: a strip of land between the Atlantic Ocean and the Senegal River. Its location is splendid. Saint-Louis is a city of hundreds of expressive faces, where the trendy boutiques, the squalid districts, and the crowded markets intermingle. The houses have two stories with exterior stairways. The finely-worked wooden balconies and verandas call to mind New Orleans.

...States of mind

We stop in the shade of a baobab. All of the symbolism and kindness of Africa are united in this single image. The air is heavy with wild scents. Far off, near a well, are groups of children: an authentic village where the scenes of life sympathize with our glance. Their outfits have the colors of the world. Some huts with thatched roofs give a proud appearance to the African landscape. Sitting by the door of his very, very modest house, an old man looks at Serge passing by and waves hello. Serge winks at me, while still running. It is understood: happiness has been found again!

...On African soil

The children are everywhere, true mosquitoes who prick you with their intense and luminous glances. In a few seconds, it is an invasion. Serge and I understand that our moments of solitude can no longer exist, that a quiet, private life no longer makes sense. We are watched, spied on at each turn. Sometimes, this becomes oppressive. But it is up to us to familiarize ourselves with the rules of another country. At the end of a day of exertions in the humid and suffocating heat, one can feel ground up like chopped meat. It is then that our patience can explode like the cork in a bottle of champagne that has been shaken too much. We then become the victim of our own fatigue. This human tide can occupy our whole mind. Will the process of osmosis ever be able to synchronize the entire human race?

...The Talibe child

The dilemma that has really been affecting us for some days is the Talibe child. This is a destitute child with a shaved head and an empty stare, dressed in moth-eaten garments. He holds a red box in his hand, intended for begging and collecting scraps of food. This child lives in fear and is paranoid about not bringing back the sum imposed by the African dervish [holy man], under whose influence he finds himself. If he should not succeed in collecting the desired amount, he will be tied up and then relentlessly beaten.

The holy man is at the same time god, medium, shaman, and spellcaster. He communicates with nature and seeks the natural unity of things and beings to uncover the spirit. He promises good fortune, protection against evil influences, health, and, of course, love. People conform to his predictions and his orders. This is why he is allowed to batter the Talibe child.

...The red box

This red box symbolizes the unbearable. It will keep following us right to the borders of Black Africa, even in our most innocent dreams. Behind this red box, each day the story of a child, unlike the others, unfolds on the road of life. How difficult it is to make the right decision when the Talibe child approaches us! Which attitude should we adopt? If we give him money, there will be an avalanche of other children who will rush to us. But if we do nothing, the child will undoubtedly be punished. So we give him some bread and a little water. There is the hint of a smile, but one senses that the child would have preferred money. We cannot change the injustices of the world, but while passing through, we modestly try to abate the sadness of the child and to return his dignity to him. Senegal, land of savage contrasts.

...Thiès, in the north of Senegal

Thiès, the second largest city of Senegal, is intersected by large streets. At first sight, it appears to be a calm and serene place. We make a stop at an orthopedic center. As always, we are welcomed by a cluster of children who run with Serge. In the course of three years, more than 6,500 prostheses have been fabricated here. They are intended for children affected by polio or other congenital deformities. They do a remarkable job of coordination, motivation, and attention to children's needs. The prosthetic workshops are organized and managed by competent people. We can only admire so much devotion and solidarity, even if much remains to be done. For we have seen a three-month-old baby here, in a condition that even the most painful words cannot describe.

We hear it said too often that people no longer believe in modern humanitarianism, that often the funds are diverted. But I can assure you that on the day when you are confronted face-to-face by a hurting child, whom you can tenderly take in your arms, you will never be able to egotistically close your eyes again. In this hospital, we perceived a real desire to save or comfort, with the limited resources at their disposal.

At the end of the day, a magnificent party is organized by the children of the hospital. All wear a sweater with this inscription: "Welcome, Serge and Nicole Roetheli." The children sing; their smiles have the colors of a rainbow.

...Dakar

Dakar, the capital of Senegal, is the center, the rallying point, of the political, economic, and cultural life of West Africa. Dakar? You like it, or not all of it, or a little bit, or seldom, or a lot, or not necessarily. But for us, Dakar represents a gamut of entertainment. We recharge our batteries with positive energy. We rediscover a colorful life.

Running, sharing, smiling: That's what the World Tour is.

...An unexpected encounter

In this office in Dakar, they are processing piles of requests for children with heart problems; frequently, these children then go to Switzerland to be operated on and saved. All of the children brought together this afternoon were operated on in our home country and then were returned to their home country. Suddenly, my eyes are fixed on a familiar face. The emotion mounts, because this face is indeed that of the young girl who was present at Massongex during our departure. Her presence had moved me to the highest degree. Affected by a painful disease called noma, which destroys the soft tissues and the bone tissues of the face, she had given me such a sad look. My culpability had been great, all the more so, because I had worn makeup for that event.

In spite of the reconstructive surgeries, this face will never be able to recapture its original appearance. Still, in spite of everything, the result is indeed remarkable. We exchange knowing smiles, before sharing tea and dancing with the children.

...Gorée, the island of slaves

Gorée was one of the principal relay points for the trading of slaves. This island, 300 meters [984 feet] wide by 900 meters [2,953 feet] long, was, for a long time, the object of numerous clashes between the Portuguese, the English, and the French. We spend a few moments moved by the dramatic history. If only the walls of the slave house could speak! It's not something for Whites to be proud of ....

...Continually running in the heat of Senegal

Run, run, run: always to make progress, to map out our long route. There is no horizon, not even a puff of wind to caress us. This heat renders the air humid and nearly unbreathable. Serge's sweat drips all the way down to the small of his back. He nonchalantly looks at me. I smile back at him; he has no idea of my most buried thoughts. While observing him from the corner of my eye, I compare him to a cowboy who never backs down when facing his adversary, when confronted by the obstacles of life. He gives me this image of strength, of the will to always want to do his utmost.

...African villages

The scenes of life are comical. The villages that we travel through are typical. They seem not to have changed since antiquity. The women relentlessly plow the ground of their ancestors. They prepare the stew and wash the clothes without ever giving up. They live in traditional houses, adobe huts with their typical thatched roofs that reveal the whole symphony of Africa. The places are inundated with children who scream, who weep, who laugh as though they had seen green men while watching us pass through. The most fantastic experience is the exchange of looks, of smiles. The color of our skin sometimes frightens the youngest.

Everything here appears so simple. The women, naked to the waist, carry cans on their heads with bewildering dexterity. Their unbowed gait renders them irresistibly beautiful. Here one feels the pulsating charm of communal life. Everyone helps one another and loves one another in a brotherly way. Very few children are abandoned or live on the street. There is always an uncle, an aunt, a next of kin to attend to the child in difficulty. It is a peaceful and serene Africa that we have been traveling through for some days now, here in the bush country. Once you draw near a city, though, it is another story.

...First mosquitoes

The cities are swarming with people; they are terribly dirty, and so many of the districts are unhealthy, especially at this time of the year. Heavy floods leave the cities "knocked out" for a few days. They are accompanied by the invasion of mosquitoes, and whenever one says mosquitoes, one also means malaria. The resistance of the parasite to different antimalarial medications has changed a lot these past years. About 800,000 cases of malaria are reported each year in Senegal; 140,000 are serious. The consequences? Seven thousand deaths per year. Senegal thus pays a heavy tribute to this infectious plague that remains the leading cause of mortality in Africa. At the present time, our World Tour must navigate between the heat, the floods, and the mosquitoes.

...Beauty in a pure state

On the Gambia River, the morning mists peel back like a woman unveiling herself. An atmosphere filled with humid scents, with momentary visions of the wild fauna. It is a place of tranquility, where time stops, where the water of the river dances with the reflections of the sun, gently rising to chase away the mists that refine this eerie landscape. Here is hidden another truth, the myth of paradise on earth. We overflow with love for these stolen visions, for this gift that nature jealously guards within itself. Serge films; I photograph.

The climatic conditions are difficult to manage. We suffer from solitude as a twosome, suffer from a lack of life, from a lack of something.... We sometimes find ourselves asking for an item that does not exist on our path: no bistro on the side of the road to break up the rhythm of our sweltering days. Weariness is stalking us; we have to continue to draw on the depths of ourselves, to watch a leaf move, to look off in the distance without showing the least sign of discouragement. We must never forget to look at what unfolds before us.

...Many faces

Before leaving Senegal, a country with multiple faces, the road passes by Niokolo-Koba National Park, one of the most important animal and plant reserves in West Africa. Created in 1954, this park forms part of a worldwide heritage and biosphere reserves under the direction of UNESCO.

Virgin forests interspersed with orchards and vast expanses dotted with baobabs—this was Senegal. Sometimes emerald green, especially in this winter season; sometimes yellow like the desert. Four rivers wind lazily through its entire territory: the Senegal, the Gambia, the Saloum, which swells where the Sine enters, and the Casamance. All have their origins in the Fouta Djalon, in Guinea. The forest storms the hills from the small valleys; the *rôniers* [trees] bring shade to the banks of the Gambia River. How enchanting!

... Three old men

We are in the last village of Senegal, at Kedougou, at the border of Guinea. African life is in full swing here, but geographically, we truly have the sensation of being cut off from the outside world.

This morning we walk to the "post office." We follow the sign to the "main post office." At the end of the road are a wooden table and a chair. This is the post office! Just to the side, three old men are sitting on the ground. Suddenly, a trembling voice asks us for alms. I pretend not to hear. It should be said that the worrisome situation in which we find ourselves renders us a little nervous. It is because in the coming days, we are going to have to face the deep jungle, with its muddy and capricious trails. No error can be afforded, neither on a physical nor on a mental level. Nobody will come to help us in case of a problem. Something else adds to our anxiety: Serge is recovering slowly from tendonitis, which turned up without warning. He has only been resting for three days. I sense that he is a little unsure of himself and very tense, though hiding that inside.

Then as Serge tries to telephone to Switzerland, I hear a second time: "Madam, alms." Vexed, I yell back at him: "You're out of luck. As for me, I only give something when someone doesn't ask for anything." Then the three men break out laughing, understanding that today the lady is not in a good mood. Suddenly, my conscience bothers me. I look at the three old men with their broad-rimmed hats, which do not let anyone catch a glimpse of their faces. I approach them. I feel overwhelmed by shame and revolt. How could I have been so mean, so insolent with them? Because the three have leprosy; they no longer have feet, no longer have hands, no longer have faces, only stumps, monstrous deformities. If I could hide in a mouse hole, I would do so....

From my pocket, I take out three coins for each one. I feel like taking them in my arms. So I do so without reservation, perhaps to exonerate myself, but at the same time, I want to protect them. They thank me. They hadn't even noticed my insolence. They nod thank you, as if I had given them the moon. It is a life lesson, a true lesson in humility! Thank you!

...Hitting the trails

I mount my motorcycle; I wave my hand. In the rearview mirror: the three old men. I cannot hold back a tear. They are going to die without having known the beauty of life. Their journey will have been one of merely suffering.

Without any clear communication, I sense that Serge is vexed by the telephone conversation that he just had with Switzerland. Problems seem to have arisen. Despite the stunning, radiant, and generous nature that greets our first steps in the jungle, our disposition hardly improves. We stupidly trade insults like the "old couple" that we are. Very miffed, I settle into a heavy silence. But deep down, I feel very guilty, because at this moment, I should be tolerant, should be listening to him, because I now can see that Serge is hurting. But, oh well, nothing doing, my temperament wins out!

We take our first break along the side of the trail. Something tells us that we should stop our trip and turn around. Then and there, like in the finale of a film, we fall into each other's arms. Serge weeps, because doubt has just taken hold of his mind. The continuation of our World Tour is perhaps in peril....

We stay in Kedougou for nine days in order to treat Serge's periostitis [inflammation around the bone].

...*A rest stop for thievery*

This evening our campsite is set up in the middle of this generous bit of nature, inhabited by strange noises. Serge finds himself in his universe here; as for me, however, I find little reassurance in this world. Of course, I know that a beast doesn't attack unless it feels threatened by a human. Nevertheless, my God, it's lovely to sleep under the stars! As objects in an immense nature, we are in direct and physical contact with heaven and earth. No matter how beautiful this sounds, this evening I feel vulnerable, because we are surrounded and closely watched by green monkeys.

We were warned to pay attention to the wild monkeys. Too often, one truly forgets that they are wild. Curious, mischievous, they are above all food thieves. Oh well, what had to happen, happened. In spite of the precautions taken, at daybreak, they pinched the bit of food that we still had. From the place where they are eating, they taunt us with bread and Vache Kiri [cheese]. This ultimately was worth a good fit of wild laughter. We needed that so much!

In harmony with the African land.

Guided by our senses; step
Upon step
Indescribable voyage
Nebula and bliss dazzling our
Every road
And sometimes a hint of nostalgia

...September 2000: Knowing how to take your time

When you arrive in a new country, it is important to take time to learn about its many facets. Ah...time! In Africa, it's better to forget your watch. Multiple interlocutors will always be there to spoil your plan: from the prefect to the assistant prefect, from the hunter to the fisherman, while passing by the notable person or the simple villager, all of them more than happy to explain the history, the customs, the legends of the place. Among women, it will be more a matter of cooking tips or of beauty secrets. It is endless, what all one can learn. Taking your time is a notion that we, Westerners, have lost. This is the apprenticeship of a forgotten wisdom.

When you try to obtain a piece of information, you must learn how to wait calmly, without expressing surprise or annoyance. In doing this, a smile is a precious seed....

...Four days of sweating blood

Today, I am happy to be able to write these lines, because the crossing between Senegal and Guinea has been a particularly trying experience. Four days of sweating blood and tears, and that is an understatement. The trails were foul, muddy, inaccessible, rocky, impassable.... We had to push, pull, carry, swear, unload, and reload the trailer. Crossing the rivers at the risk of losing everything and of being carried off by the swell of the waters. These were moments of incredible anguish! We could not have afforded even the slightest error, nor any serious wound, not even a small glitch. There would not have been any means of getting ourselves out of there. Help would have been impossible. That is to say, we have not seen a single vehicle!

We did not have a minute of respite. During these four days, I do believe, I have never prayed so much. It is incredible how you become a believer in times of adversity.... I needed to believe in a higher power, because Serge was taking considerable risks in getting the motorcycle and the trailer across the swollen rivers. What is more, the motorcycle and trailer did not withstand this shocking treatment. Six punctured tires and four broken axles. The rearview mirrors are in pieces, and the trailer hitch is shattered. A colossal amount of energy has been required to make progress, to make progress in spite of all ... at 2 km/h [1.2 mph]. What a victory!

These days of incessant struggle were not the end of our three-ring circus. The first evening, we pitched our tent in an Eden-like setting, on a plateau where the light reflects the beauty of the world...a beauty that was about to be transformed into a veritable nightmare, because hardly had we settled down when a thunderstorm of rare violence was unleashed. For a moment that seemed to last forever, we experienced a sort of end of the world with sounds and lights. Refugees, if you can call it that, in our tent of misfortune, we really thought that our end was near. I took Serge's hand, and I gripped it tightly. Serge also was afraid, which was not a good sign. Flashes of rare violence were tearing over our heads. I had a very strong thought for my family, so strong, that even at the other end of the world, my relatives had to have felt the anxiety that was ours.

I sent kisses to Clara and Steve. This may appear absurd, but it wasn't without some sense, because I could not figure out in my dazed head how we would be able to get out of there alive. In the morning, it was a radiant sun that awakened us. What a relief!

...Conakry: Moments of doubt

Finally we have arrived here in Conakry, capital of Guinea. Itinerant merchants, freewheeling children, and mothers who prepare gruel are all crammed into the chaotic streets. And the billboards? They boast modernity....

In the next four days, we are going to begin a veritable marathon. On the program are several visits to free clinics. Upon our arrival, an initial surprise awaits us: the traffic is stopped, police officers escort us, and a large group of children dressed in vivid colors embellishes our entry into the city.

We spend a long month in Conakry because of the painful tendonitis that Serge contracted on the way from Senegal to Guinea. The problem is such that only a prolonged rest can put things back in order. The days are long, very long.... Serge has completely lost his sense of where the run is headed, and I have lost my bearings. A feeling of uselessness overcomes us.

During this whole time, doubt about his recovery sets in. It worms its way into our sleep. Yet, wouldn't the adventure also be about accepting surprises of this type? But depression is certainly here, mixed with a hint of rebellion. It is a question of mental equilibrium—isn't that brilliant! How to maintain equilibrium in an adventure such as this—that is the greatest difficulty to resolve.

How is this recovery going to play out? We fear running again in the humid, suffocating heat, which is enemy number one for Serge. In such climatic conditions, he is continually dehydrated, which increases the risk of tendonitis. And tendonitis that is poorly treated will become chronic tendonitis, resulting in an inevitable operation and perhaps the end of a great dream—the end of the World Tour. Dropping out, however, is not on the agenda.

...Children from here and elsewhere

Our best supporters are the children, the schools, the messages on the Internet, the drawings, the organized games, the local runs to collect money. We are touched by these gestures from the heart, by the sincerity that this run generates around the world, by the great generosity of the children of our own country, who want to help the children of other continents. To an ever greater degree, young people are becoming aware of how giving a bit of themselves is the first step in giving aid to wounded children everywhere.

...Change of itinerary

How good it is to set out again, to have the ability to eat up the kilometers anew, and to feel the call of the road, because the road is our home, our life choice, our daily routine. It turns out that it is imperative that we reexamine our initial itinerary, because of the constant instability that reigns along the border of Guinea. In this zone, many villages have been burned and pillaged; some people have been massacred with machetes, and the women have been raped by rebels from Sierra Leone and Liberia. The forest area that we would have to pass through (Macenta) has sustained heavy human losses. The roads are closed and guarded by soldiers, and there is no possible way to enter the Ivory Coast. Guinea, though a democratic country that has never known war, is in a state of alert. We aren't at greater risk because we're Whites; the roots of the conflict are interethnic. But just the same, we are not going to tempt the devil. Our decision is made: we will leave for the opposite side of the country, then branch off into Mali, Burkina Faso, and Togo. That will cost us the "trifling sum" of 800 additional kilometers [497 miles].... This equals about a month of running....

...Like a soldier

We take to the asphalt again like an old soldier going off to combat, at the same time resigned and resolute. We have mixed feelings. They fluctuate

The jungle path between Mali and Guinea.

between enthusiasm and weariness. We're having difficulty finding a happy medium that will allow us to move forward. Serge runs like a robot that could have been programmed. The conditions of the run are demanding because of this accursed heat that makes progress more and more difficult. It affects morale. It even happens that Serge, who is by nature more tolerant than I am, becomes annoyed in certain situations. It must be said that the African, whenever he notices us, cannot help but alert the whole village. Frankly, after a while this becomes tiresome. The scenario can repeat itself dozens of times in the space of a day. I truly believe that the word *solitude* does not exist in Africa....

...Panic at Moribaya

Tonight, we scrutinize the horizon unfolding before our eyes. We contemplate the sky while offering up a small prayer. I prepare the customary meal of pasta, tuna, and a bland tomato sauce. Serge stokes the coals to accelerate the process, because we agreed on a satellite telephone call to my parents. It works! The sound waves reverberate to the farthest reaches of Africa. It is magical! I relate our day. I reassure my parents about the situation in this country. Everything is calm and peaceful in the country-side. I hang up.

We are drinking our café au lait that sets the rhythm for the end of our evening, when suddenly we hear voices; footsteps approach us. "Good evening, sir. I would like to converse with you." Here is a polite form of address that reassures us. There are ten villagers who come to warn us that the inhabitants of Moribaya are afraid of us, because it is the first time that they have seen Whites sleeping in the open country under a tent. And then the children heard us speaking on the telephone. The villagers think that we are spies and that we are communicating with the rebels. We discuss this for a long time; we show them the newspaper articles concerning us. Then they calm down. They wish us goodnight upon leaving and say that we are now under their protection. The next morning, we pass through the village of Moribaya as heroes.

...October 18, 2000: 5,000 kilometers in some part of the world

Five thousand kilometers [3,107 miles] is a figure that might appear ridiculous measured on the scale of the world, on the scale of the earth. But each step, each meter, represents an inner victory, which each day brings us a little farther along, a little nearer to our home. Serge dedicates his sweaty strides to all the children who do not have the fortune of living in a better world, who do not have our good fortune. His effort might appear useless in the eyes of certain people, but dreams, as crazy as they may be, are so beautiful to experience, as long as they are freely chosen and accepted! The rest is only a question of willpower, of love, of health, of tolerance, and of patience.

...A little prince of the road

In the distance, something out of the ordinary grabs my attention. And Serge? He runs on in silence. My curiosity will be rewarded by a very beautiful encounter with an unusual family. A father, his young wife, his son, and their two-year-old little girl are traveling with some donkeys. It has been two years since they left Dakar for an unknown destination. They just keep moving forward; that's it....

We give them a drink and a little food. This encounter at the side of the road is a reward for us. The three-year-old boy makes me think of a Buddha, of a little prince, who has come from elsewhere. His manner of leading his donkey conveys, at the same time, a strength of character and a gentle feeling. I offer him a plush toy that I had well hidden at the bottom of my luggage. I was prepared to give it up only if it felt right. Saving it for the "little prince" was the right moment! He thanks me with a nod of the head. Our paths, our destinies, are going to part, but in my heart, I will never forget this genuine family and their quest for another life, their quest for liberty.

...Encounter with ourselves

Lost in these endless landscapes, lost in the oppressive heat, lost on an endless road, lost in ourselves, lost in our run that reveals to us each day that running in Africa is not easy. Even though we chose to do this (which is true), some days, we unconsciously curse our mode of travel. There is always the same ritual, the same repetitive gestures, the same questions. What good is it to run? Serge is always at the limit of his potential, at the limit of his willpower. But he possesses this rare strength, whose source he alone knows. "If a place exists in paradise for fools, well, then we will have a choice place there," he tells me. There are bursts of laughter, and then the day continues on in silence, in the turmoil of our steps....

...Mendiana, at the police station

Mendiana, a village lost in the bush country, in the dust, the last village before Mali. We arrive exhausted, worn out by numerous nights of camping...and the hundreds of mosquito bites. The itching drives me crazy, makes me nervous. Then after the bites, there remains the fear of contracting malaria. A painful vaginal infection does not help in this humid climate infested with the most diverse germs. In these circumstances, it is best to have an unshakable faith. Weakness must be left to others. All the same, we feel very vulnerable.

After finding a room lacking everything except something vaguely resembling a bed, we go to the marketplace by motorcycle. In the central plaza, the sight is depressing. Everywhere there is nothing but trash, nothing but filth.

Suddenly, we are questioned by a totally agitated odd character: "You must come to the police station with me," he tells us. We hesitate, but then we think, perhaps it's in our best interests to follow him. At the station, we are received by the police chief. Before we can even open our mouths, he yells; he insults us. Our jaws drop. What a farce! Serge no longer holds back. He shoots back at him: "I learned that in Africa the first priority was to say hello. You have not done this, and you insult me without knowing who I am. Do you want to get into trouble?" This has no effect on the police chief, who retorts with a temper so explosive as to move mountains. He's within an inch of beating Serge up: "This evening, you will spend the night in jail!" Serge adds fuel to the fire: "Very well; if you give us a bed and something to eat, we will do fine. This will be a new experience!"

"If a place exists in paradise for fools, well, then we will have a choice place there."

We are not alone
on the African roads.

I try to calm things down; I tell the police chief that we have made a mistake. But deep inside, I absolutely do not see what we could have done wrong. After spending many months in Africa, I have come to understand that here, when you feel that things are going badly, it is better not to insist, but rather to acquiesce. It is easier said than done.... I sense the police chief changing the subject; he asks us for our papers. Of course, he finds our vaccination card missing. Never have we had to show this paper in nine months of travel. He orders us to go find it quickly, while leaving our motorcycle here. It's out of the question, Chief! Then Serge slips him a document signed by an official, which states that we are important and influential people, and that all police officers should help us and open doors for us. The police chief does not believe his eyes. He signals us to leave.... Serge is furious. But it was clear that this October 27 would not be our day.

I'm rolling down the dusty trail, when suddenly a bicycle emerges from the side and crashes into my motorcycle. The bicycle is demolished; the kid who steered it is sprawled out on the ground. Thank God, he is not wounded. But lo and behold, the occurrence is a pretext for a crowd. The people understand that the kid was at fault. His brakes failed in full descent. Nevertheless, a villager makes it clear to us that we must pay for the repair. Before the situation degenerates, we discreetly give the child a little money so that he can repair his bicycle. "You are White; you must pay," the villager tells us....

Running and repairing—
it's the same adventure.

On the trails, you
make it or you crash!

Marching, running with
All our heart,
Line of hope that
Illuminates the faces of despair

...Anguish at Bougouni

Three hundred kilometers [186 miles] of infernal trails to connect up with Mali: what a grind! I flipped the motorcycle on several occasions; the trailer fishtailed. It was necessary to repair it once again. With my knee drenched in blood, I cry. Is this pain, or rather rage that rises in me, bit by bit? Why must one always suffer to the nth degree in order to experience powerful emotions? More disturbing, Serge is not in great shape. What is brewing here? I feel him losing strength; discouragement is gaining ground. He no longer speaks, he withdraws into himself, he retreats totally into his run. We arrive anonymously in Bougouni, where he comes down with headaches and spells of dizziness, and his fever spikes. He lets slip: "Nicole, I am at the end of my rope." It's like an electric shock. He never makes such remarks.

For three days, he is bedridden. He no longer eats. I have to force him to respond. He has a high fever. He tells me not to worry: "This must be a bad sunstroke." I feel quite alone. There is no help on the horizon; the capital is 400 kilometers [248 miles] away. I panic. My husband is starting to get delirious. He is boiling hot; his body is about to catch on fire. I run out to the street to find a pharmacy; it's in vain. I finally get my hand on some fever reducer. His temperature drops, but the coming days are going to be difficult. We take to the road again, but deep in my heart, it's becoming apparent to me that the decision to stop the run is up to me. However, whoever knows Serge knows very well that he always fights, come hell or high water. "Bullheaded," some would say.... I have always admired his enthusiasm, his willpower, his force of conviction. But here, I completely disapprove, but in vain.... I'm anxious to arrive in Bamako.

...Africa

After months of battling with the elements, and with ourselves, I have the impression that we are at an impasse. Could it be that Africa has cast a spell on us? Not a single day is easy. Serge sums it up: "To run Africa is to accept a share of recklessness and folly, but in spite of our willpower and the courage of my wife, our resources no longer suffice."

...When legs refuse to move forward

Not a word passes between us. Serge is focused on his run; the heat is oppressive, damnable. It saps all of our energy, our potential. But do I have the right to complain? From the corner of my eye, I observe my runner "on the soles of the wind." He is dripping with perspiration; his lips stick together; his tongue is heavy. Way too much energy is being expended! After each segment of 4 kilometers [2.5 miles], he has to take a break, drink, and allow his pulse to return to normal. He gets tired very quickly. His morale is faltering. Never before had I seen him dread the hills so much, for Serge is a runner who rather appreciates rugged landscapes, uneven terrains that have character, that have life. This is pushing him to his limit! In the villages we pass through, we no longer find drinkable water and only very little food. We must renew ourselves with so little....

...Bamako, capital of Mali

Evening falls on Bamako with a golden light, and the cars that fill the streets set the avenue ablaze like an immense fireworks show. We feel the pulse of the city beating anew, with the ever-present tramps and begging children. Serge takes me to a charming restaurant. We rediscover the pleasures of dining, the pleasant aromas, the tastes of life. A new portion of Africa is nibbled.... On the world map, it's only the blink of an eye, but we're moving forward all the same. It feels good!

Tomorrow, the man from Valais is joining us. Gilbert and his son are coming for a few days to film some shots of our World Tour. We feel good; we are happy. Finally!

... The verdict falls

A buddy met on our journey has put an apartment at our disposal. It feels like living at home. It is divine to feel this warmth of home, this identity, which for us is lacking at times. I wake up, bubbling with energy. I prepare a true breakfast. I want to do silly things, to take my time, to please my husband, and simply be a woman for him. I call Serge but get no response. I continue to whistle. I call again. Still no response. I tell myself that he indeed has his nerve, because his breakfast has been ready and waiting for over fifteen minutes. I go back into the bedroom. Horrors! Serge is lying on the bed, almost unconscious. His body is dripping wet. He tells me that he has horrendous headaches.

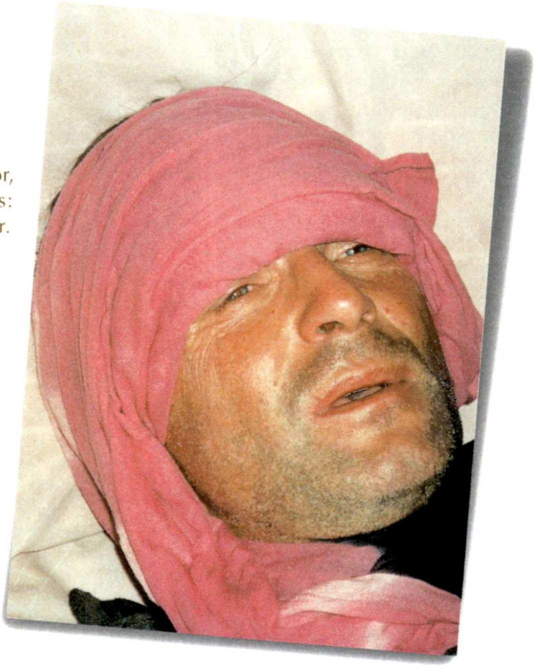

Without the attention of a doctor, death was assured. A malaria crisis: 41.6°C [106.9°F] fever.

I have to react instantly. But here I am alone in a city of two million inhabitants, without any name or telephone number of an available doctor. Another marathon starts, one of life and of love. I move heaven and earth to find someone who can help me. Serge is transported in a car. It takes more than three hours to find a doctor, for today is a holiday. Serge feels very bad. I panic. I'm afraid. Finally, a competent doctor! He examines Serge. A 41°C [105.8°F] fever! Five hours of analysis and so much indescribable anguish. I am like a lioness in a cage. The doctor approaches me.... "Your husband is infected with malaria parasites. He has contracted the most dangerous kind of malaria (falciparum) in West Africa. This type of malaria is unforgiving; it is fatal if it is not treated with good drugs." I fall to pieces, in tears, but the doctor reassures me that Serge is out of danger.

Since that day, he must always have specific drugs within arm's reach, for a crisis can come on at any time. Thank God, Serge is alive, but it was a close call! His athletic constitution undoubtedly saved him.

Black asphalt; one step
Upon another
Rejoicing, weeping
Kilometer after kilometer
Irrational trip
No doubt about that
After so much despair

Fantastic
Alternation of our steps, where
Sagacity has become master
Of the way

...The African markets

It is not easy to contain our emotions, our unease, on the market streets inundated with colors and aromas. The African markets are akin to around-the-clock theaters. And we so often stroll down streets ablaze with the sadness of human plight. Here in Africa, the majority of activities take place right on the ground, without gadgets. The children play with the dirty ground; a woman breast-feeds before our amused eyes; another scales a fish attacked by flies. There are so many shocking scenes! Or is it that we have become hypersensitive people? I love to capture this life. I still have so much to learn and to give. Here, there is no way to escape reality; you simply endure it.

...Raclette under the African stars

Tonight, our encampment is sheltered from fugitive glances, from roaring noises. The alchemy is perfect: we hear the hymn of the world, the echo of life. And just think, with infinite tenderness, Serge prepares for me... a veritable raclette [a melted cheese dish, the specialty of Valais], using a wood fire! He puts poetry into his movements. His look is full of mischief. I can sense that he is happy. The colors explode. The stars illuminate our secret garden. Aromas that could awaken the dead rise to the heavens. We lift our glasses of Coke toward Valais. We take a moment to think about all the people whom we love. As we lie down, we contemplate one more time the colorful facets of the world.

...Sometimes a stroke of luck

We arrive at Bobo-Dioulasso, the second largest city of Burkina Faso with 500,000 inhabitants. Our feelings are mixed. For several months, it has been the same thing almost every day. I dream of true exchanges with the local people, but nearly always, we are met with sadness and nonchalance. In the gaze of the people, one perceives an existential malaise.

We come to a tree-lined avenue, where some nonchalant, itinerant merchants are standing. We go down to the *l'Auberge normande* [Norman Inn]. The sign is enticing—only the sign!... But here we meet a lot of Whites on diplomatic missions. At least, in this place, we will be able to renew ourselves before resuming our African odyssey.

"Hello. My name is Charles. Are you the famous runner?"

"Perhaps not famous, but a runner, yes," Serge answers. This type of unexpected encounter is incredible. "I am from Lausanne. I followed your 'American Challenge,'" our speaker continues.

Thank you, Charles, for these lovely shared moments over the past two days. Thank you for listening... and for the Swiss chocolate!

...6,000 kilometers and a first assessment

Already 6,000 kilometers [3,728 miles] of wild beauty, of inner tears, of suffering, of powerful new sensations, but also of so much sadness encountered on the African roads. Every day it becomes a bit more apparent to us through our means of travel that a great dream is built, it is shared, it does not simply fall from the sky.

After nine months, we are experiencing some difficult moments. The people constantly approach us with the same set formula: "Hey, White man, give us some money; give us some gifts." Under these conditions, it is difficult to have a true exchange on equal footing. We are suffering from this deficit.

In certain aspects, Africa makes us despair. At the same time, it bewitches us. Oh, what a paradox!

...December 14, 2000: Ouagadougou

We have a meeting with a new humanitarian delegation. Infant malnutrition is a problem that one encounters too frequently in Africa; hence it is important to teach the mother to feed her child in good sanitary conditions. The competent people in the field set up the necessary structure for helping these discouraged and distraught mothers. The organizers also take on the responsibility of visiting the villagers in the bush country. It's a matter of informing them of the importance of schooling their children. By all accounts, it will take a very long time to persuade them....

Very few parents have long-term vision. A child in school is one less child in the fields.... And that is without taking into account that a real financial problem exists. Schooling costs a lot. When one realizes that a Burkinabe peasant annually earns the equivalent of 150 Swiss francs [about US$120], and that the tuition of a single child represents an expenditure of 50 francs [about US$40], the ratio is, of course, alarming.

In this center, more than 250 girls are schooled. Moreover, the status of girls is even more precarious than that of boys. If a girl agrees to go to school instead of assuming multiple domestic tasks, she is discredited, treated as a lazy person.... There is still a very long way to go....

...General observations

Composed of about sixty ethnicities, Burkina Faso is one of the most disadvantaged countries of the world. Its population (around ten million inhabitants) is also one of the densest on the planet (thirty-four inhabitants per square kilometer). The country faces a serious problem: deforestation. Trees represent 95 percent of its energy resources. With the intention of correcting its focus, a program entitled "One joy, one tree" is in progress. Moreover, the farmers, using archaic tools, produce sugar and peanuts for exportation.

The inhabitants of Burkina Faso practice three religions: animism (56 percent), Islam (33 percent), and Christianity (11 percent), but nearly all have remained attached to some ancestral animistic rites.

...Mutilated women

Female genital mutilations, in particular circumcision, are commonly practiced in Africa. A woman named Fantani confides to me that the situation is alarming; she informs me that the psychological and medical consequences can affect a young girl until death. How can such barbaric practices still exist in the year 2000? Where is the world going with the equality of the sexes? I am offended.

...Hygiene in Africa

At Koupela, we seek a place to eat and sleep. A surrealistic vision awaits us: everywhere there are piles of garbage, and women are washing clothes in puddles of nauseating water in which donkeys and pigs urinate. In the market stalls, pieces of decomposing meat drip in the sun; the flies are part of the decor. All around there are people—many, many people, just waiting around.

We finally find something resembling an inn, just opposite the market. Five tables adorned with pretty tablecloths; for once, we want to settle in. We order a simple meal. "You can eat everything here, because the board of health comes through once a month," the server points out to us. It's difficult to believe, because at that precise moment, the rats are boldly running around the walls of the kitchen.... You have to pick your poison: it's either open your eyes and don't eat, or else eat while keeping your eyes closed. Against all odds, the meal is well prepared. Serge devours it, but I have more trouble. So the boy takes my plate and puts it out in the courtyard. Within two seconds, dozens of vultures pounce on it. Dumbfounded, I call over the server and call his attention to the matter of hygiene.... Impassively, he tells me: "But, madam, this is Africa!" In one sentence, he sums it all up.

"But, madam, this is Africa!"

Traversing the continents
Only to dare to
Gain
Or to dare to lose everything

...Christmas under the baobabs

We cross the border of Togo without much difficulty. Serge runs an extra 10 kilometers [6 miles], because this evening we want to have a good camping experience for Christmas Eve. We settle down under two baobabs. The decorations are up. The tent symbolizes liberty, and the fire symbolizes our family, whom we miss more than usual under these circumstances. But this evening, the heavens belong to us; the stars will be Serge's children, our parents, and our friends. In spite of the distance, we are happy, for we love our life, our choice, our means of communicating with silence. On the holiday menu: potatoes and bacon with the leftover raclette from Valais. Thank you, Mama!

Serge gets the satellite telephone going. Through the miracle of sound waves, he speaks with Clara and with Steve. On the heels of this call, there will be an avalanche of calls, more than a hundred, all originating in French-speaking Switzerland. We learn that our telephone number has appeared in *Le Matin*. What a nice gesture! This will be one of the loveliest Christmases spent in a foreign place since we began our adventures around the world. The magic of solidarity!

...The man from nowhere

This evening, the sky resembles a shroud that muffles the sounds of nature. The campfire illuminates eternity. With silent steps, an old man approaches. His gestures translate a desire to communicate. The palm of his hand is like a novel. His clothes are tattered, but in his eyes one senses an endearing serenity. Some Whites who are preparing a meal, what possible significance might this have for him? In exchange for a photo, Serge offers him a pen. The old man beholds this curious object; then he tries to scribble something on his hand. He shakes his head indicating that the pen doesn't work. Serge approaches.... It is better with the tip out.... Very amused, but remaining discreet, I observe the scene. Serge writes just one word on the hand of our stranger. Bright eyes from one, tears of joy from the other. The silhouette disappears into the silence of the night and is gradually swallowed up by the tall grasses of the savanna.

...January 1, 2001: Faces in the distance

Every morning on the African road, there is a rural exodus. Dozens of women depart to the fields, walking briskly with bundles of wooden sticks that surpass the imagination atop their heads. I love to capture what is new to me, because it enriches me, makes me progress in my way of thinking. Certain faces are painful to see, faces cracked by the wounds of time, faces that can betray the suffering of hard labor. Too often they show subservience. A face can reflect the beauty of the world; it can also bespeak its other facet—misery.

...Kara

In the region of the Kabyes (stone farmers), Kara is the second largest city in Togo. Its inhabitants are remarkable farmers. Along the river that traverses the city, the gardens are cultivated meticulously. The mud-walled huts with conical roofs are connected to one another by low walls. Life is organized in a communal way inside the enclosures.

Victim of a second malaria crisis, Serge is seen by a neighborhood doctor, who administers two shots. Another bad moment, due to a very high fever....

...Child of the savanna

The sun hits us directly in the face; Serge sweats as rarely before. The women are in the fields. They carry heavy loads on their heads. Their faces betray sadness; they are wrinkled with a thousand furrows. They are noiselessly engulfed by the savanna. At the same time, the children call to us constantly. They ask us for money or gifts. Serge runs, runs in silence. He does not show any sign of discouragement and yet...I know him so well! At this moment, I feel that he is drained, without energy, without a dream.

We arrive at a police station. A barrier blocks the way, breaks our momentum. The policeman nods at us. The barrier opens as if by magic.... It is then that a child verbally attacks us: "Hey, White man, give me ten francs!" Our eyes shoot daggers at him. But nothing doing, this kid taunts us so much that Serge "blows a fuse" and chases him.... The child runs at breakneck speed and takes refuge in the midst of his family. He throws himself on the ground and squeals like a stuck pig. The child rolls his eyes as if witnessing a nightmare. The village locals, of course, observe the scene. The rascal picks himself up and arms himself with rocks to throw at us. The people of the village completely disapprove of his behavior, and some even try to reprimand him. They applaud us as we leave the place....

...7,000 kilometers

The crossing of the 7,000th kilometer [4,350th mile]: the spark of hope grows a little more each day on the roads of the world. We carry out this leg of the journey in the company of Stéphane Carrupt, who has come to run with us for two weeks. A true pal! Not a day passes without our bursting into laughter. This does us a lot of good, because right now, we must confess, we are a bit worn out, overwhelmed by the heat. This also coincides with the end of our journey through West Africa. It certainly put us through the wringer!

A poster in Togo that stresses the prevention of AIDS (SIDA).

...Dance

Music and dance make up an integral part of African life. They have rhythm in their blood. They express everything that they feel in their daily life. Through rhythmic body movements, they express laughter, tears, love, hatred, and sadness. In countries with precarious conditions, people try to compensate for their weaknesses by attributing to nature mysterious and multiple forces over which they have a magical grip. Everything is a pretext for singing, clapping hands, and swaying hips.

...January 10, 2001

Togo is the smallest of the French-speaking African states. It is stretched over 600 kilometers [373 miles], but its width does not exceed 100 kilometers [62 miles]. Bordered on the south by the Gulf of Guinea, this country offers a more agreeable topography, in any case, less monotonous than the countries previously crossed. At the center, an area of hills progressively gives way to a high plateau from which the mountains of Togo emerge. Very dependent on international economic aid, especially French aid, Togo is ranked among the poorest countries on the planet. Its principal resources come from phosphate mines and from agriculture, mainly from the cultivation of cotton, coffee, and cocoa.

The country faces huge problems with sanitation, notably impurities in the water and the lack of a coherent health policy. Numerous are the Togolese who travel several kilometers on foot each day seeking water—water that is often infested with microbes, causing significant digestive illnesses. Moreover, the country lacks rural development projects and agricultural and industrial dynamism. Mechanization is rare, and infrastructures are rather outdated. The demographic growth is exploding. Nearly 60 percent of the Togolese population is under the age of twenty.

...Lomé

Finally, here we are at Lomé! We enter the Togolese capital in the company of our buddy Stéphane, who has shared our lifestyle for the past ten days. Abutting Ghana, on the coast of the Gulf of Benin, Lomé represents, in our mind, the end of West Africa, an immense region that has been occupying our minds and spirits for the past several months. A frontier city, Lomé exudes a semblance of modernity, while preserving its powerful traditions. Here Serge has his third malaria crisis in a two-month span....

...What is it that makes us run?

What is it that can really motivate our choice of life? What is the point of so much effort, of incurring so many risks? We are not on this World Tour for money, nor for a record, nor for glory. Why, then? Well, it is difficult to give a clear answer. Perhaps it is quite simply that we have chosen to be ourselves. As Serge tries to explain: "Motivation is something personal; I simply feel quite motivated by our objective." It is perhaps also a need for a personal quest. Is it selfish of us to experience pleasure on the roads of the world? We are not going to answer that question. But it is obvious that there is a real desire for commitment to our adventure, even if I will never sacrifice my quality of life for the run. (I do not like the term *sacrifice*. Our choice of life was made freely.)

...More abandoned children

Upon our arrival at the Oasis Center, emotion immediately overpowers us. The children are gathered here, washed and fed. The majority among them have been abandoned by their parents. They found themselves thrown out on the streets, or else they ran away for various reasons. The coordinators of the center play the role of mediators while trying to restore their confidence, for the children often feel at fault. It is a matter of finding their bearings. The children generally spend three months at the center. After this, if their families are identified, a reintegration is attempted, and a follow-up is assured. Depending on their needs, financial, material, nutritional, or health aid is provided.

Today, we share a meal with about twenty children. Again we experience a powerful moment in life and much happiness.

Braving the uncertainty
Enigma everlasting
No doubt
Impertinence of our steps
New destination

...Cotonou, a city filled with activity

Upon our arrival at Cotonou, in Benin, we are greeted by an anarchic unrest. People are driving every which way, while honking their horns and confusing sidewalks with roadways.... We are overwhelmed by the traffic and the appalling pollution that tears at our lungs. The police escort us and open a path for us. We can relax and appreciate the unfamiliar that unfolds under our footsteps—a veritable open-air theater! On the avenue that leads to the center of the city, Serge takes his last strides in West Africa. In a roundabout, the children wave posters: "Thanks, Serge and Nicole." They sing a song in our honor. These moments when we connect with the children are super. For us, this is an inner victory. May the journey continue!

...The children and us

In Cotonou, we are thrust into a hospitality house that brings together about forty abandoned children, of whom nine are babies. We converse with them; we try to get to know where they are going. We are only passing through, but we try in these few moments to provide our love, friendship, good humor. The children latch on to us with an infinite tenderness. These are some moving moments that make separation more heartrending. *They* remain here with a fragile destiny, while *we* are free to leave again, heading toward new horizons.

...Child smugglers

In Togo and in Benin, a significant trafficking in children exists. This movement essentially affects young girls from six to twelve years of age, who, after having been kidnapped or sold off by their parents, are hauled to Nigeria, the Ivory Coast, or Gabon. The child smugglers have a lucrative business.... These unscrupulous people follow trails in order to avoid the border crossings, and quite often the children die from hunger, from thirst, or from mistreatment during their transfer. Those who arrive "safe and sound" will be exploited sexually or as domestics.

How can such a tragedy be avoided? Parents lacking financial resources are powerless against this scourge, which especially affects the rural areas. With no way out, they put their trust in the belief that they are placing their children as domestics supervised by tutors. This provides them with an income that most frequently is a product of theft. It is only after certain ones among them manage to escape that they find one another on the streets, where the Oasis Center begins its work to track down the smugglers.

...West Africa

West Africa, a melting pot of countries linked like a chain, sometimes a requisite stop for a picture, a cliché whose meaning appears trivial, or even anonymous, to some. With each image comes another emotion, another reflection. So many emotions shared with both young and old, who have offered us lessons in wisdom—the school of life, the sweetness of time!

The women who breast-feed along the side of the road, who doggedly work the land of their ancestors, their land. Africa—as much beauty, as much monotony as misery. West Africa has so many repeated questions, revolts, and awaited answers. It lives at two speeds; it mixes modernism and primitive life. It is colors, smells, authenticity. And just consider the looks and the permanent smiles that make up the beauty of our trip! But Africa is also this constant begging, this negative approach that makes the visitor leery. It will have marked us; it is a region of its own. What a contrast of civilization, of culture, and of religion! Africa also means magnificent dusks that set the sky ablaze to eternity. Good-bye, West Africa!

The days
Hold a promise of renewal
Evermore

Continuing to run
After what, after whom
Positive we won't
Ever forget

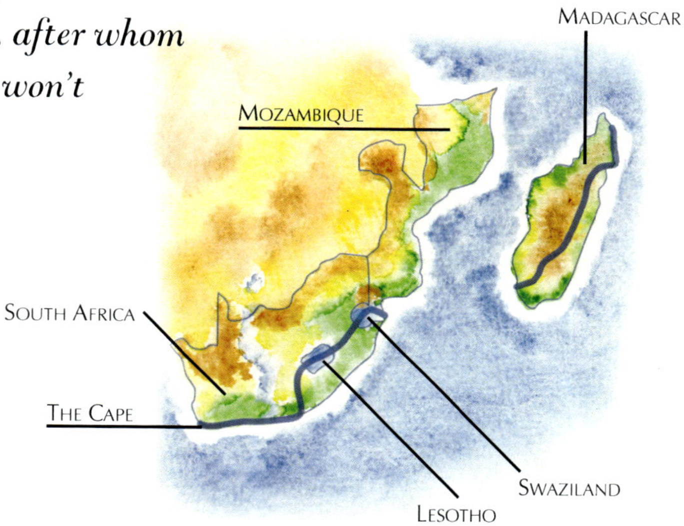

South Africa & Madagascar

...February 22, 2001: The Cape, South Africa

We are two minutes from takeoff, two minutes away from finding ourselves in the air, two minutes from leaving a year on the road behind us.

After more than twenty hours in transit, here we are on South African soil. Another world, another reality awaits us. An unpleasant surprise: the motorcycle and our luggage didn't follow us here.

The Cape, on the other hand, keeps its promises. The city offers the amateur historian the depth of a memory haunted by distant Europe. The Cape is a wonder, an idyllic location. The South African capital of the art of living, of fashion, of high cuisine, it is also the theater of a rare symbiosis between man and nature, between earth and sea, on a peninsula whose floral variety surpasses the imagination. How the Mediterranean sweetness of Africa perks us up!

...Table Mountain

Table Mountain National Park is the pearl of the Cape and provides its unbelievable character. A two-hour climb on foot or a cable car ride is a must, so fantastic is the view of the city from up there. We take in the sights and allow ourselves to experience life. We enjoy the delicate aromas that blend in with our good humor and with our regained health. We soon reach the Lion's Head. In my life, I had never, ever seen such a spectacle. It really is love at first sight. I could put down roots here. I love Cape Town.

...The Cape of Good Hope

We arrive at the Cape of Good Hope with 7,305 kilometers [4,539 miles] of the run completed. In front of the roadside sign indicating that we are indeed at the extreme southern tip of Africa, we do not overlook the expedient photo opportunity. It is here that the "Run for Kids" course resumes. Under the sun, the ocean takes on an extraordinary hue. This country charms us more every day. We are eager to get to know it better.

...American horseback ride

The run takes on the pace of an American horseback ride between the sea and the mountain. Serge's steps ring out like the light sounds of bells. They lead him into the depths of life. Vast plains, which are enlivened by tiny green hills, set the rhythm of our daily life. Our glances linger sometimes on dream houses. We are still in Africa, but an Africa quite different from the one that we have frequented until now. In a few days, we have changed worlds. The infrastructure is modern; technology is indeed present. To recharge our batteries, we could not dream of anything better! Plus, we are no longer suffering from that humid heat that was rendering us more and more vulnerable in West Africa—not a negligible point.

...But what planet do you come from?

I experience the same feeling that I had during the "American Challenge." When we had crossed the border from Mexico into California, we had passed, at that very moment, from a status of affluence to one of poverty in regard to our way of life and our gear.

The contrast differs in South Africa, however, in that two peoples—Whites and Blacks—live side by side. We mostly come into contact with Whites, who applaud our effort, encourage us, and ask us lots of questions. Blacks are packed into slums that are crammed into the slightest plot available. The roofs of their houses are tied down against the tempests with the aid of a hundred pieces of plastic held down by rocks. Their floor is made of compacted ground. Here again there are untenable social differences. And yet at first glance, this land breathes luxury; its nature is lush.

Only a hundred meters separate the rich and the poor, the Whites and the Blacks. The faces that we come across are marked by a very heavy past. They have nothing in common with the smiles and nonchalance that characterize the inhabitants of West Africa.

One major problem is quite obvious: here, alcoholism wreaks great havoc. It can provoke a certain violence. For the moment, we cross South Africa as if wrapped in cotton batting, even if running always remains a demanding activity. We respectfully listen to the advice of Whites. Each new country has its rules. It is better to conform to them. Here, we are considered a little crazy, but we happily claim the status of crazed individuals!

...The woman with a big heart

At Botrivier, an old, smiling lady greets us in a modest hotel. She opens the gate to her magnificent garden for us, as well as the door to her heart. Very sensitive to children's issues, she is touched by our manner of living. She offers us a room and a sumptuous meal. And in the morning, there's a copious breakfast on the table. On a card, she jotted her wishes for a good voyage and a long life. Thank you, Cecilia; we will not forget you!

...Strange thief

We set up our campsite at the bottom of a valley, in the heart of the virgin forest of Tsitsikamma, between a lagoon and the ocean. This evening, we are sleeping in a wooden hut under majestic trees. As a concert, we are entitled to the howls of baboons.

I get goose pimples. Time has stopped, the fire crackles, we enjoy this magical moment. We enter into close communion with ourselves, with this nature that we adore and respect. I light candles to give magic to the place. Serge occupies himself with the fire. I get out the food; I spread the goods upon the table. Barely out of the hut, I hear a commotion. Shock! An enormous male baboon has just taken his turn and gone into the cabin. Within the blink of an eye, he swipes our sustenance and comes back out with a package of *rösti* in his mouth.... What could we do? I was quite scared.

...The world is small

Serge traces out his long route; he runs, runs, runs.... His steps give meaning to his life. To me, he reflects an image of sincerity, of immense willpower to want to give his all. Through his unfailing commitment, he transmits to me the same desire to go on.

We are lost in our thoughts, plunged into silence. Suddenly, a tour bus stops. What a surprise: two familiar faces get off. It turns out to be two people who live in my native village of Ardon. They are also friends of my parents. They are visiting this country with an organized group, we in our own style. We spend a good hour along the side of the road, exchanging sentiments and our faraway memories. What a small world it is!

...Garden Road

We find ourselves on the famous Garden Road of South Africa. It is a rather narrow coastal strip wedged between the Indian Ocean and the Tsitsikamma Mountains. Randomly following creeks and estuaries, we discover magnificent beaches bordered by dunes or impenetrable forests. Long ribbons of sand interspersed with brown boulders and translucent lagoons. We reach the 8,000th kilometer (4,970th mile). A feeling of euphoria enfolds me.

Each day we discover the sweetness of the South African climate. But the heat can become burdensome. We feel as though we're in an oven. Running still remains difficult, but recuperation in these conditions is easier. Our morale remains high. Of all the countries run up to this point, South Africa will remain among our favorites. There's only this one negative note: a distinctive contrast still exists between rich and poor, between Blacks and Whites. The gulf is enormous.

...A kid in the street

We are seated at a table in a McDonald's. We appreciate these moments, because they mean air-conditioning, cleanliness, and toilet paper. In short, all those details that may appear insignificant, but acquire a great value in our adventure.

"Serge traces out his long route: he runs, runs, runs...."

Dusk arrives and the light turns golden; the cars illuminate the avenues of Port Elizabeth. Then I exchange glances with a boy in rags who begs us to give him something to eat. What an intolerable contrast! One more! And lo and behold, now the kid is chased by an employee. But the kid hides behind a wall. He awaits our exit. We offer him two liters of Coke—a modest gesture that will keep this boy of the street content... for five minutes. One child among far too many who live in poverty.

Here are some more figures. More than two million South Africans are undernourished. Fifty-three percent of the people live below the poverty line. Nine million live in shantytowns. Four million are homeless. Sixty-five percent are illiterate...and at the same time, several hundred yards away, the windsurfers and the surfers wholeheartedly enjoy themselves.

...Support for one day

The more you become imbedded in this country, the more you become conscious of the barriers that still exist inside its borders. Everything here is enclosed. You get the impression of semi-freedom. The lack of affluence for one group of society is blatant.

It is difficult to find places to camp, because there are numerous bans. Fortunately, for several days now, we have been enjoying an outburst of solidarity. We are often invited in to share soup with peasants... what a treat! The good fortune of such encounters makes up the great richness of our daily life. Here, we feel fulfilled.

...Encounter with the unexpected

The sun is suspended at its zenith; we decide to stop for lunch. We find ourselves in a private reserve where huge signs indicate the presence of lions. Seated under the foliage of a tree, we first of all notice a herd of zebras. Like in a fairy tale... a moment later, and two giraffes take a turn to make an appearance. It's a true fairyland! We are happy to note that at the dawn of the third millennium, magic endures.

...One day on the road

The wind blows hard. It spews a cold that chills the veins. I am chilled to the bone. Serge curses, because for exactly two hours he has been trying to fix the motorcycle trailer; the axle broke again.... We absolutely must find someone capable of repairing it. Serge takes refuge in a silence that conveys his anxiety. "Sometimes I wonder what possessed me to have come to this part of the world," he says. At least the landscapes that we are crossing are stunningly beautiful, which serves as a comfort. It is only at the end of a 50-kilometer [31-mile] trek that we reach the nearest city. Fate, once again, will be at this rendezvous. We find a mechanic who will repair the trailer and give it a "face-lift." But fate's joke is going to cost us dearly.

We leave Grahamstown and follow our route. When we return to retrieve our trailer, it will also be time to welcome Clara and Steve, who are joining us for the third time since our departure. We await them with immense joy. Serge is impatient; he asks himself tons of questions: how will he find them? Have they grown? What are their desires? What are their passions? There are so many answers that he does not get on a daily basis. Fortunately, there is the satellite telephone. It is an extraordinary piece of equipment that connects us to the children. In spite of the eccentricity of our lifestyle, Serge attaches a very great importance to these beloved contacts. He wouldn't want to lose them for anything in the world.

...Trekking along

After due consideration, we make the decision to change our initial itinerary; the risks related to the surrounding violence are just too great. We will thus bypass the Transkei region by a distance of some 500 kilometers [310 miles]. Transkei was an independent state, but it is now part of South Africa. The integration is difficult, because more than 80 percent of the population is unemployed. Revolt and violence are engendered by this phenomenon. No Whites live in this part of the world, which is thus uniquely dominated and controlled by the Blacks. We will go into the interior of the lands, said to have better social stability in store for us. And then, something else titillates us: we read in a newspaper that a French couple is in the process of crisscrossing Africa on foot. Let's see...

...Sadness at the other end of the earth

The earth turns; our steps follow tormented paths. The sun no longer burns so strongly. And then, this new tragedy: four friends, Valais mountain guides, have disappeared forever. How painful it is to learn of the death of someone whom you have loved, whom you have appreciated, with whom you have shared moments of life. Serge is devastated, because for him the mountain signifies the sweetness of the air and the passion for life. The accursed mountain has killed once more. For sure, the next kilometers will be dedicated to the memory of those who have disappeared and to their families.

...Clara and Steve

It's not a mirage: Clara and Steve have indeed rejoined us for a few days of happiness. They are now two adolescents, reacquainting themselves with their father. We share the joys of reunion while we let ourselves be carried away by the sweetness of their presence. These moments are always magical. The grand moments of life are a great complicity! Steve is endearing,

Clara and Steve: Serge's children.

reserved. How does he see his father? I love to watch him laughing with Serge. I well imagine that he misses him sometimes. As for Clara, she is a beautiful young girl who seems comfortable with herself, who only asks to blossom like a rose after the storm.

We have spent a few superb days together. They return now to their life, and we to our route. We are a bit sad.... So long. We love you! 8,238 kilometers [5,119 miles].

...*A pretty gift*

From the corner of her eye, Clara had observed the scene. She had offered this commentary: "Papa, you are really not romantic for having had the idea of offering a thermos to your wife for her birthday." She had added: "I hope that my friend will have better taste." Well, Clara, do you know that I have been dreaming of this gift for some time already? This one-liter thermos is invaluable in my eyes. Imagine being somewhere with no bistros to be found, and yet I am going to be able to prepare nice hot coffee every day. It's not banal. It's a thing evidently worth nothing in the eyes of certain people, but holds a true richness in our situation.

...Children in the streets

We arrive in North Aliwal, a city with animated streets. A throng of kids in rags rummages around in the waste bins. One among them licks a Popsicle stick, another a cup. Such images cause us terrible pain. But darn it, what can you do to stop such injustice? We are running for the goal of promoting a better world, but too often we are confronted by this type of unbearable situation. An immense guilt assails us each time, because we are quite aware that we cannot help them all.

We do what we can at our own level. We enter a bakery and come back out with cookies. We commence the distribution, but the inevitable occurs: the children fight and do not know how to share. From my stern demeanor, they can gather that I am not happy. Then, as if by magic, everyone calms down again, and the distribution can continue.

...Lost between the future and the past

The more we advance, the more the landscape bears a strong resemblance to that discovered a few years ago in Patagonia. Nature is frozen; the trees gradually drop their leaves. Here, 4 hectares [about 10 acres] are necessary to sustain a cow, and 1 hectare [about 2.5 acres] to sustain a sheep—proportions that astound us.

We feel quite alone faced with such a vast territory. How immense the earth is! There are very few humans and still fewer bistros to make our kilometers more enjoyable.... It is crazy how we have stuck to our habits from Valais: we stop in all the bistros that are found along our route. However, we must point out one detail: we see a bistro about every six days.... On the road of this mountain pass that carries us to an altitude of 2,000 meters (6,651 feet), we are certainly not going to find one. My thoughts are "drying up."

...Image of tenderness

The image of an old, hunched-over man is reflected in the window of a restaurant. He can hardly walk anymore with his two uneven wooden crutches. He instinctively stops in front of me, but his sight must be deficient. In his hand, which defies all age, he counts his pennies. The poor man certainly doesn't have enough money to enter the restaurant. In any case, he would be refused access. As I exit, I slip a few coins into his hand—another priceless moment.

...The resumption of life

In our hotel room, there is as much hot water as one wants, which is not displeasing to me, because a wintry cold has settled over the land. In the distance, I admire the snow-covered summits of Lesotho. From our personal effects, I take out our book *Keep On Running*.... I hadn't opened it for two years. I skim through several pages; emotion overcomes me. All of it seems, at the same time, so close and yet so far away. I can scarcely believe that we are still and evermore on the roads of the world, on the road of life, in the same state of awareness, and with the same motivation as at the time of the "American Challenge." It feels to me like reading the story of another couple on the edge of time.

...Maseru, capital of Lesotho

Maseru, the capital of Lesotho, is laid out at the bottom of a harmonious valley. Our hearts are immediately won over by the warmhearted welcome of the people. Here, in this secluded place, we rediscover Black Africa in all its splendor: chaos in the streets, constant honking. The people live, they laugh, in spite of the pervasive poverty. They have a noble and proud countenance, just like their mountains and their arid plateaus.

Seated at the door of his modest hut, an old man greets us with a wave of his hand—a simple gesture, but how noble! He meets the expectation of our dream.

This land evokes a feeling of emptiness, an emptiness born of silence, of its immeasurable expanse. The plains extend beyond the visible horizon; the shadows become blurred. I retreat into my thoughts, Serge into his own. Mine have hardly any consistency at this moment. I isolate myself in a deceitful silence. Monotony sets in. And then, this music plays in my soul: "What good fortune you have, Nicole; your life, you have chosen to live it in this fashion! The adventure that constantly adorns it only makes it more authentic." Nevertheless, it is a rainy day... 8,973 kilometers [5,576 miles] across Africa.

...Street Confrontation

Every time we arrive in a village or a city of South Africa, the same unbearable images leap before our eyes. The Black population is settled in dilapidated and unsanitary shantytowns. The houses are only heaps of chance materials. The cold pierces them constantly. What an injustice!

We stop in front of a hotel. While Serge is negotiating the price, I watch. Some children are crisscrossing the streets in the hope of meeting compassionate people. At the window of a restaurant, other children, but White in color, taunt the unfortunate Blacks. They devour their sandwiches that are dripping down on their Sunday clothes....

I will never get used to such provocations. A "little sweetheart" approaches me; his face and his hands are viciously burned. He makes me understand that he is hungry and cold. At the same moment, a police car passes; it chases him with contempt... not to mention that these police officers have his same skin color. The same blood runs in their veins. I reassure the child by glancing at him affectionately. He understands that he can come back to me. He sets off with a little coin in his hand. But already other children follow....

I push open the hotel door. I return to the comfort of my life, while he returns to the anguish of his. We try to be charitable on our journey, but it can only be manifested through modest gestures of brotherhood. If only we could change the world! ...What we want to believe is that through this run we will be ambassadors of smiles and love. It's a drop of water in an ocean, but a drop of water nevertheless....

...May 18, 2001: Passing 9,000 kilometers at Clarens

We cross the 9,000th kilometer [5,592nd mile] in the village of Clarens, named for the Swiss town where President Kruger died. The village slumbers peacefully at the base of a massif, under the imposing 2,249-meter [7,378-foot] Mount Horeb.

Our passion, our motivation, our hopes for a better tomorrow are always fixed somewhere at the bottom of our heart. To run the world is not an end in itself; to run with the banner of solidarity is a whole other thing. In our own way, we are also a little like the street children. "What we are living is not an adventure outside of time," says Serge. "It is an adventure of our time."

...Golden Gate, a national park

Our itinerary takes us through breathtaking scenery. The route seems to climb up to the sky. It winds without end. The high sandstone walls take on a golden glow at sunset against the background of the grassy savanna. The effect is striking. Serge runs like an antelope, perhaps because we find ourselves in the heart of a national park of more than 11,000 hectares [27,500 acres]. What a dream!

...While passing through one evening

I'll attempt it, but I don't promise accuracy in writing the name of the village in which we are spending the night: Phuthaditjhaba. Just try pronouncing it! On our way through, heads bow. We go into a store. The owner, of Portuguese origin, speaks French. He recounts.

The village shelters 35,000 Black inhabitants and 1,800 White inhabitants. He settled here sixteen years ago. He lived here during the time of apartheid, a word that, even today, burns your lips. Just seven years ago, a Black person did not have the right to exchange glances with a White. The restaurants were closed to Blacks; they did not have access to education nor health care. At six o'clock in the evening, a siren would howl. That meant that it was time for the Blacks to return to their homes.

Today, the Black African justly considers civilization as the common heritage of all humanity, and he demands, with an absolute right, the opportunity to contribute to its progress and to live free just like any White South African. Yet judging by the innumerable shocking images that unfold before our eyes, one must readily admit that some progress still needs to be made!

The area becomes dangerous for Whites, especially in the larger, urban areas. The Whites distrust the Blacks, just as the Blacks distrust the Whites. It's as if a heavy, leaden blanket has settled over the land—a strange land, which questions us constantly, which also disconcerts us, because the violence that undermines the country is latent; it is not obvious.

At five o'clock in the evening, the streets are empty; we hear only the noise of the wind and the leaves that flutter about. Everyone returns home. Is it a habit of life or the fear of danger? That's a question without answer....

...Some good deeds

How many times have we left a bag filled with food or clothing along the side of the road? That's our best technique not to make anyone jealous. It is a modest gesture for us, but one that symbolizes our desire to share. Once a day, we have this type of thought for a child, a woman, an elderly person. In South Africa, we have more wiggle room for maneuvering in this realm, because very few people ask us to give alms. It's easier to give without the continual begging. This facilitates generosity.

...Our favorite "chicks"

Sonia and Alexandre Poussin [the name *Poussin* means chicks] left on January 1, 2001, from the Cape of Good Hope on an epic journey that is going to take more than three years. At the pace of human footsteps, they departed, to go up the whole African continent. For several days, we have known that we were on their tracks.

We will not soon forget this cordial encounter. One might say that we've known one another for a long time. Watch out for the dialogues: words are shooting back and forth like machine-gun fire! After several hours, our eyelids become heavier and our yawns wider. It's time to go to bed.

The next day, the weather is radiant; the sun illuminates the world. Our faces also glow; they open up on a new day. With Sonia and Alexandre, we share two symbolic kilometers, a way of cementing our newborn friendship. And already our roads diverge. After a few minutes, their silhouettes are lost in the blur of the trail, which renders the image of this couple even more beautiful. To each belongs his direction, his road, his destiny. Thoughts remain that will make us continue to feel close to one another.

...My parents in Johannesburg

After sixteen months of separation, what bliss—a reunion with my parents! My emotions are at their zenith. I have awaited this moment for such a long time. To see them in good physical condition, younger than ever, fills me with joy.

During the few days that we share, we visit Kruger National Park—a world without constraints. The landscape is characterized by vast stretches of pastures where red grass and buffalo grass dominate. And along the waterways, the acacias abound. While crossing the road, animals as diverse as cape buffalos, lions, leopards, elephants, rhinoceroses, zebras, and giraffes plunge us into a magical natural world. It's majestic!

Under the shade of a baobab, we say good-bye to my parents. Have a good trip back; see you later!

At dusk, closer to the sky.

...Johannesburg

With an annual average of 25,000 murders, South Africa is the most violent country in the world. The official statistics are terrifying: 62.5 murders per 100,000 inhabitants, versus 7 per 100,000 in the United States. The Black towns are affected the most. On the entire planet, the expansive Johannesburg is the metropolis where the most murders and assaults take place. Fortunately, the countryside is much more peaceful, though you should not be naive; it's better to remain on your guard.

...The road

Taking to the road again means continuing to sample the intoxication of life. It's rediscovering the feeling of making progress; it's renewing human contact. Even though there are random encounters, the road itself guides our feet and presides over our destinies. To go in search of new horizons without ever forgetting the goal of our adventure, that is our line of sight, our target. The road is our house, our living room, our garden, our solitude. Certainly, it can prove itself to be a bitch.

"To each belongs his direction, his road, his destiny."

Here are Serge's words at the end of this day's leg of the journey: "Today, my legs were throbbing as if I were a novice at this sport. I gritted my teeth to finish this leg of the journey; I was just dragging along."

...Surprise prayer

The sun is hidden in the depths of silence. It is cold; we can't find any place to set up our tent. The landscape is encircled by wire fencing. And anyway, given the violence, camping is strongly discouraged. There's only one possibility left for us: to play the role of pilgrims and go ask for hospitality by knocking on an unknown door.

Knock, knock, knock... a door opens. A White woman answers. She invites us into the warmth. With one sentence, we understand that this evening we will sleep in peace: "It's Jesus who sends you; make yourselves at home."

At dawn we are awakened by hymns. Our hostess offers up a prayer asking God to bless us. I can hardly hold back my tears, because her words are troubling and touching. Spirituality is indeed an ingredient that has a significant place on this World Tour.

...At the pace of a runner

The road that we have been traveling for years at the speed of 12 km/h [7.4 mph] gives meaning to our life. It contributes to our quest for freedom. Traveling is the apprenticeship of the sublime as well as the sordid, of ecstasy as well as pain, of life and of death. Today, in this scenery, reminiscent of a Western, only the desperados are missing. Are we perhaps a little like desperados?

The zenith catches up with the horizon; night slips down like a bridal veil. The fire is already crackling; the water is boiling. There isn't any room for another person, but there is room for silence.

...Remaining ourselves

When we embark on an adventure such as this, it is we who determine the degree of difficulty of that which we seek. So we accept the unexpected, the vexations. What is essential is always sticking to a code of conduct, always remaining ourselves. Running across continents consists also in our accepting that we must adapt to nature, to people. It is important to create a climate of confidence, to be in harmony with ourselves.

Intoxicated by the sun, the first hours that follow the bad weather hold something just as magical as it is ephemeral. What a morning!

Stick to your road
Wagon in motion
Advancing
Zigzagging through
Incipient
Light that comes
Along
Near us ever
Donating the spark of hope to make progress in the torment of our steps

...Good-bye, South Africa!

By a long trail of 60 kilometers [37 miles], we leave South Africa for Swaziland, a country hemmed in between South Africa and Mozambique. The trucks do not brake when they see us. They raise dust with their passing. This seems to be a game for them. This road delivers a powerful force to the heart of a dense forest. You could believe you're in the middle of the Amazon.

As you leave the forest, you perceive houses clinging to the sides of mountains. The slopes are abrupt; the voids below dizzying.... As we enter the first village, there is once again a multitude of children with smiling faces and inquisitive looks who spontaneously run with us. They must indeed wonder from where we come. Spontaneously, a kind of serenity is established from this first contact. Here, Blacks again dare to look a White person right in the eye. A form of racial equilibrium is being reestablished little by little....

The countryside is not rich, but the poverty that we experience does not have the air of cruel injustice that one constantly detects in South Africa.

...Arrival in Maputo

We arrive in Maputo, the capital of Mozambique, in the midst of honking horns. About a dozen marathoners have come to accompany us for a distance of approximately 20 kilometers [12.4 miles]. The traveling merchants are set up along the avenues. The people are in high spirits. They smile, greeting us with friendly gestures. Television crews film our passage. The ambiance is fabulous.

We are directed to an NGO [nongovernmental organization], which is responsible for disadvantaged children. In addition to chronic poverty, floods have plunged the country into a state of devastation. Numerous children have been orphaned. Being taken inside such institutions always causes some very intense moments. In this center, each room has several beds. All of them have been carefully made, with teddy bears on top of the covers. How beautiful it is!

The next day we are escorted to several government ministers. The minister of sports mentions the misfortunes affecting his country: natural catastrophes, the plague of AIDS, and antipersonnel mines. The latter cause numerous amputations. We can actually visualize these tragedies while strolling through the streets of Maputo. One would readily qualify Maputo as Neapolitan in regard to the laundry hanging in all the windows. And behind each of these fabrics a story is hidden....

...Loading the motorcycle

After some days spent in Mozambique, a new destination awaits us: Madagascar. For the time being, all our attention is focused on the procedures of shipping the motorcycle. The steps are tedious. We are in a warehouse; cardboard boxes litter the ground; people run in all directions; they bump into one another; the scene is really very peculiar.... I am deep in thought, when suddenly two hearses burst in, carrying two wooden caskets. People bow their heads. Spontaneously, I join in their tears. The place is cold and gloomy; the moment is difficult. Right next door, life continues; cartons pile up; our motorcycle will perhaps be loaded....

Morrow's world
Advancing step by step
Desiring a just and better world
After
Grunt work and enlightenment
Advancing, still anticipating some choices, searching for our
Star, following our life
Clogged roads
Across our route, our destiny
Returning one day, perhaps, to our home

...July 10, 2001: Madagascar

After a good week of administrative harassment, where we were jammed into an airport awaiting a plane that did not arrive, here we are again in a third-world country. At first glance, there is no doubt about this. Madagascar, the fourth largest island in the world, is a subtle blend of Asia and of Africa. As with every time we set foot in a new country, we are totally excited by the idea of discovering it. Ravaged by poverty, illiteracy, and deplorable sanitation, the Madagascan people seem endowed with a great capacity to improve their lot in life. Immediately, a good dose of the joy of living is palpable: an ambiance like we have never felt in any other place. The Madagascan people cultivate the memory and the traditions of the Indonesian and African tribes. They are very respectful toward strangers—no solicitation or aggression. It is an epiphany.

...Tulear

Tulear, city of dust. The heat here is oppressive. What miserable images in the streets! Oxcarts, rickshaws, and the unending honking of horns reinforce this vision of anarchy. You could believe you were in the heart of the film *Le Salaire de la Peur* [*The Wages of Fear*]. The music blares until sunup. Souls wander with bottles in hand. The drunkards frequent the disreputable bars. "Tulear is the asshole of the world!" exclaims a passerby....

To be sure, a new culture is introduced to us; a new adventure begins. But first, it's necessary to repair the trailer and the motorcycle, because this time the air transport between Mozambique and Madagascar was not what you would call a success. A lot of damage and numerous problems. Fortunately, we found an experienced motorcycle repairman who repaired and detailed our vehicle. Thank heavens, everything was done for free!

The bright-colored, richly decorated rickshaws are a true fashion parade. These wooden carts pulled by robust young men give an air of cheerfulness to the city. These are the taxis of Madagascar—deeply moving images, a mode of transportation from another era. For a few supplementary coins, these men run to satisfy the client. In spite of some apprehension, we tried this means of travel. Wow, what an exotic sensation! You understand that these chauffeurs, however peculiar, adore their trade, and that they would not change it for anything in the world. They detail their carts with love and determination so that they sparkle. During the evening, they hang an oil lamp on the front. That adds a sweet touch. Already, we are attached to these people, who are so warmhearted.

...Zebu thieves

It's necessary to get your bearings, to learn to court this new Madagascan land. Arriving in a new country is like courting a beautiful girl, learning her habits, her desires, her customs of life.

We set up our tent in a thorny landscape, on hard and rocky soil. An intangible sunset, and suddenly, in an instant, this scenery regains all of its splendor and beauty.

At daybreak, noises awaken us. We perceive about twenty people, dressed as warriors, armed with real spears, who are running across the bush land. An unbelievable sight! They are in pursuit of zebu thieves, representatives of the community of Bartabas, for whom it is inconceivable to marry a young woman without bringing her his share of stolen livestock.

...July 21, 2001: 10,000th kilometer

After several days on the road, we reach the gates of Isalo National Park, a natural park covering an area of 82,000 hectares [202,540 acres], composed of thick Jurassic sandstone that forms a heavily eroded massif, scored by deep canyons. This park offers a great diversity of ecosystems. We spend a day discovering lemurs, birds, plants of remarkable adaptations, and grandiose landscapes.

Immediately after leaving the park, we cross our 10,000th kilometer [6,213th mile]. How can we not call to mind this symbolic passage, even if it is only a numeral fixed in our heads between magnificent panoramas and intimate valleys? This enthusiasm is shared with the children met on these high plateaus. These are blessed places that crystallize with the passage of time. An inner force, perhaps even spiritual, pushes us onward, nourishes our desires and our doubts.

For several days, we have been traversing incredible villages. In the evening, in the seedy bars, tongues loosen up under the effect of rum. We are told incredible stories of the smuggling of precious stones. The Madagascan substratum abounds in riches. As soon as a deposit of sapphire is discovered, there is a rush, like at the time of the American gold rush. But the sanitary conditions must be even worse. People adore the intense feelings that radiate from such places.

"What remains yet and again is to run the world on our own."

Isalo Massif, Madagascar.

...Good night!

Sleeping in the homes of the locals remains a unique experience, even if the matter of rest is not always the best. This evening, we constitute the number-one attraction in a Madagascan village perched on the highlands. A multitude of children watch our every action and movement. There is no way of isolating ourselves to tidy up, to relieve ourselves, to eat. But what matters is that we are providing a free source of entertainment. We experience the most simple expression of comfort: a roof, falafa reed walls (derived from rivinola, a traveler's tree), and a raffia mattress. The shower? A simple can. The toilets? I won't even speak of the odors! Across the way, a seedy bar blares its music until 2:00 a.m. Waking up is assured by the crowing of the roosters. We could strangle them! At 4:00 a.m., it is the dogs' turn.... Phew, at 5:00 a.m., we slumber into a coma. But lo and behold, it's already six o'clock—time to get up! Enough already! That was refreshing!

...Madagascar, we love you

On the high plateaus, there is a world of dreams, of wide open spaces, of lands without owners. The sun illuminates the terraced rice paddies; the traditional villages consist of pretty mud houses. The sun-drenched landscapes reinforce the beautiful image of Madagascar. You can admire the hard work of mankind. The lands are well worked and well tended. The isolated and protected valleys give this region a dimension of austerity and of prosperity at the same time. In the distance, the aesthetically-pleasing summits catch the eye of the shrewd climber. The gray sheer walls are tempting. The invitation taunts you, doesn't it, Serge? Madagascar, we love you! You are our diamond. Madagascan women, your elegant hats render you even more beautiful. Your features are refined; your smiles take on the form of stars.

...Deeply distressing poverty

The more we advance, the darker the film that unrolls before our eyes. The contrast between the rich and the poor is distressing, heartrending. In our heads, a veritable mix of feelings is churning. In the countryside, the people die of starvation, caused by the lack of a balanced diet. The presence of humanitarian associations is often the only help. After years of battle against poverty, the results are there, quite visible. Whole villages have appeared where there was nothing, and thousands of destitute families have rediscovered a bit of human dignity by schooling their children and obtaining a job.

We continue to traverse hamlets and villages. Along the side of the roads, the children are in real danger because of the traffic. The adobe houses, the color of red earth, of red blood, are covered with thatched roofs. You get the feeling that everything could collapse with the slightest gust of wind. The poverty is more and more ubiquitous, but it does not, in any case, erase the kindness of an extraordinary people. The big hearts of the Madagascans continue to beat intensely with emotion. Everyone puts on the most beautiful smile for our passage, from the youngest to the oldest. Smiles coupled with sincere, warmhearted encouragement. What a beautiful message!

...Street children

Poverty and misery go hand in hand here. The places are saddened by the empty gazes of children who wander in the solitude of life. The streets are clogged, the odors are suffocating, and the traveling merchants try to survive as well as they can. Children rummage in the mountain of refuse that blankets the street. We are spectators of a cruel time. The children live in conditions that are unsuitable for their development. We are coming into contact with a merciless reality. Serge and I can and want to bear witness to this "real truth." By our slightly crazy trek, we want to ensure that the future of these very vulnerable children is brightened a bit. "Don't remain spectators; become doers for a more just world." This is the motto of a humanitarian organization. This is what we try to do in our modest way.

...Antsirabe

Antsirabe is a former thermal city fallen into disuse, but it has kept its outdated aura of the colonial period. Located at an altitude of 1,400 meters [4,593 feet], it is the coldest place in Madagascar. Unfortunately, the principal activity today is the rampant begging of young children. Kids barely two years of age run after the White man.... What future do they have?

In the days that follow, we cross a multitude of valleys. Ancient villages are nestled there. The houses and their painted balconies give beauty to this wild and savage land. For fifteen days, it's been raining and raining ...and we continue to advance along our long route. Everything is blurred into a dream, into a nightmare. In spite of the cold and the certainty of being cold, I try not to complain. Moreover, how would I have the right to do that? On these highlands, the whole world walks barefoot, practically naked. The people are numbed by the cold, but they do not have the time to listen to their states of mind. Then, in admiration, I greet each of them with a wave of my hand. Another moment of sharing.

...Fear of dying alone

The gates are thrown open before us: nature seems to be carrying out experiments with captivating and stunning results. But the hard reality of these people's lives is not at all in harmony with this permanent beauty. The poverty of the population tears at our hearts. It does not prevent smiles, which are permanent for them. There is no aggressiveness toward strangers; indeed, quite the contrary.

Curiosity engenders dialogue. A seated old man looks at me persistently. I must be pleasing to him. I approach him. With the hat that he holds in his hand, he salutes me. "I have no fear of growing old, because I have found wisdom in growing old, but I am afraid of dying alone," he tells me. He takes my hand; he lifts it to his cheek. I am moved by all this sentiment. "From now on, you will not die alone. At the bottom of your heart, you will carry a smile and the gaze of a White woman, which will go with you on your long voyage." The old man sighs. My remarks inspire this conclusion from him: "What a beautiful end to the story!" I get back on my motorcycle, while leaving behind one moment of life, one of many.

...At the heart of the shantytown of Antananarivo

In the capital, Antananarivo, the poverty saddens and shocks us once again. A social mosaic presents itself to us: vendors of cigarettes and odds and ends, furious taxi drivers, traffic jams, pollution, and always so many kids in the streets, left to take care of themselves, in rough, rudimentary conditions. Before our very eyes, we again find a little more of the misery of the world.

Anta, a Madagascan delegate of the humanitarian association that welcomes us, speaks to us about her people and the difficulties they must overcome. With her team, she accomplishes extraordinary work. She gives of her life, her sincerity, and her willpower to improve the lot of her own people. She works in the heart of the shantytown of Tana, and as a dynamic leader in a center for malnutrition, she raises the awareness of mothers. The undernourished children are welcomed into the day-care nursery and receive adequate and balanced nourishment and curative and preventive medical attention. But in order to educate, confidence must be established with all urgency. On each occasion, we come out again overwhelmed by these encounters. At the same time, it is a pure joy to meet these marvelous children, courageous in the face of their very precarious destiny.

...The local restaurants

The *hôtelies* [Madagascan diners] are small popular restaurants that you find along the road. The sanitation there is always questionable. Seated in a diner, I completely lose my appetite. No, decidedly, my stomach can't take it. The flies have been stuck for ages on the slabs of meat, the hens peck at the crumbs, the cats finish off the client's dish, and the famished dogs lurk around. My morale sinks; I, who am so fond of eating! But I must get hold of myself, I know that. Anyway, in the days that follow, Serge marks his territory with violent diarrhea....

Ilakaka, Madagascar: The sapphire city, a shantytown, many poor, some rich, some very rich ...

...A heavy blow in Trafalgar

Behold, it's already eighteen months that we have been plowing along across the world in search of the human heart. Today, we experienced a beautiful day: 58 kilometers [36 miles] of travel across lavish valleys, green rice paddies that burst forth under a radiant sun, the virgin hopes of freedom. This evening, we deviated a little from our route. Nine kilometers [5.6 miles] on a trail to find a setting vibrant with beauty, a reflection of wild tranquility that strangely reminds us of Canada. On the menu is fondue, raclette! The ambiance is muffled, the aromas enticing. We are mad with joy, even if, to be quite frank, the cheese is as indigestible as it can possibly be.

It's here that a health problem is going to hit me that will have serious consequences in the future. A little fatigued, I leave Serge to go take a shower. I walk more than 100 meters [328 feet] in total darkness. I open the door of the restroom hut; I feel like vomiting and I do. What a mess! Nevertheless, I take my shower. I am unnerved, because it is impossible for me to regulate the water temperature; the boiling water almost burns me alive. I leave. Suddenly I feel very cold. I slip on a mere pullover. I decide to dry my wet hair, but right next door, there is a strong gas odor that bothers me. I feel myself becoming weak. I manage to get as far as the bed. And then, thud, I pass out.... Serge discovers me in a coma, all my limbs stiff and immobile.

Later, when I wake up, I have the impression of having experienced the most frightening thing in my life. I was no longer in control of my body, of my mind; I was no longer myself.... My body was quivering, like a true disarticulated puppet. I was convulsing; my tongue was flip-flopping. I was howling with fear, because I was aware of my overpowering reactions. My howling fits must have been shocking. I was fighting to live, not allowing myself to slip into the other world. Inside of me, I felt a force that was helping me to pull through, but my body was no longer obeying me. My voice had changed into a deep male voice.... Fortunately, Serge, my love, was there. How good it was that he protected me like a loving, affectionate spouse. I was evacuated to Antananarivo. The crisis lasted three more hours. I begged Serge not to take me to the hospital, because I was afraid of the doctors' injections. And then, I felt my composure returning.

Anta, the delegate, lovingly sprang into action. We stayed overnight with her, but I remained anguished the entire night, with a deep-seated fear of never seeing the sun, the light of life, again. In the morning, I could not walk very well; my limbs were still stiff. We called Charlie, a female doctor who works for a charitable organization. She immediately put me at ease. Anta and Charlie are two marvelously comforting women.

Then suddenly, a new crisis. Around me, I felt a wind of panic. This time, hospitalization was immediate. Tests followed; I was under constant medical supervision. After a night of rest, my composure returned, and I gradually recaptured a bit of confidence in myself. After having left the hospital, I had another crisis situation. I was overcome by anxiety. Serge took me to have my head examined. He feared psychosis. What a grind for him, because it was evident I had become "insane!" The test results: the brain lacked tone following the coma. The most probable diagnosis was that I was suffering from cerebral malaria (neuropaludism). Serge called our doctor in Switzerland. He counseled us to have me undergo a scan, which we were able to do. Thank God, thank God, thank God, no permanent damage was detected! Over the following days, I regained my health.

I refuse to even consider that the "Run for Kids" could have ended here. I want to look at the future with serenity.

"I refuse to even consider that the 'Run for Kids' could have ended here."

Last boxing match... lost!

...*Attack of a boa*

A farmer invites us to his house. His garden notably shelters an extremely rare species: the chameleon of Madagascar. Our guide reassures us. Nature and animals live in harmony in this authentic environment. Serge is enthused; he photographs more and more. As for me, I am not very reassured. But God created a man and a woman; thank God he did that!

Our guide takes a boa in his hands. He invites Serge to do the same. This critter, more than 2 meters [6.5 feet] long, has settled in his arms, when suddenly, it begins to constrict more and more tightly. Instinctively, Serge tries to unwind it. But lo and behold, the boa launches an attack of rare violence and, with its two fangs, punctures one of Serge's eyelids. Then, with a sudden strike of its tail, it breaks open the skin of Serge's cheek. I scream; my heart beats wildly. Serge's eye pisses blood. I run like a crazed person to my motorcycle to find something with which to disinfect it. Serge regains his composure. Thank God, his eye is not pierced, but you can indeed make out the two holes in his eyelid.

One more time, we've had a stroke of luck. "You see, Nicole," Serge kids me, "having been a boxer in my youth has helped me know how to take some blows." Thanks for the joke, but I was still shaking nevertheless.

...After the incident

I had difficulty regaining my composure after this incident. Serge's eye looks bad, like that of a boxer after a match that turned ugly. Tonight, we'll sleep in the village of Andasibe. A former industrial center for wood, it presents false Western airs with its railroad restaurant as retro as it can be. It is here that you can see the star lemur, also known as an indri. It can reach 70 centimeters [27.6 inches] and weigh 6 kilograms [13.2 pounds]. It is the largest of the family. Its head is black, its body black and white, and its ears like those of a big bear cub.

At the end of this exciting evening, I unfortunately have a violent crisis in the restaurant, in front of about fifty people, and this despite my medications. This time, I do not fall into a coma. Again, there's panic everywhere, a shock for all the people present. Serge is distraught. Two French doctors witness the scene. For me, it's horrible, because I am completely lucid. I can indeed perceive the looks of the people. For about thirty minutes, I scream and my eyes are completely rolled back and dilated. The doctors reassure me, by telling me that what I am experiencing at this moment is traumatizing, but absolutely not dangerous. They maintain that I am suffering the side effects of the preventive treatment of malaria. Two hours will suffice to calm me down.

There are still five days to go on the journey across the island of Madagascar; five days of anguish that bring us closer to the next large city, where we should find the medicine that is supposed to be able to cure me.

Each day, we are in contact with our doctor. According to him and his colleagues specializing in tropical illnesses, I must have been a victim of a resistant form of cerebral malaria. The germs should disappear in the span of a month with the use of antibiotics.

We arrive in Toamasina (Tamatave), the number-one commercial port on the island. The streets and the causeways are literally warped. Rickshaws plow through the city in the midst of disintegrating, decrepit buildings that are eroded by the rains. But never mind that, what is important to us is that Toamasina (Tamatave) represents the hope of finding the eagerly awaited miracle medication.

... *Where does your cheese come from?*

There's a seaside restaurant at Toamasina (Tamatave). We see the sea again after long months of running. It's a simple restaurant that has a nice ambiance. The grilled fish are excellent. We are enjoying a delicious meal, because I am feeling better; we found the medicine. While leaving, Serge, being curious, catches sight of this inscription posted on the wall: "For your austral southern galas, as many raclettes as you want." Then he turns toward a distinguished gentleman who, we suppose, must be the owner of the establishment. The dialogue commences.

> Serge: "Hello. I have a question. Where does your cheese come from? Because I am a raclette specialist."
> The owner: "From Switzerland, my country of origin."
> Serge: "Oh, my, so do we! From what area?"
> The owner: "From Valais."
> Serge: "So do we, but where in Valais?"
> The owner: "From Sion."
> Serge: "No way; well, so do we!"

Nicolas, the owner, left Switzerland twenty-five years ago. He traveled the world as a restaurant chef. In spite of everything, he remains attached to his Valais. We've circled the world; his acquaintances are ours. It's a small world!

...The mortgaged forest

The Madagascan people expect so much of the future. But this future will be compromised unless measures are taken in the areas of communication, awareness, and education. Poverty, rampant population growth, and unchecked exploitation aggravate the downward spiral toward its fatal end. The culture of slash-and-burn, the bush fires, the demolition of the forest for charcoal, and even the recent sapphire rushes are all challenging the great balances of nature. This conversion into desert wasteland reduces the hope of agricultural development. At this pace, twenty to fifty years from now, the Madagascan forests will have disappeared. But how can you blame a peasant for cultivating, for providing heat, or for cooking with those things that he finds in his own environment?

...Spirituality

Ancestors occupy an important place in the daily life of the Madagascan people. They are respected, because they represent the roots of life. Homage is paid to them every day. In numerous circumstances, the deceased are invoked. Here, death is not perceived as an end, but rather as an obligatory transition. The Madagascan people have the conviction that the dead can help the living, that they can make life easier for them. Tombs are placed on a mountain. The more important the dead person's ethnic group, the more elevated his position on the mountain. Thus he can more easily communicate with the gods.

We leave Madagascar. The odometer shows more than 11,000 kilometers [6,835 miles]. The next leg of the journey: Cairo. In spite of the difficulties, our motivation remains undiminished.

Ephemeral beauty
Guard it and preserve it
Yonder is there
Perhaps a hidden secret?
Totally powerful and divine mistress of eternity

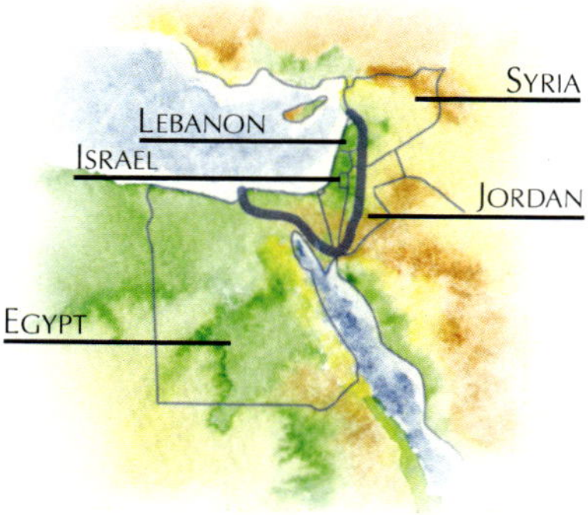

the Middle East

...September 25, 2001: Nairobi

We have a layover between the sky and the tower of glass in Nairobi. The people swarm in the animated alleys. The cloudiness is not conducive to smiles, nor to the courtesy of a hello. People's glances are fearsomely hard. Never had we experienced this in Africa. For us, danger lurks at every turn, at every crossroad. Everywhere, police officers are standing watch with pistols, billy clubs, and whips in their hands. It's a shocking contrast, given how calm Madagascar was.

By surprise and from behind, a street kid in rags tears off my plastic earring with a rare show of violence. I don't have time to react. Serge tries to catch him, but he has to come to a dead stop, because suddenly he feels as though he's being caught up in an ambush. The kid calculated his strike well, with a glass bottle in his hand. I remain flabbergasted. In the streets, a multitude of children sniff glue to survive, to forget loneliness. Here, daily existence does not belong to the weak. Nairobi will remain for us a synonym for the escalation of violence.

...Bureaucratic aberration

Arriving in a new country is like filling out a marriage application. It is disquieting; nervousness takes hold of us. Still these moments are magical. Upon arriving in Egypt, we must cross new cultural barriers; we must assimilate a new language; people's perception is different. An arrival by airplane in and of itself suggests some form of aggression. Everything is rushed.

In this time of turmoil following the events of September 11, 2001, we do not sense any animosity toward the foreigners that we are. On the contrary, the smiles are warm. We take a taxi. It rolls along at a lively pace. In the center of Cairo, you can feel the European influence. Huge illuminated billboards attest to the war being waged between Coca-Cola and Pepsi. Cairo, an incredible city of seventeen million inhabitants, will leave us dazed for a long time.

Swarming with people, this megalopolis is bursting with energy. Here there are disparate architectural details, Baroque facades, laundry suspended from the balconies.... The horns honk constantly, day as well as night.

Cairo is a labyrinth of cultures, of colors, and of smells. For us, the most difficult thing is to master Arabic. There is very little English spoken, so the matter of communication is rather a grind. The slightest detail has its importance. For example, it's impossible to decipher a bill. There is only one solution: to rely on others. I have the impression of being born a second time. We must learn everything; our reference points are left behind. The word for success: adapt.

A new journey into the silence of the Middle East begins. It is a delicious but frightening mixture. The glances of men toward a foreign woman are embarrassing, disturbing. However, what tranquillity to be able to move around without feeling the least danger! Isn't Cairo advertised as the safest large city in the world? In light of what we see, we are ready to vouch for this.

On the administrative level, it is a different story. Why do the border crossing areas almost always take on the look of a bureaucratic aberration? For an entire week, Serge has been trying to retrieve our motorcycle, in vain. Oh, all these forms! All in Arabic! Serge signs the papers without really knowing what he is doing. What a grind! Will we be able to continue to travel while constantly having to put up with so many impositions? The question is posed seriously. The logistics are really becoming complicated. It's an adventure within an adventure, but this one is so unpleasant. It's necessary to dig ever more deeply into the resources of our morale. One day, will these reserves run dry?

...The pyramids

Silence rules in this mythical place. There they are, in front of us, the three goddesses of eternity, majestically built. Aesthetics control the wisdom of man. We are in the presence of so much beauty. What a powerful feeling! It's a place of contemplation. The Sphinx watches over the silence of the

"Silence rules this mythical place."

Heat, dehydration, protection.

desert; the cat is charged with standing guard over the necropolis [city of the dead]. It is an homage to the past, to the present, and to the future. Men believed that death could be conquered, defied by the audacious labor of building these stones. A mythical zeal, an absolute belief.

...Nargileh circle

Our marathon resumes in Alexandria. This Mediterranean city doesn't really look like an Arabian city. A multiethnic mixture endows it with its distinctive character. One notices the superb rococo buildings, mementos of a luxurious epoch.

We observe the scenes of the street, the noisy bars. The nargileh circle ...is a place where men gather to smoke the shisha. The nargileh is a large water pipe. The principle consists of blowing very hard and consistently to make the water hum loudly in between thick curls of smoke. At first glance, one could think that this pipe has hallucinogenic virtues. But no, it's simply another method of smoking tobacco. For an Egyptian, smoking the shisha in the evening is an excellent means of having a social life, like drinking hot tea, like dreaming, like playing dominos. The women, however, stay at home.

This privileged moment offers us a poetic note, a bath of exoticism. 11,583 kilometers [7,197 miles].

...Among women

One woman completely veiled, letting her glance show through, refined by an application of black eyeliner, another wearing only a shawl to hide her hair, and yet another, enticing, in modern attire, all brush past one another simultaneously. And I am among them! Four women out on the same street, but where is the road of life going to take them?

...Gray dust

Gray dust: the Egypt that we are crossing lacks colors. They are effaced behind the trucks that belch out black smoke. Our run is punctuated by the unbearable honking of horns. Serge wades through refuse and manure. Never before had we seen such a demonstration of chaos and filth. Everywhere there is grease, rubble, trash of all kinds along the sides of the roads, around the houses, in the streets. The entrances to the cities are particularly vile. The majority of the buildings are decaying.

Driving is chaotic. Cautiously hunched over the handlebars, I speed along like all the cars. I feel like I'm entering a kind of spectacular bullfight. A powerless policeman regulates the traffic from the side of the roadway. In the middle of an intersection, a cart pulled by a tired donkey slows down the traffic. Say, Cleopatra, where are your reed-fitted boats with immaculate sails that floated in the wind and that glided across the all-powerful Nile in that golden age? It's a different time, with different mores.

Duration of time
Eternal
Source of terrifying
Energy
Road of the impossible
Traversing the great void

Of unique and historical sites
Following the road of thirst

Sentiments that are unworthy
Is it
Not
Alluring to discover the
Illustrious Desert of the Sinai lost between the past and the future?

...October 15, 2001: The Sinai Desert

Behold the Sinai Desert. Ouch! Already it's a vision of gray sand, of dust as far as the eye can see! Footsteps crack like a whip. The effect of the unrelenting heat immobilizes even the most daring. The eternal silence of lines without curves, long distances that wipe out even the most courageous. At the entrance to this new desert, I wonder. I hope that we won't do as the Hebrew people guided by Moses, who wandered around for forty years in this great void in search of the Promised Land. For us, *we* are the promised land. We cannot count on anybody or anything other than our instinct, our destiny.

We must find within ourselves a new equilibrium to confront the battle of straight lines without limits or curves. A fear emerges from the bottom of our guts. The desert, consumed at a rate of 12 km/h [7.4 mph], is truly a one-of-a-kind experience. Oh well, at least we know the rules of the game. Here, there is no life; the puff of wind is our only hope.

...Running toward near nothingness

Not a sound, except for Serge's breathing. The sweat drips to the bottom of his back. The beads of perspiration are transformed into an illusion—a desert mirage! Silence has become the master of my emotions. Stride after stride, it's nearly surrealistic to run toward nowhere, toward near nothingness. There's nothing on the horizon other than the horizon itself.... The contrast is striking between the ease with which my motorcycle runs at a steady pace and the unexpected, immeasurable suffering of Serge's steps. Each new meter brings this truth home. What is essential is to master the little things that may seem useless.

Frequently, with his mouth in the shape of a U, Serge ingests small amounts of water heated to 35°C [95°F]! The stakes are high. We all conceal our weaknesses in our own way. Victory belongs to those who believe in their capacity to overcome potential failure. But what does it matter: it's crazy how people are never in a good place. We now dream of rivers, canyons, forests with spicy scents that would carry us off toward a breath of cool air. In reality, the only breath of cool air consists of a wet kiss that soothes Serge as far as the next kilometer....

...To tame the imaginary

The desert is the suffocation of life. There are indeed some twigs that painfully attempt to survive, to nourish themselves from the light of day, but it is in vain. Our thoughts are sinking down into the uncertainty of the great void. They are drifting.

Nothing escapes us, not even a run-in between a grain of yellow sand and a grain of red sand.... We are on the lookout for the least unusual detail. But what is really unusual in this setting is still this strange runner, whose soles stir up the sand, the storm of life. He is the absolute master facing the test. Each time that we thrust out into a desert, I tell myself that we embody something of the ridiculous. The harshness of the landscape dies in the eternity of silence. We are alone facing our doubts, our joys, our rebellions. The desert holds a little bit of an escape up ahead. We must not turn back, but rather make a delight out of every moment of our progress. It's an action of our own choosing. It's a revelation of the self, as much physical as mental. It's about the respect of nature in all its splendor.

...Photo stop

I like to capture a look, a light smile behind my lens. A look conveys reality, the person's state of being. Often a deep helplessness is hidden there, but the camera is often a pretext for a relationship between the child and me. A wink of the eye and the game of seduction begins; the expressions explode. What could be sadder or more heartrending than the gaze of a child devoid of cheerfulness?

This magic box often renders a sublime look. I take pains not to appear intrusive. I am aware that I do not have the right to steal the soul

One of the most beautiful deserts: the Sinai.

of the people whom I photograph, their identity, their values. The faces that I have encountered and photographed have captivated our daily existence.

Running in order to encounter others and to find ourselves: this is the marvelous reward of a chosen dream. The Sinai Desert, Egypt—11,672 kilometers [7,252 miles]. One step, one kilometer after another, one day among so many others. It's not the easiest....

...The silence of God

This evening's scenery is anchored in the breath of life. We stop near an oasis. The oasis of bliss. The coffeepot whistles the song of the world, the silence of God. The water boils. The sacred mountains are sculpted by the wind of the desert. Pink, yellow, and red lights come dancing over the summits. It's a moment for contemplation, accompanied by the power and the immensity of the place. It is the warrior's resting place in this poet's corner.

I never cease admiring and listening to the silence of the desert, which gently nods off to make room for the twilight. Serge smokes his pipe. He thinks intensely about his two children. I support him with my thoughts. Clara is sixteen years old today. We love her with the intensity of our fire, which is magnificent. This evening, it fills in for you, Clara. We speak to it and ask it to protect you, as well as your brother, along the path of life. We fall asleep under the stars while clutching one of them to our heart. A thousand star kisses to you!

...Vision on the road

Silence reigns forever and ever, when suddenly we are distracted by the harmony of a fleeting image: in the middle of the great void, we gaze upon two Bedouin women in black tunics and embroidered veils that float in the wind. They gesture to us. They want to offer us water in exchange for money. We greet them with a friendly smile; we wave, but nothing more. I invite Serge to continue on our journey....

So surprised, I didn't know how to act in the presence of these women—two Bedouins with their remarkable expressions. It was an image of a rare beauty that I didn't know how to capture, to my great regret!

...The greatness of a one-of-a kind place

The Sinai is a point of convergence for the continents and a place of separation for the seas. It is mountainous and arid. There's something terrifying about it. During the day, the heat here is overwhelming; at night, it's bitterly cold. We live in a great infinity. The desert threatens. We pass through now to the heart of the mountains. It's beautiful, oh so beautiful, as rarely seen here! There's neither uniformity nor monotony. The highest peaks rise before us: Mount Moses and Mount Saint Catherine.

Few human beings live in the desert. Aside from the cities on the coast, the peninsula is inhabited by a Bedouin community that survives thanks to palm trees and date palms. They band together around water sources. Mythical and alluring figures, the Bedouins are the lords of the sands. They are also breeders of sheep, black goats, and dromedaries. In winter, they host tourists, or they go farther off to cultivate vegetables, oranges, and dates. The oil fields and road construction also offer some possibilities for work. The children go to school for two to three years, after which they help their parents, primarily by selling jewelry. During this time, the women care for the herds.

...The Saint Catherine Monastery

This old monastery is nestled at the bottom of a narrow valley, at an altitude of 1,500 meters [4,921 feet]. It is surrounded by the desertic mountains. It is a sublime place, where the spirits whisper. The Saint Catherine Monastery is an orthodox center that brings together twenty-two monks of diverse nationalities. Monastic life, which started here in the sixth century, continues uninterrupted. The monks dwell in isolated cells in the mountain. The monastery is not tied to any superior or to any patriarch. The monks form a church unto itself.

...Mount Moses

Serge could not refrain from running in "conquest" of the legendary Mount Moses, which culminates at an altitude of more than 2,000 meters [6,562 feet]. Moses is said to have received the Tablets of Law inscribed with the Ten Commandments there. Upon his return, Serge shares his impressions with me. From the pinnacle, he witnessed the setting of the sun. The view extended over the entire Sinai Peninsula, as far as the Gulf of Aqaba. At night, he came back down by a stairway of three thousand steps, cut into the rock by the monks.

...Encounter with Mary Magdalene

Accidentally taking a wrong turn on the road does have its reward: we meet Mary Magdalene, an atypical nun, at the bend of a sinuous path, in this narrow and deep valley. This woman is covered by a long black tunic. She's wearing a white cloth on her head. She leans on a pilgrim staff, and an old faded bag hangs on her back.

Sister Mary Magdalene has been a recluse, all alone in this desert, for seventeen years. With her own hands and from the native granite stones, she constructed her little chapel, as well as her house. She admits that sometimes solitude weighs upon her. She would like for the church to agree to let another nun come to keep her company. Twice a month, she walks as far as the village of Saint Catherine, where she buys provisions. I offer to carry her bag. She stops, surprised and quite moved; she tells me that in the span of seventeen years, this is the first time that someone has made her such an offer.

She continues to chat and recount her incredible stories. At a place twenty minutes from here, a Bedouin strangled his own sister because he had impregnated her. Of course, it was all her fault! Anyway, Mary Magdalene is not fond of the Bedouins. Even though she has lived side by side with them for so many years, they continue to ask her for money and cigarettes.

On the other hand, never has the idea occurred to them to ask her how she is getting along.

She offers another example. Thanks to collected water, Mary Magdalene cultivates grape vines. Unfortunately, they are regularly eaten by the black goats. One day, a Bedouin is said to have shouted at her, "Mary Magdalene, you have to buy glue and put it on the grape bunches; in this way the goats will remain stuck to them forever!" Serge offered to fill up her bag with 10 kilograms [22 pounds] of food. For two hours, he carries her provisions, the equivalent of enough food to survive for a month. This fortuitous encounter fills us with bliss.

The Sinai Desert is now behind us. I am bursting with love for this holy land. We leave behind a bit of our heart. 12,065 kilometers [7,497 miles]. Good-bye, Egypt; hello, Jordan!

The Sinai: left, right... straight ahead!

Just never
Overlook the truth
Rare beauty of eternity
Drive ever onward; do not deny the obvious
And note that this is a magical and
Nonpareil place in the world

...November 8, 2001: Between two seas

While making our entry into Jordan, a country wedged between two seas, the one Red and the other Dead, we follow in the footsteps of Lawrence of Arabia. We succumb to the charm of the citadel of Petra: each stone was hewn by the madness of man.

There's also charm in an encounter during our crossing of the desert of Wadi Rum. We befriend a family of Bedouin livestock breeders. Here, it's sweetness of life that prevails. What a lesson in humility!

In the capital, Amman, two worlds live side by side. The modern women at the wheel of their cars cross paths with those who are veiled and pulling a donkey.

...Dānā

Dānā has preserved its picturesque aspect. This village is perched on a hill overhanging a narrow valley and deep gorges. Once again, we are fascinated by such intense, concentrated scenery. Two Bedouins, in the way of welcome, offer us hot tea with infinite kindness. A meal follows under a tent. Wisdom and a mastery of simple things are shared sentiments.

In Jordan, altitude differences are masters. The steepness of the slopes deters the most daring. The fragility of the infinitely small lost in the immensity fascinates us. This evening, the sky is purple and mauve. Serge serves me a strong sweet tea on a slow and sweet evening. A curious Bedouin pays us a visit. Silence dominates the expanse where the dry twigs of a fire crackle and dance on the surrounding walls. There's nothing left to do except to stretch out our sleeping bags and to make note of these few hours in the eternity of the desert under the benevolence of the heavenly canopy.

...Few smiles

The Jordanian population seems more reserved to us than the Egyptian population. The glances are distrustful. In certain circumstances, we feel that Westerners are frankly not welcome. Relationships are cold. There is a distance between us, a distance, but never aggressiveness. I have never perceived the slightest smile on the faces of the women. Is it simply modesty in the face of the image that we represent? At this moment, the country seems to be impervious to the outside world; you hardly meet any tourists.

...Short detour via Syria

What is there to say about Syria? We cannot pretend to understand this country, because our trek here only amounts to about 150 kilometers [93 miles] of our journey. Along the edge of the road, the atmosphere is a little sad. The houses resemble dying carcasses in the gray dust. The people appear poorer than in Jordan; there are more beggars, especially women who live in difficult conditions. Young children work in the street selling knickknacks. Our journey unfolds to the rhythm of honking horns.

The whole country is under high military alert. We must resort to setting up our camp among all the rubble and filth. It does not take long for the soldiers to show up and point their submachine guns in our faces. The darkness adds to our fear. Fortunately, their intentions are not bad. The soldiers have never experienced such a situation. Just think about it—strangers who choose to sleep in such a vile corner! A senior officer speaks to us in French. He recommends that we leave this place, because strange things happen around here. We continue to negotiate. After a while, the soldiers agree to protect us for the entire night.... We promise them that we will leave the place at dawn. Thus, everything returns to normal. Fully reassured, we fall asleep like babies, despite the icy cold. 12,622 kilometers [7,843 miles].

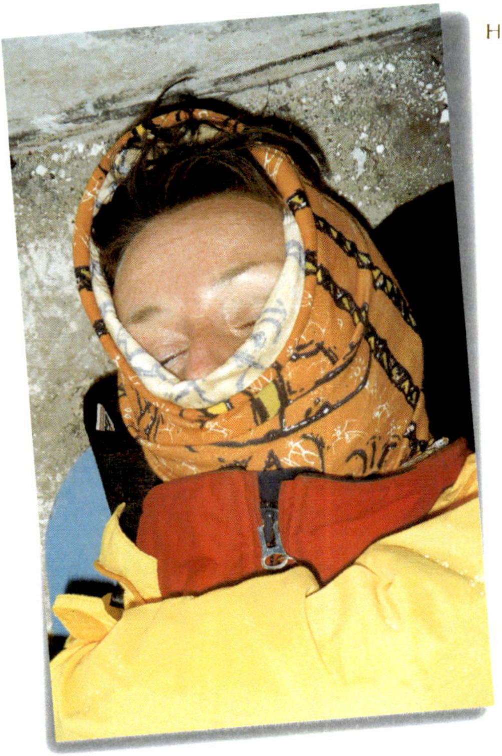

Hot, cold... it matters little; I'm sleeping.

Little glimmer of hope that
Elucidates despair
Braving life
Amid harmony
Never
Open the door to helplessness
Never leave me in dismay

...Soon it'll be Christmas in Lebanon

The border crossing between Syria and Lebanon unfolds calmly and uneventfully, without corruption. We are accustomed to different, more eventful customs negotiations during our border crossings. Numerous are the Lebanese who welcome us. This signifies a broader spirit of open-mindedness than we have experienced until now. In the distance, we see snow-covered mountain peaks. Winter is gently settling in, making room for the cold and for the rain that slaps us in the face. The trees unveil their rich autumnal colors; the clayey soil of the fields has been plowed as far as the eye can see.

The most beautiful feeling of our first night spent in Lebanon is what we experience in the Christian quarter. Christmas is approaching: the store windows are illuminated and richly decorated. For ten minutes, we are glued in front of one of them, staring wide-eyed, just like the children that we still are. We secretly hope for a beautiful Christmas gift.... And then, there are these mixed scents, the aromas of coffee and hot bread. In the restaurants, we notice couples holding hands in a charming picture of life. After two months spent in Muslim countries, we have withdrawn into ourselves a bit. We felt the effects of a lack of life—a way of thinking that isn't like ours. But obviously, we respect these other values. We don't have a monopoly on the best values. To travel is, first of all, to tolerate.

...*Snowstorm*

On the mountains close to Beirut, we encounter our first snow of the "Run for Kids." The motorcycle is in trouble, and so am I! As for Serge, his race has more and more in common with ice-skating, to such a degree that we resolve to return to our point of departure, since the mountain pass that we would have to cross is too heavily covered in snow. A quasi-polar cold accompanies us for several days. We make our advance through natural settings that are certainly magnificent, but diabolically testing. The silence adds to the ambiance, having become, at the same time, heavy and enigmatic. This is not the time to admire the famous cedars of Lebanon!

...*Traveling*

The more you travel, the more you become aware of the lack of tolerance of humans toward humans, of the lack of respect toward nature. And then, religions often divide instead of uniting. The world turns too quickly. This overly rapid evolution weakens the fulfillment of so many human beings. Not all humans have the means of remaining masters of their emotions, of their responsibilities. Travel provides the freedom of surrender, of exaltation. It leads us up the slopes of intoxication. The realities that we confront place us on the tracks of life. There are only two possible paths: one track guides us toward what is right, the other toward uncertainty. Our steps, our convictions guide us in the direction of the wind. Traveling at our own rhythm is putting us in a position of constant soul-searching.

The year 2001 is drawing to a close, and our planet is becoming more impoverished at an alarming rate. Just look at the lands we've crossed, at the many faces humiliated by daily suffering! Just look at the children dying of hunger, of cold, of grief, carrying on a daily battle for a place in mountains of filth! Just look at the women fighting for their identity, mutilated by religious or social convictions, by taboos! Just look at the unjust conflicts that castigate the people! The people only ask to be free, to live in peace.

...December 2001

On the outskirts of Beirut, the sky sinks like lead to the sea. About a dozen scouts take up Serge's stride to accompany us to the center of the city. We also join up with Lebanese journalists, as well as a few of their colleagues who have come here expressly from Switzerland.

As Christmas dawns, there's nothing but effervescence, with decorations and garlands appearing and turkeys roasting. The expenditures are extravagant. Christmas symbolizes family, love, sharing, celebrating. But on the other side of the world, simply a little more distant on the geographical map, battles are raging, old men flee, children are maimed, women are without defense. It's almost Christmas....

At home in Switzerland, the children are preparing to unwrap their gifts, and the adults are preparing the festival meal. But then why, on this Christmas, will there not be decency and tolerance? Serge and I look at the moon; we pray, because a child should not die without experiencing laughter, playing, dreams, and love. I would like for people everywhere on the continent to stop a moment and to have a fervent thought for all the people who will not experience the festivities. For them, Christmas will be a day like any other day: a day of cold, of hunger, and perhaps...of death.

...Nadim, fourteen years old, prisoner

The place is dismal. Children, adults, and elderly people are crammed into this prison north of Beirut. What a bizarre "privilege" to be the first female authorized to enter into this exclusively male place!

The imposing entry door is opened. Behind us, many secondary doors slam shut with a noise heavy with meaning. A strong odor pervades this place. And then, it's the moment to exchange first glances with the prisoners. I am tense. What is the correct attitude to adopt in circumstances such as these? To remain natural, that's what suits me best.

To a group of about ten prisoners assembled around us, Serge suggests the game *pompes* [a game of muscle exercises]. They take to it enthusiastically. Then a young boy advances toward Serge. He hands him a picture of his own inspiration. The subject: a bird in a cage.... In a broken voice, Nadim, a fourteen-year-old, says these words: "I drew this bird in a cage because *you* are free and *I* am not. I won't be free for a long time...." We are speechless; our jaws drop. It's incredible to imagine that this adolescent has only a shattered life on his horizon. However, it's not our place to judge. We can only sympathize with the misfortune of Nadim, perpetrator of the murder of his own father. It was a crime of honor: his father had raped Nadim's sister. One rape, one murder, one prisoner: three tragedies.

Nadim, you alone can judge your deed. In any case, your bird in a cage will have a special place in our personal belongings, and each time we glance at your drawing, we will fondly think of you.

Message from a child locked up in a Beirut prison for having killed his father, who had raped his sister: "To Serge! If the days pass and we should not meet again, this small caged bird will remind you of your trip to the Roumieh Prison where we met! Nadim, December 10, 2001."

Insufferable images
Never
Deny the suffering of the
Impoverished people who
Are truly the people abandoned by the world

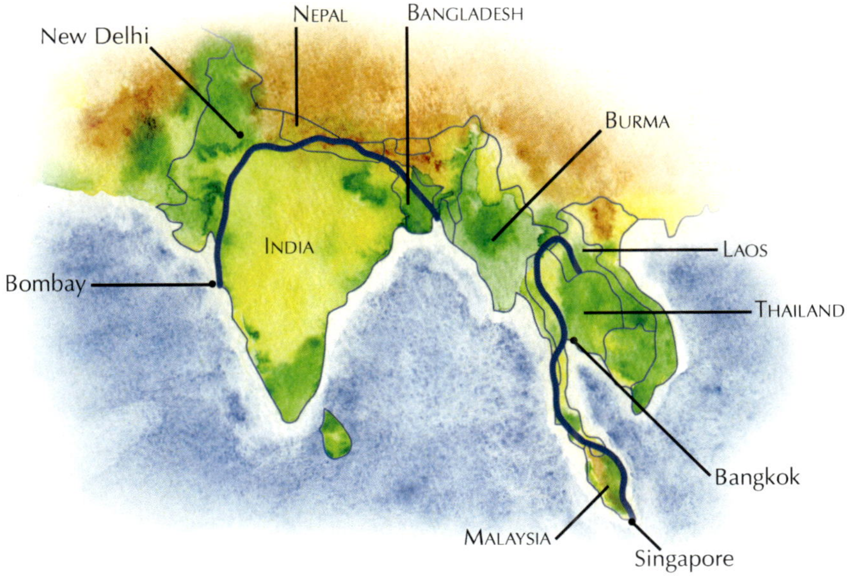

Asia

...A mob of images

A great number of poor, a few rich, a "bouquet garni" of religions, a few millennia of history, and an atomic bomb. The thrill seekers will not be disappointed. It's a departure into the unknown, a start on new adventures. For me, there's more apprehension than usual. India troubles me, will always trouble me. In a few seconds, we will touch down into a mob of images, into the true core of life: Bombay, India.

...Bombay, fifteen million inhabitants

Our first contact with India takes place with tactfulness. It is five o'clock in the morning; Bombay is asleep in its dreams. But an initial shock: hundreds of people sleep right on the ground, their bodies nearly naked. In the streets, the old London-style buses—vestiges of the English presence—drive about. The colonial houses give an anachronistic character to the city. At first glance, Bombay fascinates and frightens.

...Feminine elegance

It's life within life, a permanent beating of the heart. Nothing but colors. The women are of a bewitching beauty, with an incredible dignity. They wear their saris (traditional garments) with elegance. They walk through the mob with joy and gracefulness; nothing stops them. They hold their bodies, their heads erect. They are beautiful and majestic.

Our motorcycle is still stuck in customs. Hassles forevermore! It's an indescribable, useless strain. However, we know that this is part of the journey.

We make use of this long wait by immersing ourselves a little more in the ambiance that reigns over a main square in this neighborhood. The people stroll around. As a bonus, we enjoy a magnificent sunset. It is an enchantment of luminous smiles, of faces of rare beauty. And in addition, the children are irresistible! They are the symbol of life, of assured continuity.

How can one resist these smiles bursting with mischief? Serge smokes his pipe like a wise man, and suddenly two small kids climb on his knees. They want to have fun with the stranger. These are irresistible moments. Now a flock of kids rushes up. The passersby are amused by the spectacle.

...*Christmas 2001: Luxury and poverty*

It's Christmas Eve.... An old, hunched-over lady strolls in the street. No one acknowledges her in the least. The poor people are deprived of everything. Here, each one forges ahead in his or her daily routine. Poverty rubs shoulders with luxury. The rich are really rich; the poor are really poor. This seems to be in their nature. This difference between social classes is shocking. On the basis of our own values, we could re-create the world at every intersection, at every turn of the road. The beggars are ubiquitous, but never aggressive. Even if we don't give them anything, sometimes the outline of a smile forms on their faces. We must find a good balance in order not to disappoint.

...*Moments of life*

Serge has left again for the customs office. I decide to wander in the teeming streets, filled with alarming contrasts. I take a seat at a sidewalk café. I order a fresh juice. That done, I capture the raw emotions close up. I don't miss a single instant of the scenes of life that unfold before me—the true spectacle of life. Contrary to my anxieties, to my prejudices, this first contact with India fills me with euphoria.

Just across from me, a merchant of dreams offers silk scarves for sale. The scarves reflect the multiplicity of the colors of India. I look at him, and we make eye contact. A woman passes by. She greets me with a smile that could rouse the dead. I feel hypnotized by the intensity of her gaze. Here, the women are the goddesses of the earth, the doves of the sky.

...*A faded rose*

The veritable scourge that leaps to our eyes: the street children, left to themselves. They live on garbage and breathe the fumes of pollution all day long. They are defenseless. Yet, in spite of that, their faces reflect the charm of generous childhood!

A young girl with ebony hair and a sweet smile follows me down this street teeming with suspect odors. She asks for my first name; she hands me a faded rose. I cannot resist so much tenderness. I go to buy her a packet of candies. My shell cracks a bit, but I don't give her any money. She gives me a kiss. I have difficulty holding back my tears. I have to run away. The people are totally irresistible.

...*On the road*

We are leaving Bombay today. A motley crowd strolls the chaotic and jam-packed streets. It's fascinating and repulsive in turns. It's not easy to force one's way through with a motorcycle in the midst of so many carts operated by hand or drawn by horses. Serge runs in a disorderly manner. The women, draped in saris, wear fresh jasmine in their braided hair. The beggars grab at the passersby to obtain a coin. The men chew betel that they spit in red squirts, painting stripes on the sidewalks and asphalt. The spectacle is constant. It's a trying first day at 34°C [93°F]. We have earned our ticket to India!

...*January 1, 2002: Traveling, traveling ...*

We are nomads of the road, from the comfort of stopping in the evening to the exaltation of departing in the early morning. We ask ourselves: do we have to follow the path of our dreams? A dream for a good cause? After thousands of kilometers over this scorched earth in search of the smiles of children, of the elderly, in search of emotions, those of others and our own, our thoughts are absorbed by the meaning given to the pursuit of our journey. A new year begins.

"The people are totally irresistible..."

BUT...between Bombay and New Delhi, there are trucks twenty-four hours a day.

...Infernal road

We follow the dorsal fin of the country that connects Bombay to New Delhi by a road of infernal traffic. It is an incredible calvary! Good God, it's dangerous! What's more, there is construction that considerably slows down the flow of traffic. This has a bit of the feel of a corridor of death.... Moreover, today, an accident claimed twenty-five lives. For Serge, it's like Dante's *Inferno*. You breathe in exhaust fumes, filling your entire lungs. But thank goodness, for once the truck drivers are not fanatics! They respect us.

The deeper we travel into the interior of the country, the more we become conscious of the fact that we are dealing with a country of contradictions. We pass from happiness to the sordid, from ecstasy to pain. The people walk barefoot on the earth scorched by the sun. India is troubling, difficult to define for the moment. The gap is too big to comprehend. It's a mixture of scorn and grace that emanates. We are compelled to respect what we see. It's necessary to utilize the weaponry of words and images to express the social conditions of the people.

I feel like I'm a character in a comic strip. Do you want to see the real scenes of life, images laid bare? Then you have to come here. The roads of India bring together the most unbelievable images. I have never before seen anything like it. Hundreds of people perform the same ritual every morning at the same place, at the same moment. Scattered or aligned on the sidewalks, so many "do their business" with their butts in the air, letting their yellowish excrement drip in front of us without the least restraint.... The children bluntly squat with their butts resting on their own excrement. It's the carousel of life and multiple odors....

Although these scenes might be downright shocking, this spectacle moves me when I think that we, Westerners, try to find a tree, a place that gives us a sense of security in order not to suffer the embarrassment of being seen....

...The perception of the people

I wander in the animated, polluted streets. I have mixed feelings. I am at times irritated in the face of so much misery. I have the impression of walking along an endless ribbon of poverty. We have to learn to conduct ourselves differently when confronted with so much human distress. In spite of everything, the people seem to be in a good mood, as they go about their daily life. We move about in a deeply distressing universe. A master word dictates our steps: humility. There are so many things to learn from watching others.

The people are curious, interested in the motorcycle and our gear. They seek to understand our voluntary endeavor. The questions gush forth, with respect and intelligence. Sometimes, stopped at the side of the road, we have the impression of giving a press conference. It's always necessary to be well prepared, giving so much of our time and our energy. It's not always easy, but it's more worthwhile to be receptive. Solitude doesn't exist on this road of thirst. It's also the first country where anyone asks why we're running. And then something unheard-of happens! A family gives us some rupees so that we can treat ourselves to lodging for the night. Another Indian, not very well-off, paid for our two meals at noon. What an unexpected situation! We are rather embarrassed. It's as if the world were a bit topsy-turvy.

...Haircut and shave

Sometimes, we want to hole up like rats, no longer going out, just closing the door of our room, saying good-bye, see you tomorrow. The atmosphere can easily become burdensome, full of contradictions. Actions and gestures are watched closely, to the smallest detail. I even blow a fuse, for Christ's sake! The alleys of India are always crammed, streaming with colors, teeming with life. And the odors, oh my, the odors!

We enter a sordid neighborhood. Everywhere there are traveling merchants, people who urinate on the sidewalks, spitters who stripe the road, and the dying right there on the bare ground, forsaken by everyone. And then, suddenly, in the midst of this vile setting, there's a pretty flower shop, an orange juice vendor. While strolling around, we look for a barber. The choices are many, not that we were expecting a "Jacques Dessange" salon.... It's the first step that's difficult. Darn it! In any case, we don't have a choice. A luminous sign attracts our attention. Everything takes place in the street, on the sidewalk. So we might as well accept being part of the spectacle! A stocky barber, with a handlebar mustache, welcomes us with a big smile. He invites Serge to sit down and prepares some outdated "instruments of torture." Oh no, I wouldn't want to be in my husband's seat! But lo and behold, the work is done cheerfully. And wouldn't you know: everyone comes to watch. Serge plays his role as a circus clown. The people laugh: two strangers here... it's difficult to believe!

The cut and shave take an hour. The barber pampers Serge in every sense. The final result is surprising, especially for the modest sum of 90 Swiss centimes [about 72 cents]....

...Ahmedabad

After having traversed Baroda, a city in the western part of India, we're here in Ahmedabad. At the turn of the century, the Muslims considered this city the most beautiful city in the world. For my tastes, they exaggerated a little.... It's here that Gandhi settled upon his return from South Africa. He founded his ashram here in 1917. Ahmedabad was the principal center of resistance to the English. 13,447 kilometers [8,356 miles].

...The man without a name

India is surprising, exciting, fascinating. The scenes of daily life are beyond us. A shaggy-haired man of an indeterminate age, in rags, his bare feet cracked, holds some intestines, some guts, in his hands. In the blink of an eye, he devours them in front of us like a wild beast would do.... Completely repulsed by this compelling and stupefying image, we continue on our way....

To speak of roads in India is to speak of truck traffic, pollution, honking horns, accidents, sacred cows, thousands of pedestrians, motorcycles, bicycles, goats, monkeys, elephants, and sometimes camels. Thousands of people live or survive alongside the roads. We come into contact with them every day, and yet, could we truly get used to this? Certainly not. But that, too, is part of life.

...Difficult exchange

Only 3 percent of the indigenous Indian population speak English. It is consequently difficult to communicate. India has fifteen official languages. Around four thousand unofficial dialects exist—enough to get lost. Only one solution remains: to communicate with gestures. I have become a perfect imitator. But I'm not going to tell you about the comical gestures! When you pose a question to an Indian, he responds by moving his head in all directions. So, is it yes, or is it no? You never know. But the beauty of the gesture is still there....

Roads clogged starting
At dawn
Just as I wind my way down the
Avenues with caution and determination
Sidewalks of shame
Truffled [filled] with
Human misery
Along with Serge, in unison, we are exposed to a
New reality of the human condition

...January 20, 2002

Rajasthan is a vast, arid region, a true desert. More than fifty-five million inhabitants reside in this territory, which is two-thirds the size of France. The population is essentially rural, and all the castes are represented. The colors play an ever-changing symphony, based on the mood of the sun. We enter a universe of sweetness and gentleness. It's a tranquil landscape composed of hills covered with magnificent trees. Serge runs in rhythm with the changing slopes. We make our way to the heart of Rajasthan.

...Beautiful Udaipur

We arrive via the clogged arteries and turn into the narrow streets, thirsting for life and color. The houses are bleached with lime and have balconies and terraces on the roof. They give the appearance of a tranquil life. Udaipur immediately appears to be a relaxing city. Moreover, it is cradled by history. The temples, as well as their occupants, the Sadhus, fascinate us. These Sadhus are great sages, esteemed as saints by virtue of their spiritual knowledge and their exemplary conduct. These religious beggars have an appearance that is often eccentric.

A Sadhu in India.

Daybreak. From a terrace, I contemplate the morning awakening of the city. In the distance, the mists dissipate over the lake. Planted on an island is the prestigious palace of the Maharajah. He is said to be bankrupt. Rumor has it, he no longer possesses anything other than a Rolls-Royce to turn others pale with envy...along with two old luxurious Cadillacs, 150 servants, an elephant, and a private hotel in London.... So, long live the bankrupt!

Unquestionably, Udaipur is one of the most beautiful cities we have traversed since our departure.

...Pushkar, 14,000th kilometer

Pushkar is yet another wonder! This city of Rajasthan is a veritable jewel, a masterpiece! The colonial architecture dominates. The houses are white, inundated with light. Situated close to a lake, this place exudes a diabolical charm. Having arrived here, as if by magic, you forget who you are, and where you come from. All the beauty of the world emanates from this city. A haven of peace after days of frenzy at every moment.

Fourteen thousand kilometers [8,699 miles], stride upon stride, and now, what treasures are stored! We move forward on a road that is often demanding. It sets the rhythm of our daily life. A race through time—our time.

...One more leg of the journey

The sun rises over the city with its slumbering vestiges, its lost illusions. The people stretch out after their bad night spent on the sidewalks of shame, of distress. The women sweep with such gusto that the air becomes opaque with dust. The children "do their business" in the midst of the confusion. Deafening traffic jostles at the intersection: vehicles loaded with merchandise, minibuses packed with peasants, both men and women, leaving for the fields. There are as many continually honking horns as there are vehicles going around the constant flow of mopeds, motorbikes, and rickshaws. Skillfully, the drivers authorize themselves to make acrobatic forays onto the sidewalks. It's hard to even move; it's a traffic jam.

A truck hits my trailer and damages the back license plate. As an excuse, the road hog laughs.... I'm exasperated. Out of rage, I dismount my motorcycle and kick the blue truck. And then I regain my senses.... I think of my papa, from whom I inherited this temperament.... Like father, like daughter! By battering my license plate, I have the feeling that it is my dad who has been attacked. Oh, Papa, I miss you! However, I find that our relationships are enriched and are more moving, when the people we love are not close at hand. They are for us, for me, companions on the road.

...The weight of tradition

India does not reveal itself spontaneously to the foreigners who visit. Here, the weight of tradition marks all aspects of social and daily life. It's very perceptible. Now and then, you have the impression of experiencing an initiatory voyage stamped with spirituality. "In India, if you do not pray, you have lost," writes Henri Michaux. It's true that this vast land is equipped with a spiritual and religious mechanism very different from ours. The religions here are mixed together. It's impossible for us to know with which denomination the people whom we encounter are affiliated. Besides, it's perhaps better not to try too hard to understand. India is mystical, period.

Perhaps we are even perceived as spiritual leaders. A lot of people believe that we are fulfilling a mission by traveling around in this manner. There is respect given with regard to our fashion of travel. Someday, we might be taken for the new sacred cows of India....

...Female slaves

The living conditions of women in the countryside are frightfully hard. The majority receive a meager education, to put it lightly. The status of women is established from birth; girls are considered a burden. Their status is akin to slavery. They are the ones who carry the bundles of wood and the water buckets, the ones who perform the thankless duties, who prepare the meals, and who bear the brunt of daily tasks.

Suddenly, we are shouted at by this woman who must have briskly attained eighty years of age. She is breaking up stones, using a heavy sledgehammer. I approach her without any abrupt movement. Her face is dusty, shy, and wrinkled to a depth that says volumes about her long existence. For quite some time, this woman has been old enough to rest, to be supported by her relatives. But no, each blow of the sledge represents her life, her history, her status. I hand her some rupees. She categorically refuses. I am amazed by so much nobility, but deep down in my heart, I know that I cannot leave without giving her this money. I leave it a few meters from her in order not to offend her. This old woman inspires in me the greatest respect, the greatest humility.

...Tie game at Uttar Pradesh

We are indeed far from a fairy tale! After the nonchalance of Pushkar, we plunge anew into the sordid, into the pain, into the "horn-honking mania," into the suffocation from trucks that spit black smoke with every acceleration. Everywhere there are people, pigs, sacred cows, filth, and an infernal, milling throng. Sometimes, this continuous commotion becomes unbearable. People cling to the buses like prisoners in a Black Maria [paddy wagon]; others spit out the windows. Having experienced a well-formed spit cross my face, I can assure you that it's disgusting! There's nothing refined, nothing aesthetically pleasing about it.

We cannot take a step without dozens of people riding on Serge's heels and thousands of bicycles dive-bombing the back wheels of the motorcycle. Serge stops only a moment to wipe his brow, to drink some water, or to tell me something, and already it's like a beehive. India is at our feet, under our nose; she encircles us, and we can't even move the smallest eyelash anymore. Our living space has been invaded; they cruelly deprive us of oxygen. I sometimes feel that we are going to be trampled to death. There's no respect for personal space. It's as if India wished she could get into our shorts....

Morale-wise, I've hit rock bottom like nowhere else. I am at the end of my rope. I am aware that the coming days will be identical: India will not change for us, and it can hardly change us. The end result: it's a tie! Therefore, "Run for Kids" goes on!

...The Taj Mahal

The Taj Mahal is one of the most renowned monuments in the world. It's a dazzling and almost surreal sight. A mausoleum of white marble appears at the far end of a long garden. It towers up with elegance, which gives it a colossal feel. We are totally overcome with emotion. The Taj Mahal is dedicated to love, a love that the emperor lost. Devastated by grief, he made a vow to construct a monument in memory of his dearly departed. Since no architect in the kingdom was capable of conceiving such a project, he summoned the most renowned Persian architect. Then he killed the latter's fiancée, so that together they could share the same terrible grief. It was in the intensity of this grief that the Taj Mahal was supposedly conceived.

...It was bound to happen

It was bound to happen due to repeated anarchic and acrobatic driving. Once again, a car cuts in too abruptly after having passed a truck. It hits

Serge square on. He falls on the burning asphalt, with deep skin abrasions, bruises, contusions, and a hairline fracture of the elbow.

Far more than this incident, which could have been far more serious, it's the reaction of the people that astounds us, even incenses us. Imagine the situation. The road hog doesn't even stop; however, someone inside the car turns around. It takes only a few seconds for a crowd to form, dozens of people. Serge is on the ground. We hear laughter and chuckles, but nobody offers to help. For them, it's a complimentary scene from the movies! We disinfect the wounds, then Serge rides along on the motorcycle as far as the next village. We are angry, disgusted. We have but one desire: to stop the race. We long to flee from such a sea of inhumanity. How fragile our existence is!...We are fed up with it, totally fed up!

Nevertheless... we will return to finish this leg of the journey three days later!

There's nothing better than a stay in India to test your physical and emotional endurance. Well, then, I can honestly admit, I've reached the limits of my endurance concerning acceptance. For some time now, I have been feeling as if I were in prison, admittedly a prison without bars. We are no longer master of our movements, of our expressions, of our own privacy. We are spied on, examined under a microscope. Looking doesn't suffice; they touch us constantly. I no longer feel that I am a woman; I have become a vulgar piece of merchandise exposed to hundreds of identical gazes: mouths gaping and eyes staring. My mental and physical equilibrium is faltering. Even so, we're at 14,538 kilometers [9,033 miles]....

...The tragedy of exploited children

Mortality remains a major issue in the countryside. Nearly three hundred thousand children die each year from diarrhea. More than 65 percent of the babies of rural families die of malnutrition. Moreover, the exploitation of children in the labor force remains a calamity. One estimate is that fifty-five million children work for employers other than their parents. The children, abandoned by life, will never experience real childhood.

...*Sacred cows*

We can't leave India without talking about the sacred cows. We're always amazed to see these cows in the middle of the streets. The cars create air currents conducive to dispelling the flies.... These cows are not abandoned. They have owners who have come to understand what a good thing it is to graze the cows on municipal lawns: cheap fodder! The cows are the goddesses of India. They represent the symbol of maternity, of charity, and of piety. They are omnipresent. In short, you've got it made to be a cow in India! But pay attention where you put your feet....

India has been a tough country, among the toughest. We have been oppressed by the heat and by the throngs, crushed by the masses, gripped by the noise, impressed by the religious rituals. Abruptly, the race took another turn. It no longer allowed us to communicate with the people as was our custom. Too much, it was too much! We leave this congested India, enshrouded in poverty.

"There's nothing better than a stay in India to test your physical and emotional endurance."

She bears her destiny.

N*ew country*
E*xclaiming*
P*assing beyond the commonplace*
A*llure of the mountains*
L*egendary and mythical summits*

...March 2002: The India-Nepal border

As a result of the accident where Serge was a hit-and-run victim, we decide to modify our itinerary. We allow ourselves to disappear into the labyrinths of the country roads. There are still so many people, but there is far less traffic. This means less danger for us. We arrive at the India-Nepal border. After four hours of customs formalities, we set foot in a new country. Hubbub is the rule; there's confusion everywhere! The border is situated in the low plains, but the authentic Nepal has to be sought out at a higher altitude. 15,000 kilometers [9,320 miles].

...Is this it [the true Nepal]?

We set up our campsite at the edge of the Karnali River. It's a dormer window overlooking a virgin landscape, in the heart of an austere nature. The sun will soon be hidden. This evening, we are at peace with ourselves again. We rediscover our solidarity with nature. We behold the sky. It's so beautiful! Our fire dances; it crackles. This cowboy atmosphere gives me a kick. Strange noises respond to the silence.

We rekindle the embers, because it's cold. While going to wash at the river, we're stunned! We discern... a Bengal tiger. This is not a myth; this animal is at home here, as it is in India and in Bangladesh. While it tries to hide in the tall grass, Serge films it. Rather ill at ease, we decide to pack up and leave more quickly than planned....

...Terai

We follow the narrow strip of land, 50 kilometers [31 miles] wide, situated between the foothills of the Himalayas to the north and the immense alluvial plain of the Ganges to the south. In these hills, the local life is still full of authenticity and reflects the warm kindness that makes up the charm of the Nepalese population. It's not rare to run across a band of monkeys or a pack of wild dogs. After a trying period, our trip acquires new life. We enter a universe where everything is synonymous with a happy-go-lucky attitude. The cheerfulness of the children is a gift. The traditional houses that portray tranquillity are clinging like mountaineers to the flanks of the mountains. The slopes are steep; they have a view toward the summits. It's an adventurous terrain that leaves room for real discovery, for infinite ecstasy.

Dazzling smiles, radiant glances: we literally fall in love, as the residents of Quebec would say. We can again communicate with our eyes; our gestures can again be expressive. Our contact with the children is fabulous. In front of each hut, we notice a swarm of children younger than five years of age. On the average, families have five to eight children. The untamed children of the mountains are back! They are beautiful. They greet us with a simple hello and good-bye. Between nature and the people, the symbiosis is perfect. We are privileged to experience a little bit of the unity of the world. We had been warned: "When you set foot in Nepal, it's for life." This is confirmed day by day.

...Pokhara

In 1962, Pokhara had barely more than 5,000 inhabitants; today, it's the second largest city in Nepal, with 150,000 inhabitants. With the passing of the years, the influx of tourists has enabled its rapid climb to prosperity. In itself, the city doesn't offer much of interest. It's another thing when you approach Lake Phewa. The shadows of the hills are generously reflected there. And if you're lucky and the weather is clear, you can discern the celestial 8,078-meter [26,502-foot] Annapurna.

The main street has the characteristics of a city of the Far West from the 1950s. For me, it's time for a few days of rest. Serge is fed up with the asphalt. He needs to revitalize himself by running several marathons at high altitude. This will be a change from the asphalt, from the traffic, and from the pollution. This is how he feels the vibrations of the real Nepal. Serge adores everything that is excessive. He is uncompromising with himself. However, he never hesitates to blame himself, when it's necessary.

My life as a "single person" permits me to read, first and foremost, *Annapurna* by Maurice Herzog. I discover a striking truth tied to a true-life tragedy. Without a doubt, it's one of the greatest adventures of our time.

Nepal and its neighbor, Tibet, have the highest elevations in the world. Within Nepal's forbidden borders, eight of the fourteen highest summits on Earth are found. Tiny land of legends, wedged between two giants, China and India, Nepal is a mythical crossroads on the historic salt and silk route.

...The receptacle of the gods

It's impossible to escape the magnetism of the Nepalese summits. When you contemplate these snow-covered monsters more than 8,000 meters [26,247 feet] in height, you can't help but feel respect. The "goddesses of eternity" tower up without mockery, without deception. They supervise the world and entice the experienced Western mountain climbers. For the Nepalese, these mountains are sacred. They belong to popular mythology and are esteemed as the receptacle of the gods. In the Tibetan language, Everest [29,035 feet] is called "Goddess, mother of the land."

These mountains give us amazing courage. They are, at the moment, our driving force. They have so much power over us, over our senses. Our gaze hovers in the distance; it is imbued with these immortal images.

The rough life in the high valleys of Nepal.

...Life on the high plateaus

The people of the high plateaus exude a natural sensitivity. Their faces reflect the light of day and the furrows of hard work. Each day has its demands. The Nepalese devote themselves completely to their land and their cattle. In front of his hut, an old man with a sage face greets us. At this altitude, life is harsh, austere. But an impression of well-being, of tranquillity, shines through nonetheless, a perfect symbiosis between man and nature. What strikes our experienced eyes are all these hills tamed by humans. Very simple houses with flat roofs, made of stones that are sometimes poorly hewn and coated with dirt, complete the living tableau.

Nepal is a magical land refined by the sweetness of its inhabitants, who are devoid of all aggressiveness. It's a remote landscape that we embraced instantaneously.

...What's your name?

In places that seem very, very remote to us, we are delighted to observe that so many children go to school already at a young age. It's said that the country is on the right path. But we don't pretend to know the reality. Is there a right to an education? We just don't know. However, one thing is certain: the inequality between Nepalese boys and girls is nothing compared to what we were able to observe in India.

The schoolchildren can be distinguished by their mandatory uniforms: for the boys, a tie, which gives them an air of sanctity, and for the girls, a red or white ribbon in their ebony hair. The children appear quite studious. Proof of this comes in the form of this slightly brash boy who advances toward us. He is eager to put his English into practice, I suppose. He asks the routine questions: "How are you? What's your name? Where are you from?" Serge takes him by surprise by saying that we are Japanese. The boy opens his eyes wide, quite disconcerted, but in any case, he would not doubt the word of a stranger. We sense that he's perturbed.... "But no, my little dear, we come from Switzerland, a country with beautiful mountains like yours. Er...a very beautiful country!" And lo and behold, now he runs away at breakneck speed. We lose sight of him in the blur of the horizon that grows ever more distant.

...A noble people

The steep dirt roads stream down from everywhere and rise up to the sky.... The women carry baskets of wood and dried leaves. They do this just like Sherpas: a big leather strap encircles their heads.

All the plateaus are worked with fervor to shape them into layered terraces. The rice paddies glisten under the spring sun. Running on these roads outside the tourist circuit offers a veritable richness of human contact. We feel the pulse of the local population. This countryside is well maintained in the image of a noble people who exude the wisdom of time. Here, time does not belong to those who are stressed; it is given to those who savor the moment of grace. 15,791 kilometers [9,812 miles].

...Center for the handicapped in Katmandu

In Katmandu, we spend a day in a marvelous hospital perched on a hill, a hospital dedicated to handicapped children. The majority of the stays are of a long duration. Since the creation of this center, more than fifteen thousand children have been treated here, thanks to generous contributions and to a network of solidarity.

I will never forget one child, confined to his bed for fourteen years. He can't move. He waits; he seems to understand his destiny. And I will also never forget his smile when I approached him to give him a kiss on his damp forehead and to show him his picture on the camera monitor. Our glances met, and we loved each other. His eyes were shining like diamonds, but his destiny was sealed by pain and joy.

...April 2002: Forced return to Switzerland

Nepal is truly a charming land, as much from its balance of nature as from the openness of its inhabitants. Unfortunately, it's more and more difficult for me to appreciate each moment that life offers us. Although I don't speak too much about it, my health status remains precarious. I suffer frequently from episodes of cerebral malaria. These crises can hit me whenever, wherever. It's becoming more and more of a handicap.

It's impossible for me to continue like this. The doctor from the French embassy, whom I consulted, has prescribed that I take the first plane back to Switzerland in order to undergo tests there. It's not easy, however, to find a seat on the rare flights to Europe, because Nepal is in a full state of political turmoil. A state of siege has been declared. The country is at maximum alert.

I have a hard time accepting such a verdict of going back to Switzerland, which can mean never returning here and having to put an end to our adventure. I can hardly believe that. The greatest uncertainty takes hold of us. In these very painful moments, Serge encourages me. He takes all things into account. He asks me to think about myself first, about my health.

When the plane takes off, I refuse to look at the ground. I'm too afraid of never setting foot on that soil again.

...At the hospital in Sion

It's hard to return to your own country under such circumstances. At the Sion hospital, they know me, they rally around me, they comfort me. I feel so vulnerable. I find my parents filled with anxiety, even though they try not to show it too much. Serge's children are also very attentive.

For ten days, I undergo test after test. The diagnosis is not good: malaria is having disturbing effects on my body. I lack iron and various vitamins, I'm suffering from anemia, and I have crisis after crisis. The doctors who hurry to my bedside are pessimistic. I have the distinct feeling that they are somewhat panic-stricken. And what doesn't help at all is that I live in the anguish of not being able to travel again. I am well aware of being dependent on the verdict of the doctors.

In the end, it's my mom who gives me the strength to rise again: "My dear daughter, I want you to take to the road again, because it's your whole life. I wouldn't want that to change for anything in the world." Her words of encouragement have a healing effect. A few days later, we are able to leave again for Nepal! I am not cured, but my health status has stabilized.

...On the road again

We left for an even better return, because we are not returning to an unknown land. It's a little bit as if we were returning home, rediscovering our house on two wheels, rediscovering the land of Buddha, rediscovering a multitude of smiles, and regaining our enthusiasm. I still feel a little weak but so fortunate to return to the roads of the world, to rediscover our complicity with the road, the only universe that I know really well, and that we share with the people we encounter.

Equilibrium between humans, nature, and the heavens.

...*Tibetans in Nepal*

Monks in purple robes with shaved heads live side by side with Sadhus and Tibetan women in their *chubas* (traditional outfits). The latter turn their prayer wheels while sharing in the life of the Nepalese.

Because of Chinese repression, more than twenty thousand Tibetans live in Nepal today. They don't all have the same social status. Some, already rich in Tibet, were able to bring their wealth to their new country, while those who find themselves in the refugee camps live in very precarious—indeed tragic—conditions, feeling completely abandoned by the world. However, they have a talent for commerce. They are excellent businesspeople. But their success in the production of rugs, and in business in general, arouses the hostility of the Nepalese.

The Tibetans, with whom we make contact, have a look that immediately lights up whenever we speak with them about Tibet and their spiritual leader, the Dalai Lama. They thirst for knowledge. They also want to manage totally on their own, without the least bit of outside help.

...A religious ritual

In these mountains where silence sings, we stop along the side of the road to take a break, because here the altitude difference is mistress. She alone dictates the tempo of Serge's steps. Suddenly, a man, coming from I don't know where, approaches us. In the middle of his forehead he has an immense red dot. Without saying a word, he continuously hits his forehead in front of every tree that he finds on his path. I don't know how long he's going to perform this ritual, but I can tell you that it's an image that exudes the power of an incredible spiritual belief. Already on several occasions, we have witnessed similar scenes, since we have been on Nepalese soil. These scenes represent so many moments of grace.

...More liberated women?

In Nepal, the women give me an impression of non-submissiveness. They appear more liberated than in India. They speak out more freely. The women of the plateaus smoke with disconcerting freedom. Occasionally, an old peasant awkwardly offers me a bit of hashish. In these areas of the countryside, drugs have now started to wreak havoc in the lives of the Nepalese. Through contact with tourists, they have taken up the habit of consuming drugs regularly. But a lot of monitoring is carried out in buses and on trails. Surprisingly, the older a woman is, the more she smokes. I don't know if this corresponds to social status. Women here seem to have more independence and an air of nobility, which nobody can confuse. But perhaps this is only a small part of the truth.

...Cremation at Pashupatinath

Pashupatinath, one of the most sacred places in Nepal, is located 5 kilometers [3 miles] from Katmandu. Human cremations take place here every day. A pilgrimage town, on the bank of the Golden Temple, bathed by the Baghmati River, which flows into the Ganges. We enter a world far beyond the ordinary.

It's disturbing, intriguing, and horrifying at the same time. On a stretcher, a lifeless body is lying, draped in a red shroud decorated with flowers. Is this a man or a woman, an old or a young person? Some twenty people surround the mystery person and stand guard in prayer.

The pyre has been prepared in a shed made of old corrugated sheet metal, where some strange monkeys move about. First of all, the body is placed facing the sacred river, then it is discreetly disrobed. In Hindu philosophy, since you arrive into life naked, you must depart into death naked. The clothes, as well as the flowers, are thrown into the water. I can't help but weep. Ablutions ensue, then the body is hoisted onto the pyre. Silence reigns; the atmosphere is grave. Two bare-chested men step forward with a strap over their shoulders. We don't know the significance of that. The face of the departed is then revealed. It's the face of a woman. One of the men, the eldest son, holds a torch in his hand. After having completed three circuits around the deceased, he prepares himself to set fire to the pyre. The fire takes hold near her face. Imagine, setting his own mother on fire... the man sobs uncontrollably.

Life came; life departed under a gray sky laden with melancholy. The flames are already high; a strong odor fills the air. At the end of an hour, the body decomposes before our eyes. Sensitive souls stay away.... In the Hindu tradition, the eldest son will have to shave his head and isolate himself in the family house, in a room designated for this purpose. He will stay there alone for thirteen days, sleeping on the ground and preparing his own food. He will be able to receive visitors—close friends and family. The thirteen days are required, so that the body of his mother can reach Nirvana. Afterward, as a sign of mourning, the eldest son will have to wear white clothing for a year.

...June 4, 2002: Heavy hearts

How can we not bring up the manner of greeting in Nepal? Hands joined while bowing, that's how we are welcomed across the whole country. Everywhere we are greeted with *namaste,* a word that means "happy to meet you," as well as "good-bye." But the exact meaning is: "May all your virtues be blessed and protected by the gods." It's as simple as that! Here people smile at one another, speak to one another, exchange ideas with one another, and are concerned about one another. Nepal is a blessed country.

We leave Nepal with heavy hearts. We're filled with sympathy for this land lost in the immensity of its mountains. We have basked in the immense kindness of its people. Despite the harshness of its living conditions, this land preserves the strength of genuine communion with nature. Nepal has offered us immortal moments.

...New detour through India

To reach Bangladesh, we revisit India for a week, in its eastern part, heading toward Darjeeling. From our campsite, we admire the moon that colors the wild and melancholy valley that extends before us with blue and reddish hues. Then the heavenly orb disappears in an increasingly heavy fog. Visibility is dangerously reduced. We make the best of it by lighting the fire. It's always a magical moment, synonymous with warmth, with inner tranquillity, with peace. Our thoughts take flight, and we fall asleep with our families so far away.

This morning, the sky is laden with uncertainties; the clouds rumble. The traffic is chaotic, suicidal. We are smoked like hams by the trucks that emit black carbide. There's no doubt about it; we are back in India.

Then a new day begins with the ascent of a hill that's unbelievably steep and painful for Serge. The wind is violent and icy cold. It is accompanied by gusts of rain. Making progress is difficult in this monsoon season. A child emerges from the forest. He looks at us in silence for a moment before leaving again in search of his scattered cattle. The vegetation is lush. The houses are buttressed on the sides of the nearby hills.

Lo and behold, we finally arrive in Darjeeling ("lightning place" in the Tibetan language). The city is constructed in tiers, from 1,800 to 2,400 meters [5,906 to 7,974 feet] in altitude. It owes its reputation to the tea that is imported into Europe. This evening, Darjeeling is shrouded in sadness. In the streets, slums and human life are crammed together.

...Buddhist temple and home for the elderly

We thought it was an impossibility, but in fact, we are enraptured to be able to enter a Buddhist monastery, while approximately a hundred monks, all dressed in purple, heads shaved, devote themselves to a session of meditation. As a group, they put into practice the ideal of renunciation and of wisdom, as preached by Buddha.

The immense room is richly decorated with symbolic images, divinities, protectors unknown to us. For more than two hours, the monks memorize numerous texts, a daily training that is followed by theological debates that sometimes continue late into the night. We are deeply moved. What beauty there is in these actions! Everything here exudes a perfect harmony. Our delight borders on ecstasy.

Situated on a hill, the home for the elderly can be reached only on foot. It is literally surrounded by a forest of prayer banners. The atmosphere of this place is unique. We are invited to attend the daily prayer and meditation. It's as if someone were wrapping us in a blanket of silence and serenity. These elderly Tibetans pray twice a day, which is the equivalent of four hours. A unique concept: young children share their daily life. They are here to learn the different levels of Buddhist schooling. It's a haven of peace! What phenomenal moments! 16,726 kilometers [10,393 miles].

Bathed by the monsoon
Across the floods
Not able to do anything
Giant mudslides; the menace
Lives on
Along with the fear of the incidents that this
Denotes
Especially property damage
Sentient of the danger that is ever present
Humidity, that's for sure

...Feet in the water

The first phrase that comes to mind to describe this country is "too much." We customarily prepare ourselves, physically and mentally, before entering a new country. One thing is sure: Bangladesh isn't a country that can be approached as the others. We are grabbed by the throat from the very first moment. We knew that the region was inundated with rain, but it is inundated just as much by a sea of humanity.... It's impossible to stay afloat; there are people everywhere, and I mean, everywhere. We are literally submerged, suffocated. By the hundreds, the people cling to us, certainly without any maliciousness, but even so, it is an issue. Bangladesh is India to the tenth power!

The dirt roads are inundated by the torrential rains. The monsoon rages with an extremely violent intensity, knocking down everything in its path. The children play in the muck. There's filth everywhere. The traffic is congested. You have to be extremely skilled to drive and run in this immeasurable mess. These practical difficulties are counterbalanced by the great kindness of the people. They are warm, smiling, and receptive to strangers. We are observed like nowhere else. It's almost as if E.T. were landing....

It's raining; the faces are masked by the worries of life. The inhabitants are lacking in material goods. They have their feet in the water, and their houses are inundated. In spite of everything, they still manage to smile. This year, the harvest will be good... or bad. And life will go on. What an incredible philosophy! We have something to learn....

...Being put to the test

Bangladesh is an excellent school for learning patience. We don't make much progress; the stops are endless and systematic. On the road, it's better to be equipped with a big horn and good karma! Bangladesh is one of the poorest countries on the planet. How can you describe, on paper, the poverty, the odors from frying food, the masses of people, the suffocating climate, the dampness? There are so many aspects that stick with us. How about these salesmen who are hawking their two-rupee "marvels!" We have been thrown back into an archaic world.

In the most difficult moments, I find myself daydreaming that I am in a club, or in the middle of a cottage, where I'm drinking my tea, while playing bridge, as in the colonial days.... It was just a dream!

...Street schooling

Dhaka is a city that is smothered from the weight of twelve million inhabitants, the majority of whom live very, very precariously. The poverty is palpable on all the sidewalks. It is obviously the principal cause of hunger and malnutrition. Several international charitable operations are present in the area. Thus, it's this system that brings the first gestures of help to the street children. It has created codes and a communicative language, with the intention of developing their competencies. These children, rather than isolating themselves, gather together in gangs. Medical care and games are two of the ways used to approach them. Moreover, three centers offer a secure environment, where the children are invited to come, whenever they please, to rest up, to get food, and to bathe.

Bangladesh is a country scourged by poverty, but blooming with the kindness of its people.

...July 2, 2002: Singapore

Singapore. After an interval of several days, the contrast with Bangladesh is complete. Here, where the Chinese presence represents more than 80 percent of the population, everything is organized, contained, orchestrated, without the slightest wrong note. As much as the people were omnipresent—indeed oppressively so—in the last few countries we traversed, here they come across as cold and individualistic. The almighty dollar seems to have made a place for itself in the sun.... It's an atmosphere that doesn't appeal to us!

And it's a sterile city where everything is prohibited. It's best to watch your step. Isn't Singapore known throughout the entire world for imposing the stiffest fines? Crushing a cigarette butt in the street is 500 Swiss francs [about US$400]. Spitting on the ground costs 30 francs [about US$24]. And all importation of chewing gum is considered a "constant nuisance" and it's strictly prohibited. Chewing this "drug" in public places constitutes an offense subject to a fine of 10,000 francs [about US$8,000]!

The authorities of Singapore don't take half measures. With their voracious appetite for cleanliness and modernity, they intend to make a definite break with the past, however glorious it was. In their urban plan, they set out to destroy all the old areas in order to make room for gigantic skyscrapers. Singapore resolutely displays itself as a city of the future....
Our run resumes to the tempo of the heat and the dampness of the east coast, heading in the direction of Malaysia.

Maledict heat
Along with its humidity
Lamentation is
Assured
Yet it's useless to think about it
Seeing perfectly well that we are
Impotent against it
And yet, we must overcome all doubt

...Infernal heat

With our arrival in this first country of Southeast Asia, it's like the beginning of a new era. We gradually find our bearings again. The Malaysian people are known for their legendary discretion. This really does us a lot of good, because the seas of humanity, which we have known for the past several months, have managed to exhaust us.

We sense that this country is at its boiling point. On the one hand, it flaunts its electronic products, its freeways, and its glass buildings in a resolutely modern manner. On the other hand, it offers generous open spaces and inhabitants who are proud of their traditions that are tied to a significant ethnic diversity (Indians, Tamils, Malays, Chinese).

Along the east coast, the road winds through a dense, lush, and adventuresome jungle.

For some, this is paradise; for us, the heat, laden with humidity, is a sizeable obstacle. We traverse fishing villages and deserted beaches bordered by coconut trees. The lapping waves dance at times on the blue ocean. And then there's the jungle, a thick, dense, almost virgin jungle. If only we could appreciate this picturesque scenery! But the fact is, the heat is unbearable. For Serge, it's horrible! It is imperative that we find a solution, because we're not going to make it like this.

This damnable humid heat sticks to our clothing; it oppresses us day and night; it dazes us, even mentally. For some days now, we have continuously been at the limit of our physical and mental capacities. I can't do it anymore! As for Serge, it's a completely different story. Only his great experience permits him to progress. You should see the look on his face! In spite of all this, every 2 kilometers [1.25 miles] he is compelled to stop his run abruptly, lest his head explode. He continually bathes in his own "juice." He is marinating like a leg of lamb on a wood fire.... His feet are bruised and white, as though they had been immersed in a bathtub for hours. We're losing our mental grip.... While writing these lines, I am very worried about the future of our run. I pray that more favorable elements will come to our aid (a headwind, a cloudy sky, less heat). Otherwise...

...The tortoises of Rantau Abang

Our short stopover of just one evening will not permit us to view the turtles, but at least we will be able to enrich our knowledge of them. The heaviest females can weigh as much as 750 kilograms [1,650 pounds]. They essentially come here to lay their eggs during the heart of summer. They come up on the beach, dig a hole, and lay about a hundred eggs the size of a Ping-Pong ball. Then, they cover the hole and return to the sea. The operation lasts around three hours. Seventy percent of the eggs are removed and placed in "nurseries," in order to reestablish the tortoise population that has suffered a lot these past years from intensive fishing methods and from pollution.

...Always on the road

With our eyes barely open, and in the solemn dark of night, our reflexes surpass our subconscious. Our motions are already robotic; they are mechanically ready to overcome one more day in this humid heat. This locale is not a place for meditation upon awakening; we are already anesthetized by the heat.

As quickly as possible, we swallow a lukewarm Coke and two cookies, which automatically stick to our palate. Serge stretches like a cat for ten minutes, an obligatory ritual before the departure of this new marathon, which promises to be infernal. His face is anxious, his muscles are already dehydrated. I feel that he has not recuperated well from the strenuous effort of the previous day. We know that we are going to have a helluva time getting through today!

Fortunately, "greasy spoons" appear at regular intervals along the roadside. There we quench our thirst as well as possible. But we don't linger in them, because we still have a long road ahead of us. It's as though we're sucked up by the black tar. We hardly talk anymore; we exchange knowing glances. The road quickly reestablishes its right of superiority. Moreover, it exasperates me. This road is a demanding mistress. Today, she would do better to deliver some cooling sensations....

Nothing is going well... vexed!

...The absence of wind

How many times, in his career as a guide, coming back from a trek in the high mountains, has Serge complained: "The headwind—what a grind! We didn't have any visibility on the ridge. It numbed our hands, our fingers. It forced us to give up!" Well, here, the roles are reversed. Such a headwind would be our best ally. We open our mouths in the shape of a U, seeking a hypothetical breath of air. Running in such a climate requires nearly superhuman resources.

The horizon is unending. This heat makes the air unbreathable. Silence has become master; words no longer have meaning. Pearls of perspiration glisten under this leaden sun.

...A composite people

The Malaysians practice great discretion with foreigners. It is difficult to make contact with them. This does not prevent them from issuing meaningful smiles as a form of welcome.

We are struck by the prominence of the ethnic mix. Those of Chinese descent and native Malays are members of the most substantial communities. In spite of centuries of living together, side by side, the distance between them is perceptible. The political and economic equilibrium is delicate, yet tempered by a common desire for well-being. The Chinese dominate Malaysian commerce; their women wear slit tunics and eat pork. The men drink alcohol. On the Malay side, the practice of Islam dictates specific clothing restrictions. The Muslim women wear their scarves carefully tied on their heads. But contrary to what we were able to see in other Muslim countries, they can assert themselves, and they can afford the little pleasures of daily life. Many of them drive cars and motorbikes. They meet with their friends at restaurants.

"The horizon is unending. This heat makes the air unbreathable."

How hard it is to run... a bout of the blues!

...August 4, 2002: 18,000 kilometers

Eighteen thousand kilometers [11,185 miles] translates into an indisputable excitement. With kindness, we scratch the surface of the earth. Eighteen thousand kilometers against all odds. Eighteen thousand kilometers to say that our steps are always connected with those of the "Run for Kids." Our humanitarian partner has abandoned the project. Disappointed and hurt, our morale takes a hard blow from it.... Nevertheless, the race continues.

Territory of courtesy
How unfortunate that
An indelicate debauchery exists
In
Lambent Thailand
Amid a thousand different faces
No
Doubt, this is a developing country

...August 10, 2002: The extreme south

Here's a forgotten area of Thailand, lost at the bottom end of a world map, in the extreme south. A Thailand where hardly any tourist stops, but it's here, nevertheless, that Serge's strides now set the cadence. In situations such as these, it occurs to me that I've had more than enough. What's the purpose of so much effort, of so much perspiration? There's time for just one question, and then we set out again....

I cannot wait to discover a livelier area. This one is so monotonous.

Our adventure is lived in close contact with nature. We must come to terms with her. Sometimes she takes us along a little too far. She teaches us to be humble. She can prove to be humiliating. She surprises us, dazzles us, and affects us.

Thailand, such as we are discovering it since beginning in the south, leads us to infer that the same contradictions exist as in other areas with a rapid tourist explosion. It's a logical transformation. Our first 700 kilometers [435 miles] on her soil are not a source of ecstasy: 700 kilometers of an almost straight road laid out through a jumble of vegetation. It's a depressing road! And then, there's always this same humid and suffocating heat. Nevertheless, we cross our fingers and wonder if the curiosity that always drives us to go on and on might have some beautiful surprises in store for us.

...A strange face-to-face encounter

Today, we had a narrow escape! By the skin of our teeth, we avoided the bite of an extremely venomous serpent, the green mamba. A bite that allows only the slightest chance of survival....

Serge is running, always at the same pace, and I am lost in my thoughts... when suddenly I have just enough time to scream: "Look out!" There's a green mamba a few centimeters from the motorcycle tire and near Serge's ankles! Serge holds his breath; he remains immobile. The snake is in the attack mode; it's maximum alert time. It moves, its head alert, its tongue darting back and forth. Panic! Serge shrinks back; the snake watches us. I cowardly hit the gas, accelerating the motorcycle and leaving Serge alone to make his own decision.... He moves back a little more, and at that precise moment, a car hits the snake. A second vehicle will finish it off. Oh, thank God! Serge is sweating; my face is pale. We realize how lucky we were. Never before, in two and a half years, had we been in such a dangerous situation.

...On the menu: Snake!

The only item on the menu, I kid you not, is snake! The meals: blood and entrails of vipers, cobras, and royal cobras. The Chinese are very fond of these, because according to them, they're good for your health and virility. Dozens of intertwined snakes are displayed in cages in front of prospective consumers. The cobras are picked up with poles to be hung in a kind of kitchen open to outsiders' eyes. They are then dressed alive. The blood of these reptiles fetches a handsome price. The skin is sold to tanners. As for the meat, it is prepared in soup. Bon appétit!

...Hello, swallows

Krabi is a pleasant port around which some wooden houses have been built. From the beach, the panorama is awe-inspiring. The rocky outcroppings jut up from the sea against a hazy background that gives a wild and pristine character to the place. A prized activity of the inhabitants is to capture swallow eggs. The Thai people climb the rock faces at the peril of their own lives. They attribute aphrodisiacal virtues to these eggs.... Midway up the wall of a cave, an altar has been built that allows for imploring the gods. The swallow builds her nest with her saliva. When one takes this nest away from her, she constructs a second one. But the third time, she doesn't have enough saliva and her nestlings die.

...Phuket and prostitution

Phuket stretches out for more than 50 kilometers [31 miles], from north to south. Hills and valleys occupy the center of the island. Its heavenly beaches offer a veritable symphony. For us, arriving in Phuket means renewing ties with civilization after weeks of solitude. Certainly, the reputation of this city is rather shady. Above all, people mention its girly bars. It seems that this type of bar is multiplying.

The poor countries are always poor in many ways: lack of education, inadequate schooling, deplorable hygiene, no drinkable water, no electricity, corrupt government, dubious justice. In Thailand, the deficiencies in the matter of schooling are especially notable in the rural areas. Lacking money, the parents often opt to sell one of their children, especially the girls, to pimps who recuperate their "capital" in less than a month by making these poor kids "work" in the Patpong clubs [red-light districts] of Phuket or Bangkok. Once their beauty has faded, these enslaved children return to their village... physically and psychologically ruined.

...The little house of spirits

Next to each house, a miniature colorful pagoda stands atop a pillar. This abode shelters the spirit of the house. Indeed, when the construction of a building is contemplated in Thailand, the first thing to do is to find a suitable place to build the little house where the spirits will be able to find refuge. For the choice of location, it's necessary to seek the advice of a knowledgeable person. The spiritual abode includes an external terrace intended to receive offerings. Each evening, a bouquet of flowers, some incense sticks, and several candles are placed there. This is an example of a religion that mixes Hinduism, Buddhism, and Animism.

...The monsoon

I look outside. I stare. Torrents of rain inundate the landscape. It's a dream without color. The wind joins in, and the trees bend down. It's a stormy day, giving rise to a monsoon. The odors of the ground rise to the surface. A ray of sunshine, and it's time to leave. We are a bit lacking in courage. There's only one step to take. Taking it means accepting that we'll certainly get soaked to the bone! Oh well, it's our choice. Sheltered under the eaves of their makeshift houses, the people greet us with beautiful smiles.

A successive parade of rain, followed by sunshine and then moist heat: The weather is difficult to bear. At times, it feels like you're in a toaster or a sauna. It's difficult to relax in these conditions. However, we have chosen to have a different lifestyle, to take the side roads. No one forces us to do what we're doing. It would relieve us to be able to complain sometimes, but to whom and for what?

...September 28, 2002: Bangkok

It's the wild, the famous, the frantic, the thrilling, the ambitious city of angels. This metropolis shelters 10 percent of the Thai population and 90 percent of the cars registered in the entire country! It's a stifled and stifling city, a city mushrooming with chaotic construction. It's a city of impurities, a diabolical city. Bangkok is like a streamer that is weaving its way in and out, between people and clogged streets. A horrendous suburbia of stress. But human folly is always fascinating. One doesn't get tired of the superb temples, nor of this nocturnal life that's not at all dreary. All of that compensates for the heat, the dust, the pollution, and the noise level at the end of the day....

For us, Bangkok also represents the arrival of Gilbert Pitteloud and his son Stéphane, who are coming to take pictures for the World Tour.

We also have the pleasure of being received by the Swiss ambassador to Thailand, Hans-Peter Erismann. He is a charming man, a most pleasant conversationalist, who receives us with great sensitivity. We share a copious meal in his residence, with everything elegantly presented. This day delights us and improves our mindset.

... *The dance of words*

Making oneself understood in Thailand is synonymous to negotiating an obstacle course. Very few of the people speak English. We have become veritable mimes; our gestures are most whimsical. We ask for tea; they serve us rice. We ask for coffee; they serve us eggs. We ask for nothing; someone automatically brings us something.... The only thing that is ever brought to us without error is the bill! Communication is a major element in such a voyage. But here we are a little like Tarzan and Jane in a jungle of words!

... *The Chinese in Thailand*

The Chinese arrived en masse over the course of the last two centuries, notably to escape famine, and after that, to escape communism. Starting with nothing, they began as laborers or rickshaw drivers. Guided by their spirit of enterprise, their strong sense of community and organization, and, above all, their unrelenting persistence, they today control almost the entire banking sector. Their integration has been facilitated by the absence of a religious barrier, contrary to the situation in Malaysia or in Indonesia. Moreover, a lot of mixed marriages take place in Thailand. It is difficult to distinguish the Thais from the Chinese. There is, however, one clue: the Thais respond with a smile; the Chinese don't display their emotions.... "The Chinese are here to succeed," said a Thai!

The 20,000th kilometer [12,427th mile] of the run across Europe, Africa, the Middle East, and Asia is completed. This milestone is crossed without any fanfare, in the solitude of our steps.

Soon we will have crossed 2,000 kilometers [1,243 miles] of a monotonous Thailand—monotonous because it doesn't bring with it any relief. The road, in these conditions, is as boring as possible. On the human side, it's a string of sweetness and smiles. But as incredible as it might seem, we encounter very few children. We scarcely attract the glance of others. Each one follows his line of conduct, his own discipline. Each one is master of his convictions.

As for us, we will soon see the end of Thailand....

...Chiang Rai

Capital of the province of the same name, Chiang Rai is an insignificant city that opens the gates of the Golden Triangle. It occupies a strategic position on the outermost edge of Thailand and has gotten a reputation... for the production of opium!

In two days, we will be in Laos.

Laos: Sweetness of a caress in
A pure state where each has his
Own
Sagacity of good manners

...On the Mekong

The last Asian country on our course, Laos opens her arms to us. To tell the truth, the crossing of the border doesn't happen without the perpetual bureaucratic hassles. To cross the Mekong (Yellow) River, we have no choice other than to use a ferry. I won't tell you the cost of the transaction—a true swindle, ostensibly authorized! Just think about it: a foreign motorcycle, a windfall for corrupt customs officials! For the ten minutes that the crossing lasts, I have time to imagine that if the Mekong could speak, it would recount terrifying stories.

On the other bank, the atmosphere is rather seedy. We are hardly reassured. We can't wait to go farther into the country and to discover some more savory aspects.

In the countryside, green predominates everywhere, a green that becomes dazzling after the monsoon. We make contact again with a mountain population. The faces once more reveal the harshness of existence in this remote place. Enslaved faces, mischievous faces. Always and everywhere, the children are able to smile.

...Opium smoker

The children are extraordinary traveling companions. Our encounters are fleeting, but on each occasion we stamp their beautiful smiles in our memories. This is how these kids will travel with us part of the way....

One must continuously keep an eye fixed on the beauty: the beauty of the people and the beauty of nature. For this reason, we experience enormous pleasure here in the heart of the Laotian mountains. We stop and appreciate each moment, because the route is still quite long. Here, we admire the colorful traditional clothing of the peasants working in the fields. There's an old person smoking her opium pipe. Her teeth are black and rotten from too much smoking. Is she smoking to forget her daily life?

A city built at the confluence of the Mekong and the Nam Kane rivers, Luang Prabang is destined to have a brilliant economic future if the current pace of growth continues. It is also home to the most significant religious monuments in Laos.

At sunrise, hundreds of *bonzes* (monks) walk in procession down the main street. It's the hour of alms. All of them then return to their respective temples enriched with a ball of sticky rice.

In the north of Laos, between floods, landslides, and collapsed bridges, only the Mekong River remains passable.

What's your name?

…Evening spider

In this very precipitous region, it takes us a long time to find a more or less suitable place to park the motorcycle and pitch our tent. It's truly a horrendous jungle, a mass of undergrowth, an incredible mess! And then, lo and behold, the smoke of the fire that we had just lit made the bad decision to come full force at our faces. To top it all off, we now have a visitor: a huge spider! I have a frantic desire to kill it, but then I would have to dare to get closer to it.... God created man in his image, woman with her fears.... Serge, as a fine man, sensitive to the animal world, convinces me to leave it undisturbed in its familiar milieu. Good night!

…Arrival of tourists

Closed for a long time to the outside world, Laos has a little over five million inhabitants. Its people still haven't succumbed to the artificial charms of civilization. But what will it be like in a few years? Tourism is exploding. Of all the places we have traversed in Asia, it's here that we encounter the most foreign travelers. Will Laos succeed in preserving its tranquil nonchalance? The awakening could be painful. From what we can learn, the people have already lost a few of their hospitable qualities. Fortunately, there are the children, who spontaneously greet us with the local hello: *"Sabaï dii!"*

Vientiane, capital of Laos, is connected to Thailand by the Friendship Bridge and is the final leg of our journey on Asian ground. Having no skyscrapers and no shantytowns either, Vientiane has the appearance of a county seat in the colonial days.

If we should remember only one thing from our passage in Laos, it would undoubtedly be the beauty of its landscapes, its dazzling slopes, its mountains so magnificent that they would make a mountaineer from our own homeland jealous.

...December 8, 2002: Asia is behind us

A year of running on Asian roads has come to an end. I learned a major lesson in Asia: we still have a ways to go to attain the openness of spirit and the wisdom of the people we encountered.... We have been in daily contact with people who are certainly poor in material goods but have an unimaginable spiritual richness. Rarely does an Asian raise his voice or yell at his neighbor. Respect for others is always the order of the day.

On the practical level, we have almost constantly suffered from the suffocating, overwhelming heat. We are impatient to find a climate more favorable for Serge's run.

Australia extends its arms to us!

At twelve kilometers per hour
Upon the asphalt; one
Step in front of the other
Traversing endless
Routes
And discovering ourselves; our chosen
Lifestyle
Illustrates our destiny
And then we start again tomorrow,
and the day after
tomorrow, and . . .

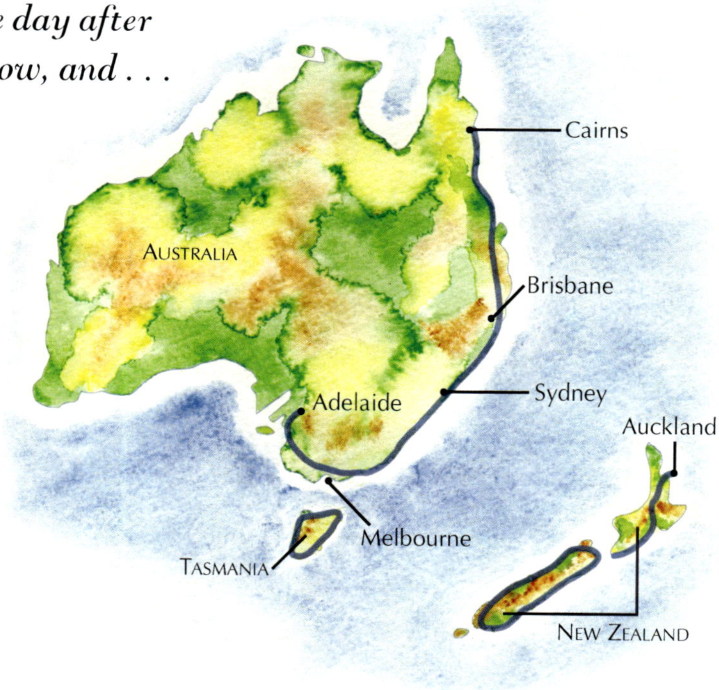

Oceania

...The saga continues

I am in the Bangkok airport; Serge is running like the wind. Our motorcycle and the trailer will not be on the same flight with us. The agent who handled our case cheated us. Even worse: his company doubled the shipping charge! We scream bloody murder; it is truly authorized fraud.

Our plane takes off in less than an hour; we are in a total catch-22. We have no other solution: we have to pay cash! And God only knows how long it will take us to get back our vehicle, once it has cleared customs! Each time it's the same mess. Changing countries is nearly always complicated, but changing continents is a saga of nutcases!

We are here: one foot in Australia, the other in complications! After having filled out various forms, we move along toward the baggage claim area. There a customs dog sniffs our possessions. But what can he possibly have? Or rather, what do we have that interests him to this degree? In no time at all, they drag us off high-handedly. I don't understand anything; my self-composure falls apart noticeably. I tell myself: "I only hope someone didn't slip a little bag of drugs into our luggage!" This type of story doesn't happen only to others. Someone rummages through our personal effects. There's nothing to report, except for two lunch sandwiches taken onto the plane, which I had slipped into my bag without any bad intentions.... But the rule is categorical: all importation of food is prohibited. There's no longer any leniency. The fine is stiff—220 Swiss francs [about US$176]! I cry out in rage. Welcome to Australia!

...Kafka at customs

Something positive to start things off: our equipment arrived on Australian soil, but six days late. A supposed time discrepancy.... On the negative side, it's stored for the moment with the local authorities. Getting it back is like going on a crusade! After several administrative hassles, the motorcycle passes the required inspection tests. But wouldn't you know, the agents detect a residue of dirt on the back of a tire! We're not out of the woods yet.

How do we do it? What do we do? There's no response, no help. Serge is sent from one office to another. "Excuse me, but this is not within our department; figure it out yourself!" Moreover, they talk to us so rapidly! It's difficult to understand the subtleties of the language. And there's no question of having things repeated!

Serge loses control. He cries out: "Might there be at least one Australian to help me?" It's in vain; there's no response. The office closing hour is drawing nigh. A man approaches us: "Sir, we're closing for the weekend.... " This is the last straw! But Serge keeps his cool. After a half hour of discussion, the government clerk agrees to help us. We now know what we have to do. A truck must come to fetch the motorcycle, so that it can be transported to an authorized garage, where it will be disinfected with a special product....

A small detail, but this process costs a fortune! All of this to avoid any contamination, because the tiniest piece of dirt could contain parasites. OK, but before being loaded, hadn't the motorcycle passed through a fumigation area?

Next, the motorcycle must be at customs again before noon, so that Madame Inspector can move along with us and make sure that we are paying for the truck, the transportation, the qualified personnel, the hours of travel, the paperwork....

Aside from these "minute details," everything's going great, your ladyship! ...In a few days, it will be Christmas....

...Christmas

It's the third Christmas away from our families, but we feel so close to them. The shopping frenzy is the same here as it is at home in Europe, with the difference that we see neither lights nor garlands along the streets.

This evening, we will light a symbolic candle, for a moment of peace in the world. Our modest contribution.

...December 28, 2002: Cairns

Cairns: the symbol of the Great Barrier Reef and the first leg of our journey on Australian soil. This will still happen in 2002! It's a new start for the discovery of a continent that, in surface area, is nearly as vast as the United States and fourteen times larger than France.

It's summer; the weather is good. The "uniform of the day" is light clothing. We prudently take to the road again. For this first day, 25 kilometers [15.5 miles] will suffice. Time to find our bearings again; time for Serge to get his leg muscles back in shape.

We regain confidence in this slightly chaotic World Tour. A new wind is blowing: let's go conquer new frontiers, new horizons! 21,000 kilometers [13,038 miles]. Each thousand kilometers has its story, its share of suffering and of rewards. We're on the way to the 22,000th! It's one step in front of the other in the morning silence.

...January 1, 2003

The first day of the year, the first wild kangaroo. He jumped like a grasshopper in the vastness of the sugarcane fields. A fleeting vision of a wild world. Happy New Year!

...We question ourselves

We are surprised by the Australians' lack of verbal communication, as much among themselves as with us. Simply saying "hello" already seems like quite a chore. We hardly dare to ask them for information, because we really have the impression that we're disturbing them. Are they all like this? It's too early to say. They are expeditious, to that I can attest! We will wait to see whether their attitudes change. Of course, when one has just spent a year in Asia ...

...First campsite

The tent is up; we will soon settle down under a semi-thick blanket, near a river where perhaps crocodiles doze.... We are surrounded by a multitude of birds, especially multicolored parrots. It's a place that is shrouded in the mystery of wildlife. We adore this perfect communion between ourselves and nature, so whole and so generous. It's she who dictates our life tempo. This evening, we will enjoy our first true *cervelas* [sausage]. What a shame! It will be completely charred by the gas flames! Lack of practice! Here wood fires are strictly prohibited. It should be said that Australia has not experienced such a drought in 130 years.

...A restless night

My night has been restless. Unceasingly, animals wandered around in the darkness, very close to us. We heard the sharp snap of breaking twigs. We recognized the jumps of the kangaroos; only they gave me a sense of security. As for the other noises: they're a mystery! We were warned: we must pay close attention to the crocodiles. This year, they mate only infrequently in the rivers, because of the lack of water. So, they climb up on the river-banks....

We must also reckon with the possibility of shark attacks. These large predators have changed in legal status from a hunted species to a protected species. To this list must also be added the spiders called "Lydney Tunnel Web," the most dangerous among the Australian spiders. This creature is equipped with fangs that are large enough and powerful enough to pierce through leather pants. And if antivenom is not injected within hours... Keep away from the jelly fish, too! It's not for naught that we see very few swimmers. Lastly, Australia has several species of snakes among the most dangerous in the world. We are determined to remain alert!

...Airlie Beach

Located 150 kilometers to the north of Mackay, Airlie Beach is the main point of departure for the islands and the Great Barrier Reef. More than seventy-four little islands are scattered offshore. From here, we have a beautiful view of the turquoise sea and the bay bordered by palm trees and eucalyptus trees. The ambiance is youthful and laid back. In fact, the transition between the monotonous road, the landscape united by the sugarcane fields, and the bay of Airlie Beach is abrupt.

To the right are sugarcane fields. To the left are sugarcane fields. In front of us and behind us, there are still sugarcane fields. As far as the eye can see, as far as the wind can blow, there are sugarcane fields evermore!

The long ribbons of road are terrible for morale. The black tar exudes heat.... Today, the sun is beating down. I have the impression that Serge is like a cockroach that you crush without reserve on this asphalt ribbon. He perspires like a wild mountain stream. His saliva resembles papier-mâché.... This level of running is decidedly not a child's game!

...Intimate raclette

Our solidarity is our only benchmark.

The day is hot as a furnace, a day of phantasms: a can of well-chilled Coke within reach! In the distance, in the far-off distance, the landscape disintegrates. This evening, to reward our abundant efforts, it's the whole shebang: a raclette that's indeed from our own native land, jealously guarded at the bottom of our luggage. We don't lose contact with our roots! The cheese, the *cornichons* [pickles], the pepper; everything is there. Who is going to take the biggest potato with the biggest helping of melted cheese? We watch each other closely; we gently bicker. It's a true hunting party! We look at each other. We joke around. We have fun like children!

...22,000 kilometers

We zigzag; we wind around; we move forward. This road is our daily lifeline, a chosen lifeline. 22,000 kilometers [13,670 miles] is perhaps only a numeral, but for us it represents so many real-life stories!

We have experienced monstrous depressions, pains, outrages, joys, and happiness. This passage of the 22,000-kilometer milestone has shot optimism into our heads, our bodies, and Serge's legs. We still feel as free as ever!

...St. Lawrence

A shortcut drawn from my captain's log: "A small outback village that is dying. Wild West scenery. Deserted road. People at the windows. Wooden doors that slam. A violent wind that sweeps the street. Innumerable pieces of bric-a-brac. Cowboys who quench their thirst at the pub. The required, customary hat. Will they draw?"

The bush country is not far off.

...Too alone

We are withdrawing into ourselves, as though we were clams. It is still so difficult to start a conversation with the Australians. Perhaps this will change upon approaching the big cities.

We really miss the human contact. We have had ample servings of contact these past three years, sometimes to the point of suffering from it, that's how suffocating it was. Right now, our rhythm is perhaps too tranquil. Certainly, the people are nice, but the spark is missing for the communication to be genuine communication. Perhaps it's that with the passage of time, we have become more insatiable.

Here's a gas station, and ten souls who live here, a pervading feeling of isolation. We are received like dogs at this campsite. We've barely arrived when the manager (female) exclaims: "I suppose that with your strange-

*"We zigzag:
we wind around:
we move forward."*

0 ...1,000 ...40,912 kilometers [25,422 miles], and sixty-four pairs of shoes!

looking contraption, you're going to request a free room?" Mouth agape, Serge lets her talk. "I am fed up with tourists on bikes, on motorcycles, or in cars, who ask me to offer them a free room. If it were up to them, I would have to make everything around here available for free!"

"As for me, I'm not asking you for anything," Serge calmly tells her, "only a bit of sympathy in your remarks and a paid camping spot for this evening." Furious, we take off. On the counter, Serge leaves a note in English, explaining the purpose of our World Tour.

We go to sleep frustrated, angry. How are we going to build something positive with such a lack of tolerance? In books or during conferences, adventurers often make you dream. It is sometimes more difficult to dream when you're out in the field....

...*Brisbane*

After more than 2,000 kilometers [1,243 miles] of running on Australian soil, we enter Brisbane, the capital of Queensland. Situated 25 kilometers [15.5 miles] from the sea, this first large city on the eastern coast of Australia plunges us into a noisy milieu caused by the honking horns and traffic jams that characterize large cities. We progress along the broad avenues, which are beautifully enlivened by borders of parks and floral gardens.

In 1829, Brisbane became the largest penal colony on the Australian continent, with a thousand convicts. An imposing bridge connects the northern and southern districts of the city. Tropical Brisbane offers a curious mixture of modern metropolis and colonial past, a distinctive alchemy. The spires of Victorian churches and the palm trees are reflected in the bluish glass facades of the tall buildings.

At city hall, a friendly reception awaits us. In a written message, the mayor has extended to us his welcome wishes.

...*Glamorous Gold Coast*

The state of Queensland, three times as large as France, is bordered by an endless coast, interspersed here and there with lagoons. Offshore, more than 2 kilometers [1.25 miles] away, the Great Barrier Reef juts out of the water, classified as the eighth wonder of the world.

This shoreline is home to the famous and glamorous Gold Coast, a seaside resort preferred by Australians, which is also one of the largest resorts in the South Pacific. It's a paradise for devotees of surfing, windsurfing, riding personal watercraft, and for others, parasailing. One piece of advice for future vacationers: you'd better bring along your credit card!

We regularly stop over for the night at the hotel-pubs, where a "cowboy" atmosphere reigns. On the ground floor is the saloon with its—how should I say it—clients of ill repute: lots of alcohol, smoke, and slot machines. And on the second floor are the rooms: modest, unfurnished, but very practical for people like us. They're inexpensive. On the other hand, they offer a minimum of comfort ...or no comfort at all!

It's the best place to experience a little bit of life in Australia. After having traversed many deserts of sand, we now have the feeling of traversing a human desert, so tranquilly does life unfold here. Each person is at home, seated in front of the television and eating hamburgers. After five o'clock in the afternoon, nothing moves. You might think it's curfew time: the roads are deserted; dead leaves flutter about in the light air; a door bangs. We are traversing a world that belongs to a single time: the past.

...March 21, 2003

It's the first day ...of autumn! Oh yes, we are indeed in the southern hemisphere! In Switzerland, the meadows must be starting to turn green....

Today is the end of a difficult leg for Serge. Completely dehydrated, he is in need of nourishment. Forty kilometers [25 miles] without any breeze blowing is taxing. He has only one desire: to find an air-conditioned place and drink, and drink some more.

We settle down in a McDonald's. It's a guarantee of finding a little coolness and some toilet paper (not a negligible detail). There we also have the opportunity to meet a few people, like these three little darlings who are licking their ice cream. Serge can't resist his desire to photograph these children. It's a beautiful image of sweetness. Click, click ...

All of a sudden, the atmosphere becomes tense. We are being watched. I grasp the situation. I speak sharply to Serge: "Surely the people believe that we are taking photos for a TV network." (The Australians are distrustful, especially after the Bali tragedy.) I was not mistaken. The kids' parents come forth. "Could you tell us why you are photographing our children?" they ask. Serge explains our adventure, giving them a text explaining it in English, but now they are even more distrustful, because on the paper it states that we have two Internet sites. This harmless photo will not find a place in our souvenir album....

...Sydney!

We arrive in Sydney via straight-line arteries. The traffic is dense; people are braking haphazardly. With difficulty, I work my way through a zigzag course to rejoin the wide avenues, all the while using the motorcycle and the trailer as barriers in order to protect Serge. Running and following a motorcycle in this type of colossal metropolis prohibits him from relaxing his vigilance.

I am completely stressed, nervous, lacking confidence. But what does that matter?! I am so happy to be in the heart of a city like Sydney. Sydney represents one of the great rewards of this World Tour. She opens her arteries, her parks, her buildings, her opera to us.... Sydney has all the temptations!

The first thing that strikes us upon arriving is the impression of grandeur, a feeling of being overpowered. Sydney is a city with very eclectic architecture. The polished lines of the glass and steel skyscrapers offer contrast to the solid structures of Victorian buildings. Sydney is synonymous with beauty.

Lines of cars move at a steady pace. I have goose bumps. We are looking for a precise address, but first of all, we have to turn right, go straight, take the first left, then the second right, pass under the bridge, find the railroad line again, turn at the roundabout, and especially at that place, not make a mistake after the traffic lights... in order to finally arrive at the home of our friends Martine and Xavier, a cool Swiss couple who settled here.

...24,115 kilometers

Our book, *Keep On Running*, which relates the "American Challenge," concludes with this sentence: "While the band is playing at full force, Serge leans toward me and whispers in my ear: 'Nicole, how about starting all over again?'" Well, at this precise moment, on some part of the coast of Sydney, we have just crossed our 24,115th kilometer [14,984th mile] since

On the other side of the world, the Sydney Opera House: 24,115 kilometers [14,984 miles] of running over the course of three years and two months.

our departure from Switzerland in February 2000. Exactly the equivalent of the "American Challenge!" I don't hide a single ounce of my personal satisfaction. A new milestone has been crossed.

And if Serge would now pose the same question: "Nicole, how about starting all over again?" I would answer him with another question, without the least hesitation: "How about if we continue?" Our slightly crazy wager is far from being won. But more than ever, in spite of all the difficulties, we are determined to keep going.

...Sydney (again)

Xavier and Martine have given up their Swiss security, family, and friends to come settle in Australia. They are a dynamic and athletic couple. At their home, we feel as though we are at home.

Yes, truly, Sydney is a superb reward. It truly does us good to feel anew the heartbeat of a city that exudes the joy of living. Even the little details have such importance: lovers who smooch on a public bench, businessmen in ties with cell phones in hand, a display of flowers along the side of a road, an old lady who painfully crosses the road. Cosmopolitan Sydney abounds in colors, in aromas, in disparate buildings. And on its doorstep, about forty beaches and coves entice the fanatics of the most diverse aquatic sports.

But already we're turning our back on Sydney. It's always difficult to let go of a strong symbol, to tell yourself that you will perhaps never return to a beloved place. Many people with whom we have shared extraordinary moments are present when I start the engine and Serge finishes his final warm-up exercises. "Good-bye!" I have tears in my eyes. The day will inevitably be a bit melancholy....

On this Easter Sunday, the streets of Sydney are deserted. In spite of a slightly heavy heart, I am happy to take to the road again. It's a good time for expressing my gratitude to Serge, who, thanks to his skills as a runner, has allowed me to experience an uncommon human adventure for years, something far beyond the ordinary, a life that fills me with joy.

...Victoria

The smallest of Australia's mainland states is a fertile garden of lush landscapes and verdant hills. The summits are lost in the clouds; the climate is cooler and more humid than in the north. Moreover, pine trees planted by the early colonists, as well as the old European-style houses, give the region a very British character. You cannot think of Victoria without also thinking of rich vineyards and of the breadbasket of Australia.

...*Lost in the bush country*

At the end of this leg of the journey, with our campsite set up, we leave to take a leisurely walk in the nearby bush country. We appreciate these moments of winding down that are a transition between the efforts of the day and the time of eating and then going to bed. It's the time for indulging in the ambient silence, for taking stock of the day, for assessing our state of health and our mental equilibrium, and for thinking of the people we love. For this, the forest is a favorable place for reflection.

We walk; we talk; we sing. Carried away by our joy of living and our nonchalance, we suddenly realize that time has passed quickly. The sun has just bid us farewell; night is falling. We move forward on a winding path; we speed up our steps... darn! Should we go right or left? The noises are amplified. My steps are not so confident; my mouth is pasty. It's starting to get colder. "Serge, you are indeed a mountain guide, aren't you?..." We search; we try to remember the tiniest detail. We are at odds with one another, each with his own theory.... I begin to think that we're going to spend the night outdoors.

It takes us five hours to find our way home again. Home? It's a motorcycle, a trailer, luggage, and stars as a make-shift bedroom! It's our manner of spending the night two-thirds of the time, with the inns and the hotels being the exception.

Tomorrow will be another day. We will set out again on the good road.

...*Time passes, life goes on*

The transition is rapid: we suddenly emerge into a more rugged landscape. The immense forests of eucalyptus offer a spectacle in strong contrast to what we have seen during these past weeks. There's a waft of perfume, like an aroma we already know. It's strange; it feels as though we were in Canada. Often, we can't help but compare a place of travel with other regions of the world. We have so many images in our heads. Today, it's raining on this intoxicating road.

Time passes, and life goes on; in a moment of weakness, nostalgia grabs hold of us for a time. This adventure is indeed an adventure.... Certainly, ours is not extreme, but it is demanding all the same. It is lived without regret, but we can't avoid the moments of melancholy, even of discouragement.

What will be left of this adventure? Some moments of pure happiness, some rare shared moments, friendships, a lot of desires, but also quite a few memories of prohibited areas, blurred moments, doubts, fears. The trip is too formidable, too powerful for us to emerge from it untouched. Besides, that's not the goal! We are experiencing tolerance and humility on a daily basis. Everything is learned.

Traveling is also respecting whomever you run into. It is so easy to experience the exotic, the total change of scene, to discover the image of a country that reaffirms your own preconceived notions, to consider only the good sides. But it is much more difficult to be fair when you should be, to admit a country's faults and its weaknesses. Traveling is an art of living, of knowing who to be and what to do.

...June 3, 2003: Melbourne the beautiful

Under a battering rain, our morale soaked to the core, we don't talk to each other very much today. Each is left alone with his or her own thoughts. Suddenly, a car makes a U-turn. A side window rolls down; an old gentleman smiles at us and asks us whether we're having a problem, because today you really shouldn't put a dog outside! In a few words, we tell him about our adventure. Touched, the gentleman spontaneously hands us a few coins. Right away, the sky suddenly seems less threatening, less hostile. We continue down our road and soon arrive in Melbourne, in the extreme southern part of Australia.

We take a break in this city. It's also the time to settle the administrative issues associated with our transfer by boat to the smallest Australian state, Tasmania.

"Traveling is an art of living, of knowing who to be and what to do."

Effective protection against the daily rains.

Built on the northeast bank of the Yarra River, Melbourne is more rustic and less snobbish than Sydney. In 1956, it was the venue for the Olympic Games. To think that the memory of this event is still emulated today! The Australians are sports fanatics. Already at the break of dawn, the entire population sets out in motion. Alone or in groups, the Australians are devoted to jogging, to bicycling, to walking. Others, more daring, surf the waves at six o'clock in the morning!

Tasmania: Promised land
According to what is written
So often about this route
Mirage of this strange land
Along with the pursuit of a veritable feat
Now our gaze turns
Immediately to another world
And we try to forget the cold of Tasmania

...June 10, 2003: Remote land

Again there's a feeling of arriving at the end of the world! We are now separated from the Australian continent after a choppy, twelve-hour boat crossing. It's six-thirty in the morning and totally dark; the temperature doesn't exceed 2°C [35°F]. The wind is sharp. We get off the boat. The port resembles a battlefield. Tasmania is known for having one of the strictest customs offices in the world. We were warned and have taken all precautions. The monitoring is in fact strict, but without a problem, our luggage passes through like a letter at the post office.

Everything is still dormant, engulfed in the morning mists.

We disembark in Devonport. At first glance, nothing stands out. The city is separated by a river that gives it its unique character. In the bottom of the bay, we can still see our boat—the *Spirit of Tasmania*. Already, it awaits new passengers. It's a distinctive sight!

On the other side, in the background, there's a series of hills and plateaus. Devonport is a city with very British characteristics.

Someone knocks on our door. What door? That of our camping trailer.... Today, we didn't feel like—let's just say that I didn't feel like—pitching our tent. I found an easy excuse because of the cold, but to tell the truth, I just simply had a moment of "weakness," the desire to pamper myself in a bit of comfort.

…*Deloraine, an authentic village*

We depart at eight-thirty in the morning. I am camouflaged in thick layers of clothing. The cold is tenacious. It is a helluva incentive to keep us moving forward. Since our arrival in Tasmania, we have very strongly felt the effects of the violent and icy winds coming from the South Pole. (We are only 2,500 kilometers [1,553 miles] from Antarctica.)

At the end of a long leg of 54 kilometers [34 miles], we arrive in a picturesque village with a name that lilts through the air like a pretty musical note: "Deloraine." Through the window panes of houses, we look with envy at the big wood logs burning in the fireplaces. How warm it must be inside!

Tomorrow, we will not depart, because an insidious ache unexpectedly came creeping into the back of Serge's right knee.

…*Breakdown and storm*

There's no need to poke your nose outside the tent; we can hear all too well that the storm hasn't weakened. It's raging like a hurricane. And yet we must go on …over yonder, farther, always farther. We have a cup of steaming hot coffee, and it's already time to leave. What rotten luck! The motorcycle has a mind of its own. It won't start! After an hour of unsuccessful attempts, we are forced to resign ourselves to the fact that today we will stay put. Stuck in this hamlet, where there's not a soul moving about.

We unload our equipment on the side of the road. A part of it flies away as a result of a strong gust of glacial wind. We have to leave for the "hunt." …Faced with the impossibility of finding the reason for the breakdown, Serge hitches a ride to go to a little larger village 10 kilometers [6 miles] away. I stay alone, my hair windblown, my enthusiasm sapped. To think that the motorcycle had just undergone a complete overhaul! What madness!

Serge doesn't find a mechanic, but a guy who knows something about motorcycles and agrees to come take a look. After two hours of trial and error, he finally finds the cause of the breakdown: a problem in the carburetor. It's not too serious, but as quickly as possible, we have to order some parts from Switzerland, without which the problem could be aggravated. We place a phone call to our friend Michel Seppey in Uvrier, and we benefit from his excellent advice on how to get the motorcycle back in good running condition.

But for today, we don't have a choice: we go back into the tent, into the cold. Time doesn't count. Time has only one priority: its acceleration....

..."The other island"

Tasmanie (Tasmania) rhymes with "little house on the prairie." Here, there are great encounters with an unspoiled nature. There's a perfect, harmonious division between fertile, tillable land and grazing land for sheep. The inhabitants have a true devotion to their land and to their livestock. They are farmers who cultivate the good fortune of having protected land. The 450,000 inhabitants of Tasmania consider themselves to be different from other Australians. When they speak of the continent, they say "the other island."

Along with raising livestock, tourism is the second primary contributor to the island's economy. On these lands, the British of an earlier epoch re-created the old England with its villages composed of cottages and farms. Tourism and livestock, however, aren't enough to keep the Tasmanian youth on the island. A lot of the young people leave the island for the metropolises on the continent.

This morning, I lack energy. A dense, misty fog affects my morale. I grudgingly slip into my pants. Serge knows me all too well. "Do you want to run in my place?" he says to me. I get it: we are inseparable partners.

The land, the rock, and the wind form an indivisible landscape trilogy. The trees are large and strong. They are resistant to the winds and to the winter cold, and they impatiently await the arrival of spring to revitalize their branches.

Running from one village to another is something exciting: we feel like treasure hunters. Our treasure today will be finding a roof for the night. The sky is surreal and eerie. Damn rain!

In the land of frogs!

...Another breakdown

In a pounding rainstorm we disembark upon the wide avenues of Hobart, the capital of Tasmania. We can't see any of the surrounding scenery; it feels as if the ocean were raining down on us. Everything went well for us until this 31st kilometer [19th mile], and then suddenly, nothing worked anymore. It's like roulette. The motorcycle suddenly stopped dead. Obviously, in these circumstances, one doesn't choose the place—right in the middle of a bridge, on a road with five lanes!

I am stuck. I try in vain to push the motorcycle, but it is way too heavy for me. The ultimate bad luck, for Serge had to go another way, because it was impossible for him to run on the bridge: it's prohibited. And wouldn't you know, it was the one and only time we've been separated! After an endless wait, Serge arrives. We push the motorcycle to a more suitable place. But it's raining again, just like every day! And we are chilled to the bone. Serge's legs are like needles that are knitting on their own. My lips must be blue! My teeth are chattering. In a few minutes, we have gone from an acceptable "humdrum day" to a deplorable situation.

We take to the road again after an hour's stop, but our heart isn't in it anymore. We arrive at a campsite. Serge is standing in front of a locked door: "Closed for the season." Damn! It's one of those days! Our morale drops as low as the temperature. I'm shivering from head to toe. And to think that several hours ago, I was already fantasizing, dreaming of a steaming hot shower.... Well, old pal, you'll have to wait some more! I've had it up to here!

A lady followed us. She must have wondered upon seeing us.... Overcome with pity, she addresses us with kindness and asks us to follow her, because she can rent us an inexpensive apartment. She leads us into the apartment. I look at Serge. It's way too luxurious for us, on our budget, but well, okay...

The woman understood our distress. The next day, upon getting up, we find a kind note slipped under the door: "For your incredible adventure, we offer you the apartment for as long as you want, free of charge." This hospitality goes straight to our heart, a gesture that every *baroudeur* [traveling warrior] dreams will happen to him some day.

...Wind of rare force

After finally having a comfortable night, we're getting ready to take to the road again. Hobart is a haven of peace, lodged at the foot of Mount Wellington. On the summits, the snow has made its appearance. How beautiful it is!

But lo and behold, the door is barely ajar before the wind assails us, playing a dirty trick on us. It is sovereign. It dominates people and nature. It bends everything in its path. It slips like an eel into our ears, into our nostrils. It slows down our steps, deadens our senses. It's not without similarities to its cousin from Patagonia, the *puelche* [prairie wind] of the desert. However, we don't have a choice: let the wind be free and master, we will be its slaves!

...Port Arthur, the penal colony

Port Arthur was established in 1830 in the middle of the forest as a road-work project intended for convicts. The repeat offenders were sent there. For the British authorities of that time period, it was an ideal penal colony, because it wasn't connected to the rest of Tasmania except by a narrow stretch of land, merely several meters wide, guarded by a pack of ferocious dogs. As for the waters that surrounded it, they were infested with sharks. Many accounts of cruelty and infamy are tied to this place, which today has become a tourist center.

It appears that the convicts could learn a trade all the same, a trade necessary for the construction of the new colony. After the evening meal, reading courses were offered. Once their sentence had been served, certain prisoners received a small plot of land; others were placed as domestics or forced to do the most backbreaking tasks on the plantations. The colony was closed in 1877, after some twelve thousand prisoners had purged their crimes there.

...How immense it is!

The immensity of the Tasmanian territory is a windfall for the fauna. It allows for all kinds of contrasts between pastures, barren hills, and snow-covered summits. The tranquil beauty of the villages we traverse and the architectural splendor of the houses lost in the warm winds make

Tasmania an out-of-the-ordinary destination for those who love wide open spaces, fauna and flora, untamed rivers, and cold, wet gorges.

We now go into the deep interior of the country, into the wild part of the west coast, one of the last unspoiled regions on the planet. Its lands are difficult to reach. They are home to almost impenetrable vegetation. It is said about thirty specimens of the Tasmanian tiger were found here again, after having been officially placed on the extinct list in the 1930s.

We lose our bearings, and yet we are but four hours by car from Hobart. It's incredible how everything acquires another dimension while running. It's now been a week that our route has been passing through irresistible solitude. The road, in these conditions, is an absolute mistress. She makes us lose our bearings.

It starts to rain again; it's cold. Fortunately, we find a "pub-hotel" a few kilometers farther up the road. Too bad, tonight we will have to take a detour from our habits. Spending the night in the tent this evening is completely out of the question; I am completely wiped out. Today, I clenched my teeth all day long; I have rarely been so cold. I hurry to open the door of our room and what a surprise: "comfy," antique furnishings and a big bathtub as a bonus! I only need a few seconds to undress and plunge into a steaming hot bath. Hmm! From the kitchen, pleasant aromas waft up to us. We are dying of hunger. This excitement puts us in a good mood. We fall asleep in the sweetness of a caress, all reinvigorated.

...Full speed ahead

While studying the map, we notice that we can take an unpaved side road that will save us 11 kilometers [6.8 miles]. It's a work road for hauling wood. But rather than a shortcut, it's a trail to hell! The wind slaps us, as in a nightmare. One can hear only the sound of the engine. I feel like a conqueror. Now the terrain is getting bad; it's becoming muddy, and my wheels spin on the incline. I am, nevertheless, determined to conquer my fear. Being determined won't be enough: in the blink of an eye, I find myself pitched headfirst into the mud, with the trailer turned upside down and the luggage split open in the sludge. My motorcycle looks like a dead bull.

Serge scratches his head.... I don't have any trouble believing that he would have done better.... The result: grimy clothes, a buckled wheel, and a shabby mud flap. And the world, well, it continues to turn....

...Madagascar, it's been two years

Once again, the air is glacial, the horizon so distant that it's lost in the mists. It starts to rain, and each time that it rains, in order to garner courage, I allow my thoughts to fly away toward Madagascar. Never will I forget that woman, walking barefooted in a pounding rainstorm and carrying her naked baby on her back.

My first impulse had been to stop, to get off my motorcycle, to give her some warm clothes, and to offer her a package of cookies. And yet ... I hadn't done anything. I was too preoccupied with my battle against the wet cold, so I had selfishly continued on my way. It's been nearly two years since this woman crossed my path, but her face and her child left an indelible scar on me. Even today, I regret my cowardice. How difficult it is sometimes to do good deeds that help others....

So one day I want to return to that country that we loved so much, where the children addressed us by saying: "Hello, *vasa*"; hello, White man.

...27,000 kilometers

The most spectacular route in Australia runs along 200 kilometers [124 miles] of cliffs and deserted beaches. One can see some amazing rock formations close to the coast. Erosion has excavated the cliffs and has created "seastacks" [islets shaped like haystacks], isolated from the terra firma. The famous "Twelve Apostles" look like sentinels of rock keeping watch offshore. The sea constantly restructures the profile of this coast. By isolating them from the mainland, it allows only the hardest rocks to survive, and they, too, will eventually collapse from the violence of the elements.

The tall eucalyptus trees exhibit trunks that are gnarled and tortured by the winds coming onshore, these winds that create plumes of foam upon the rolling waves that emerge from the depths of the ocean. It's on this mythical route that we pass the milestone marking 27,000 kilometers [16,777 miles] of running. It's a new opportunity for saying thanks to life.

...Death didn't want us

I'm still trembling. Today, the light was dazzling, the mood light; the straight-line roads were disappearing into a naked landscape. Serge was running like a feather that takes flight into the sky. But just think, this feather could have flown away forever! We had the greatest scare of our lives. This life, so very dear, and we almost lost it by not remaining vigilant, without even realizing it.

This light with a thousand reflections, this supernatural road, we had only one desire: to film it, capture it from every angle. Not for a second did we imagine our error. We are so accustomed to being on the road that our vigilance completely failed us. Serge crouched down, the camera stuck to his eye, while I continued on my route at a snail's pace. Neither he nor I realized that Serge was in the wrong lane of high-speed traffic. Suddenly, a large truck, at least 20 tons, appeared out of nowhere from a hairpin curve. I heard the sound of the horn; I looked in my rearview mirrors, and I cried out in anguish. I knew for sure that Serge had been run over by the truck. Serge dead; yes, I was sure of it. Nobody could survive such an impact. I stopped my motorcycle; I went back. Serge was there. I thought I was seeing a mirage. I exclaimed: "How is it that you miraculously survived?"

"For the simple reason that the driver had superhuman reflexes; he took the risk of moving completely to the other lane of the road." Fortunately, nobody was coming toward us. The truck disappeared on the horizon, leaving us speechless.

Our monumental error resulted from bad reflexes, because in Australia, we obviously drive along on the left side of the road, but our reflexes, which are resolute, reason otherwise. We had barely escaped death, just barely! Today, the road didn't want to take us, to mow us down in the middle of the race; it wanted us to continue on the course that we had mapped out for ourselves. I have no difficulty believing that Someone up above is protecting us.

...The Aborigines

Broaching the subject of Aborigines in Australia is a delicate matter. You sense quite a strong reticence. The Aboriginal population composes a community that is stretched out, torn, caught between two worlds, between thousand-year-old traditions and modernity. The Aborigines of the cities are most often unemployed. Unemployment leads to terrible consequences, one of which—alcoholism—is three times higher than in the rest of the Australian population. The Aborigines are poorly qualified for the workforce. "The only true religion of the Whites, work, is not theirs," wrote Judith Wright in 1915.

In the last few years, the Aborigines have been progressively going back to their lands, to unspoiled nature, in spite of the unsanitary conditions of the living facilities. This life turns out to be much more compatible with their deep aspirations. They can thus cultivate their art, their know-how... that the White man then exploits in his luxurious galleries, under the pretext that this helps the Aboriginal community. No way! There's still a long way to go, before the Aborigines will no longer be considered "a third-world community on the edge of a developed country."

The arrival of the English colonists in 1788 resulted in the expulsion of the Aborigines from their lands, the destruction of a part of their cultural traditions, and their social disintegration. Furthermore, the English passed on to them diseases against which they had no immunity. The clash of the two cultures inflicted a trauma on the Aboriginal population, from which it is only now beginning to recover.

The colonists considered Australia a country without an owner. In certain places, the colonists practiced "the Aboriginal hunt" or systematic poisoning, with the ardent intention of exterminating the community. In 1828, extermination was officially sanctioned. The more "fortunate" among the Aborigines were "penned up" on prison-like reservations. They were forced to take European names and to wear Western clothing.

When the past resurfaces through the presence of a book on a bookshelf, when you absorb the history of this ravaged people, then only one word comes to your lips: shame. For a White, there isn't anything to be proud of. But it doesn't seem as though the Australians will be apologizing to the Aborigines anytime soon. And yet, weren't there many present at the Sydney stadium and in front of their television sets in 2000 to applaud Cathy Freeman, an Aborigine, an Olympic track and field champion?

...The end of the fourth continent

Australia is behind us; in front of us, the unknown takes shape. We have experienced Australia at the rhythm of distances, of infinite horizons. An immense country that we can't pretend to know. We have merely scratched the surface.

...New humanitarian challenge

We never would have imagined that one day we would return to Fairbanks, Alaska, the terminus of our "American Challenge." It's a formidable stroke of luck, a coincidence, fate! It's been six years already ... and nothing has changed here. Oh, to be sure, this arrival is nothing like our arrival on December 4, 1997! On that day, the thermometer read -32°C [-26°F]. In that astral cold, we had just managed some handshakes, and then we had hastened back to the warmth. These images remain forever etched in our memories.

Alaska is again on our itinerary. People from here didn't forget us, in particular Ron Zamber and his wife, Suzan. Ron is an eminent ophthalmologic surgeon who has more than eight thousand operations to his credit. Regularly, he takes leave with all his equipment and his assistants to practice his profession in third-world countries. He makes his expertise available to the most destitute, giving them back a glimmer of hope called sight.

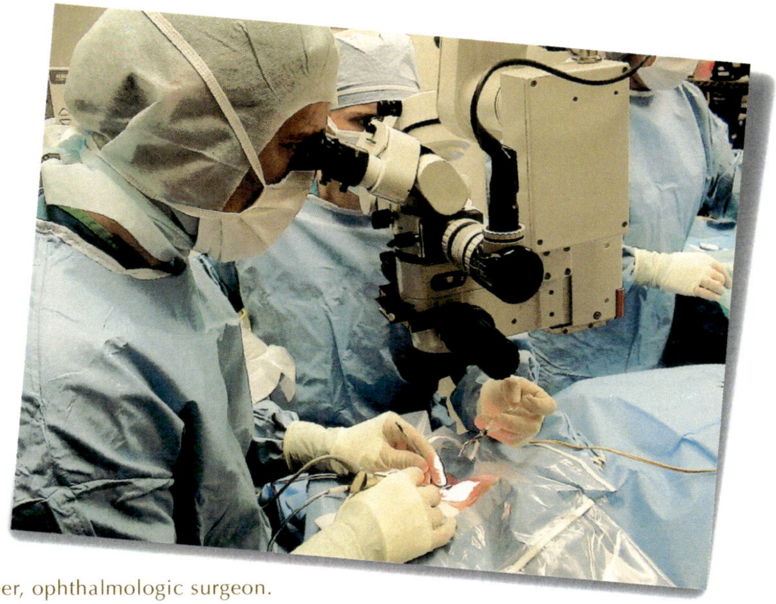

Ron Zamber, ophthalmologic surgeon.

For 150 Swiss francs [about US$120], Ron can give sight back to a person suffering from cataracts. Suzan accompanies her husband regularly to the intervention sites. But prior to that, she takes care of the administrative aspects, such as authorization requests and searching for qualified on-site personnel. Ron has already operated in Ecuador, Malawi, and Nepal.

Since our passage through Alaska in December 1997, we have kept in contact with Ron Zamber. He asked us to return here, just before we were ready to embark for New Zealand. We come to an agreement that the "Run for Kids" will continue with the goal of collecting funds for the furtherance of Ron's work.

Thus, our run can resume with this beautiful ideal of giving support. How right we were not to lose hope! We are overjoyed!

...He recovers his sight

The scene unfolds in Nepal. Under a suffocating heat, an old man with a wrinkled face is seated. His hands tremble. In barely an hour, he will be operated on by Ron Zamber. This man has never in his life enjoyed the gift of sight; he doesn't know our world and doesn't know any colors. He is accompanied by his wife, whom he has never seen.

The operation goes well for him; he opens his eyes.... There aren't words to describe it. He looks around; he looks at a face: "My wife, you are even more beautiful than before." A woman whom he had never seen! His tears flow. And how about ours?

From now on, the "Run for Kids" will take its rightful place in the effort to raise consciousness about the work of Ron and his team.

Our collaboration is set in place.

*New departure where the people resemble one another;
one sole purpose*
*Enter the unknown, the immensity, intersected
by sublime landscapes*
Where purity lives in a pure state: New Zealand

Zigzagging
En route toward the unexpected
Amid plains and mountains
Lasting forever, a journey
Across the land, in search of oneself
No
Doubt, we are married to the world, now and forever

...September 20, 2003: Auckland

After the endless waits in airports and two days of flights that bring us back from Fairbanks, we are received in Auckland like nowhere else. We have barely deplaned, and already they put a cup of coffee in our hands. How kind! The only city in the world wedged between two seas (the Tasmanian Sea and the Pacific Ocean), Auckland is also surrounded by forty-eight inactive volcanoes. We will begin the discovery of this new country in two days, the time needed to get back our motorcycle and trailer.

What strikes us the most when entering Auckland is the mixture of races. All cultures and religions seem to be represented here and to blend together harmoniously, which, at first glance, reveals an aptitude for tolerance on the part of the New Zealanders. The funniest thing for us is talking successively with an Asian, an Indian, an African, and a Syrian, and being able to say to our conversation partners: "We passed through your country on our run." Obviously, this necessitates some explanations each time!

In the span of ten days, the New Zealanders make countless beautiful gestures of goodwill toward us. One day, an old lady crosses the street to serve us fresh orange juice and four lovely slices of cake: what a dream! Another day, a gentleman invites us to drink coffee in his shop. The welcome is impressive. This gives us a helluva shot in the arm. Just as much as the collaboration established with the surgeon Ron Zamber fills us with joy. Running with the idea of being bearers of a humanitarian message constitutes an additional source of motivation.

...Waitti

Waitti is a city of 6,600 inhabitants. It was one of the principal destinations of the gold and silver rush around 1870. Today, the mines are worked by means of bulldozers, which is not without consequences for the environment. In 2001, a part of the city collapsed. Even nowadays, the deposits yield revenues of around a million dollars a week.

...From Rotorua to Wellington

We continue to be welcomed like royalty on a regular basis, notably in Rotorua, a thermal spa where you smell the sulfur from a distance. We're hardly settled here, and they're catering to us; they offer us two free buffets, two passes to visit the geysers, a massage for Serge, and a Maori show! What an incredibly kind gesture!

After having traversed the entire North Island, having traveled exactly 911 kilometers [566 miles], we arrive in the capital, Wellington. The city is encircled by hills. It can't help but call to mind European cities. Wellington is called "Windy City" by the New Zealanders, because the wind blows here the whole year. We don't linger long. Now comes the departure for the South Island!

...The Maori culture

Day by day, we learn a little more about the Maori culture and the history of these indigenous people. In contrast to the Aborigines of Australia, the Maoris are well integrated in New Zealand. This community has the tradition of painting the face and the body with colored lines and curvilinear shapes that symbolize the important stages of life, from birth to death. The Maoris are recognized worldwide for their artistic talents, especially in the realms of sculpture and painting. Yet another congenial feature: the Maoris greet one another by touching noses!

For a successful wedding night, the husband must find his name inscribed on the hands of his wife....

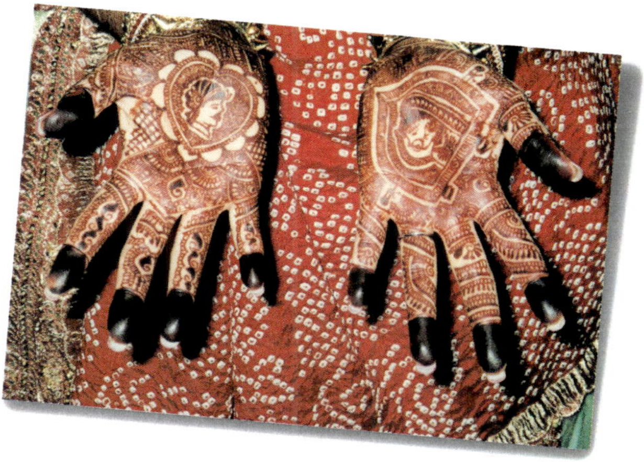

...Electronic message at the 29,000th kilometer

We have to do battle on a regular basis against the elements. For several days already, the hostile element goes by the name of wind. But now, it's a fierce, howling wind. In spite of everything, we don't dislike this kind of situation. What kind of adventure would it be, if it were not spiced with the unexpected? Certainly, at this moment, we must hold tight; it could be sheer hell. But once again, when we choose to live our dreams, what should we complain about?

Picton is the first city on the South Island when arriving by ferry from Wellington. A modest village of three thousand inhabitants, its population can reach twenty thousand during the tourist season. Here we complete the 29,000th kilometer [18,020th mile]—29,000 opportunities for contemplation, for emotion, for encounters, for discoveries.

We make progress in the storm, but it's perhaps in these difficult moments that we realize how privileged we are. Our lifestyle is our choice! Alas, that's not the case for one little boy, who sent us an e-mail.

This eight-year-old Parisian is suffering from a rare and dramatic disease that makes him age prematurely. Physiologically, he appears to be thirty. Just imagine! This child, through an intermediary acquaintance, wants us to send him some advertising pens from the countries that we're traversing. "Little fellow, we don't know your name, or your face, or your eyes. We just know your request, your age, your painful disease. Know that you can count on us. All the pens will be preciously and jealously guarded in our luggage. The next few days of running will be dedicated to you, only to you. Good-bye, Nicole and Serge."

...Daniel and Christelle from Vevey

We take a short break after 22 kilometers [13.6 miles] of running; we're mentally out of it. We can't manage to catch up with the horizon. The sky is filled with white clouds shaped like slumbering swans. A light breeze is blowing that carries with it an odor of cattle. The only noises piercing the silence come from a flock of crows and from a flock of sheep. In the distance, a familiar silhouette, a cyclist, is approaching. Eventually, he's side by side with us. It's a Spaniard who's traveling around. We exchange some invaluable information.

Two other silhouettes are moving in our direction. We don't pay much attention to them, because we're savoring the chatter of our impassioned cyclist. A man and woman now arrive in our proximity. "Hello, Serge, how are you?" Surprise! But who are these two people? "We are from Vevey....

We read your book, *Keep On Running...* down to the minutest detail before leaving on our tour, utilizing the local means of transport." It's incredible all the same!

Serge proposes to Daniel (that's his name), that they should run a few miles with us. Initially hesitant, our new friend turns to his companion, Christelle. "OK, let's go!" This leg of the journey ends at the local coffee shop. Our dialogues abound; we don't feel the fatigue anymore. It's now time to leave one another. May the wind of New Zealand blow in your direction! Good-bye!

...Land of contrasts

The South Island displays such terribly trying changes in elevation that it represents a true challenge. After many days, many turns, and endless kilometers, we've finally arrived here in Franz-Joseph-Glacier, a village populated by 320 inhabitants. The scenery is lavish. We are in the mountains; the glacier is very close. Now we understand even better the allusion made to Switzerland when it's compared to New Zealand.

It's been a few days. We again crossed a tropical kind of forest, and this evening we nearly touch the eternal snows. We fall asleep in this exceptional place, while breathing air reminiscent of the Alps.

...December 10, 2003: 30,000th kilometer

The kilometers: we don't know what that means anymore....

The only thing that we do know: the months, the years, and the kilometers spent on the roads of the world.

It's because every day we begin again at point zero.

It's that before us, the door to the last 10,000 kilometers is opening up.

It's that our runs, since the "American Challenge," have brought in, up to this point, nearly 300,000 francs [about US$240,000] for the benefit of underprivileged children.

It's that dreams exist and that we are living them.

The only thing that we don't know is what tomorrow will hold. And that's the adventure!

...The slow pace

Isn't happiness found by taking it slow? This slow pace sometimes wears me down, especially at this moment. The straight-line roads are atrocious. It is difficult to conquer this infinitely huge horizon. No matter how many times we look ahead of us, we can't resist, so we lift our heads, and then there's this indomitable line that doesn't stop taunting us. This way back up along the east coast is very monotonous. And the monotony is conducive to silence. So we've each retreated into our own thoughts. What good is it to talk? We know our questions, our responses.... Today, the vast space is master of the situation.

...The difference is in the ostrich

This morning, waking up is difficult; I have no desire to get up. However, there's no question of sinking back to sleep. I drink my coffee while looking outside. As always, Serge does his warm-up exercises. There's another monotonous day in sight. "Be satisfied with the present moment." Easier said than done ...

We have only completed a hundred meters, when Serge says to me: "I don't have the drive today." Lo and behold, we are both in the same frame of mind. That's promising! It will be a matter of digging into our mental resources.

The grasses undulate; the fields are like the hair of angels. The sheep bleat when we pass by; the farm ostriches accompany us gracefully in a running motion. Inspired, although not feeling very fit, Serge yells to me: "How I would love to be an ostrich today." We burst out laughing.

We are taking a break along the side of the road. The tires of the trucks stir up the drizzle, which splashes back at us full force. Without any hang-up, Serge devours a big piece of chocolate. Look! We're close by a cemetery and on a large billboard is written: "You can buy your Christmas gifts here." I die laughing. The billboard poster has some humor.

...Christmas 2003

Christmas takes place without fanfare, garlands, or lights. We look at the stars one more time. As always, they stand in for our families so far away. Merry Christmas!

No trumpets or garlands for New Year's either. We are content with an intimate meal. Our gift to humbly celebrate this passage is a piece of salmon! The adventure continues. Next year... we will return... home! Happy 2004!

...Iraqi pain

This maid left, fleeing her country, Iraq. She lost everything: her business, her family, her money. Above all, she lost her past and her future. Her look is sad, but her eyes are so lovely. She is happy to be able to express her sentiments to us, total strangers that we are. She confides that the Americans have come to their aid, but at what price? She stifles the words of hatred. She is surviving here, but what will her future hold?

...New destination

Lo and behold, the time has come to think about the administrative papers that must be filled out in light of our upcoming departure for the American continent. For the motorcycle and the trailer, the decisions are made months in advance. Serge knows the procedure, but each time the laws and regulations change. Once again, it's necessary to run in rhythm with the police offices, customs, and others. It's a true obstacle course!

C*ompeting*
H*umanely*
I*deas*
L*aunched*
E*ach one individually*

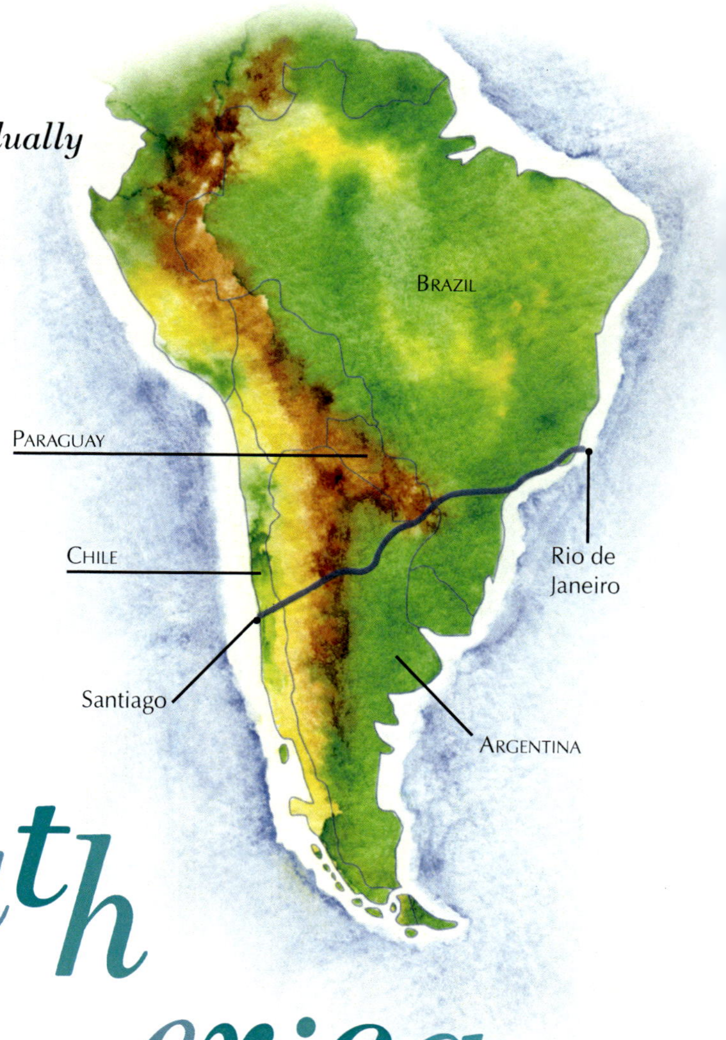

South America

...Returning to Santiago

A mixture of joy and new apprehensions: such are our sentiments on the eve of rediscovering South America. Yes, rediscovering, because it's in Santiago that we had a layover in 1994, on the route that took us to Ushuaia, the starting point for the "American Challenge." It's from here that we will take to the road again. It's a bit as if we were starting again from point zero. For that, we would have to rejuvenate by about ten years... Well, no... the wheel continues to turn for us, too.

This new contact with South America couldn't start any better. I am sitting, wedged in a chair, waiting for the next flight. The jet lag is taking its toll. Opposite me, a little girl with golden hair looks at me intently. "Look, Papa," she says, "Look, the lady has painted eyes; how pretty that is. Papa, look, her eyes have the same color as the world." How can such a young girl speak like an open book? She approaches me and hands me some chocolate, saying: "It's for you." Irresistible; I fall apart for this kid. Welcome to South America!

...Santiago

Immediately, it's effervescence. Yes, Santiago sets life ablaze. Here, everything is transformed into a spectacle: it's a big top, a circus in an uproar, street spectacles everywhere, music, a crazy liveliness. In particular, the Plaza de Armas, the nerve center of the city, is a jewel of elegance. The buildings, with their architectural diversity, echo this elegance. One might say that they indulge in a fiercely fought competition: the highest, the most beautiful, the most aesthetically pleasing. Modern and old find their place here.

I benefit quite a bit more than Serge from these few days of absolute idleness. For his part, as with each time we change continents, he bustles about to sort through all kinds of administrative red tape. I settle down on a terrace, and I let time fly by. I look at the procession of life that passes by; it's a permanent beehive, certainly a beehive with many contrasts, as always in the South American countries. The gap between rich and poor is enormous.

And then there are these imposing, penetrating stares. In contrast to so many other countries, where the people have the habit of looking down when they speak, here they look us straight in the eye. The men are like mighty bulls! It's a truly bizarre impression. Attitudes that can put you ill at ease, if you do not make the decision, as a woman, to respond with the same frank and direct look. It is in your best interest to set your boundaries, because machismo is in the air! The women are not left behind. Many are true Amazons. They seem to have evened out the playing field. So much the better for them!

...Grandma Louisa

On the eve of leaving on this long ascent through South America, I have a very strong thought about my grandma Louisa. She died some years ago. During the "American Challenge," I had telephoned her from this magical city. I remember it as though it were yesterday. She said to me: "You are where?" and I responded: "Grandmother, we're in Santiago." It was impossible for her to pronounce this word, which was barbaric to her. Our Louisa is no more. We are going to take to the road again without her. So many memories!

We delayed our departure for a day, because we still haven't found our equilibrium. Once we're on the road again, it will be for good, so it's better to take care of all the details now. We also took advantage of this extra day to grant interviews to a Chilean national television channel and to several newspaper journalists.

...Some foot deodorant

During this first leg of the journey, we have to thread our way through the middle of indescribable traffic. I swear to you that it's better to be attentive to the motorcycle handlebars in these conditions! And I'm not telling you what this represents for Serge!

With the passing of the kilometers, one after the other, while leaving this city nearly as populous as all of Switzerland, our anxiety flies away. At the 22nd kilometer [13.6th mile], a surprise: a television crew is following our progress. It's all the warmth of the people of South America that comes along.... Journalists and technicians have the great idea of bringing us a bottle of cold water, a cap, and... deodorant for Serge's feet! In a quite natural gesture, thinking that this product is intended to suppress bad body odors, Serge sprays some on his whole body... except on his feet! Wild bursts of laughter! Without a doubt, this image will have been the best scene filmed and an excellent free publicity stunt for the deodorant! This just goes to show you that bad odors don't just make people flee, they can also make people laugh....

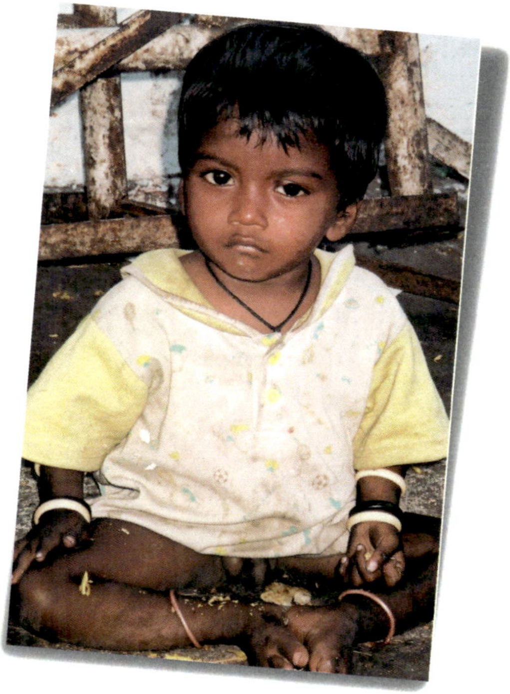

A child's look is unique.

Amid the pursuit
Real dream
Growing
Expectation and hope
Nascent and at
Times
Imaginary
New explorations and discoveries
Again

...The old man of the cordillera

It's the country of wind, of the tango, of steak. Thirty-one thousand kilometers [19,263 miles]! It's better than 30,000, not as good as 32,000....

We're seeking a roof and a bed, because this evening the temperature is going to drop. Serge is searching frantically.... As for me, I await the verdict! I approach an old gentleman. His face is marked by years of hard labor. His destiny is catching up with him. He sweeps the street and stirs up the dust. I start the conversation in Spanish...a semblance of Spanish!

He tells me: "Everyone here is mean."

I ask him: "And you, are you also mean?"

He responds: "Absolutely not; I am the only decent man in this land." I smile at him and offer him a new cap. He immediately hides this very precious item, while declaring that he will put it on come Sunday, the Lord's day. How touching he is! He looks at me again: "You have a funny motorcycle."

"Well, you see, that's my house." This response doesn't satisfy him. He still wants to know if I am transporting a television or a radio in my trailer. At the same time, a very pretty girl passes by close to us. I try another subject: "Did you notice how pretty she is?" I'm expecting a comment.

"What do you mean, 'The Cordillera de los Andes'?"

I laugh heartily. We smile at each other. The old gentleman charmed me in the time span of a fortuitous conversation on the street corner.

We're going to have to clean our four and a half rooms again ... our trailer!

"You have a funny motorcycle."

...At 3,185 meters

We experience an exceptional day among the first imposing slopes of the Cordillera de los Andes. It's as if you're climbing to the moon. How majestic! On the summits, the luminance is magical. It takes your breath away. How can something like this exist? It's too beautiful! The mountain plays on her charms; she undresses shamelessly. Her divine shapes move about before our eyes.

Never before had we climbed such a spectacular road. What can appear unreal is, however, quite real. Serge is the first to make a note of that.... But today, fortunately, he's in form to conquer it...the *cordillera*! He calculates his steps like a cat. At this altitude, it's best to conserve his energy. This evening, we will sleep at an altitude of 3,185 meters [10,449 feet]. We will let ourselves be rocked to sleep by the fatigue of this magical phase of the journey.

..."You can't pass"

To pull oneself up to the heights of the *cordillera* is doing something; to go back down isn't any easier for a runner. His knees are put to the test.

The landscapes are so awesome on this side. The mountains have character. They size us up. We're well aware that they are the strongest. The Valais blood that runs in my veins is strongly permeated by this relationship with the forces of nature. We are lost in our thoughts, when suddenly we hear: "Stop, you can't pass." We're at a military post, and it's no joke! Their looks are stolid. We know we're in a jam. We are sufficiently experienced in South America to know that our behavior must be beyond reproach. We make our point for ten minutes, but an exemption is out of the question: this road isn't made for running.

I'm fuming, but I don't show it. I prefer to stay out of the way and let Serge negotiate. There's nothing to be done. The soldiers are uncompromising: we must turn back. This will indeed be the first time since the beginning of our World Tour. So Serge goes straight out for a bluff. He demands a written interdiction. "I absolutely must have a written document, because we have to render an account to the president of our country...." Then, he adds: "It's really embarrassing for the public image of Argentina, because this will be the first country in four years that would prevent us from continuing our route as planned."

This surprise bluff doesn't immediately have any effect. It's still necessary to wait patiently for nearly two hours before the leader stops deliberating... His verdict: the barrier opens, as if by magic.... A move that's accompanied by this paternal advice: "Be careful!"

...Valentine's Day 2004: Always a couple

How many times have we been asked how we manage to be successful in our life as a couple, while living as we do on the roads of adventure! I must indeed admit that this manner of living has its demands. But doesn't a "normal" life have some, too? We don't have a miracle formula. It is evident, all the same, that our success results from a few very simple factors. Mutual respect is the foremost of virtues. We learned how to deal with our tempo long ago: for Serge it's the rapid tempo of a runner, and for me, it's the tempo of the slowest motorcycle driver on the planet.... That's already a whole agenda in itself.

And then, it's also necessary to learn how to deal with the unexpected, with the lack of comfort. So many situations can put us in a context of aggressiveness. Living together twenty-four hours a day for five years necessitates, in any case, a good dose of humor. To each, his own formula! We can sometimes lose the desire to please each other. One thing is sure: like everyone, we sometimes have to endure the daily routine.

...Mendoza

Mendoza is the endpoint of our first major leg of the journey starting at Santiago, Chile. To get here, in addition to the Cordillera de los Andes, we crossed wastelands and numerous villages. The last kilometers to reach the heart of the city have been very trying, with the pollution from hydrocarbon emissions becoming more and more pervasive.

Mendoza is an obligatory pivotal point for those who want to cross the *cordillera* in this area. This sprawling city is located not far from the mythical Cerro Aconcagua, the highest spot in the Americas. Contrary to what we would have imagined, the change of scenery is not as marked as we would have hoped. We could nearly believe that we were in certain neighborhoods of European cities. It's not a coincidence, because the inhabitants of Mendoza have Spanish and Italian ancestries. A lot are active in the cultivation of vines. They are, of course, not the same ones that you find completely intoxicated on the streets of the city all day long....

...February 17, 2004: Serge on the summit of Aconcagua

After a run that is approaching more than 31,000 kilometers [19,263 miles]... Serge felt the call of the mountain: to make the World Tour pass by its highest point. On this February 17, 2004, he just reached the summit of Aconcagua, which culminates at 6,959 meters [22,831 feet]. I'll let him narrate this adventure within our adventure:

"In my heart, I remain a mountain guide. I left the base camp of Aconcagua by the normal way (Plaza de Mulas, 4,300 meters) at six o'clock in the morning. I arrived at the summit after seven hours and fifteen minutes of climbing, passing by these high-altitude camps: Camp Canada, Nido de Condores, Berlin, Independencia, and then ending with La Traversia and La Canaleta.

The World Tour passing by its highest point, the summit of Aconcagua, at 6,959 meters [22,831 feet], in a single stage: base camp, summit, return, as a daily marathon... just in passing...

"While filming with my little camera, I recorded my first impressions on the summit. Too much emotion... I thanked Nicole. I realized that I had carried a little of the heart of my daughter, Clara, and of my son, Steve, in my light backpack.... I thought of Mama, to whom I owe my love of the mountains, of my brother Yves, also a mountain guide, of Gilbert, of Ron, of Suzan, and of so many other friends.

"Before being frozen by the effects of a temperature of -35°C [-31°F] and a fearsome wind, I went all the way back down to the base camp in one stretch.

"It's a stretch totally unlike the others! It's a marathon for which the main difficulty resided in the constant search for oxygen.

"The highest mountain in the world after those of the Himalayan chain, Aconcagua was conquered for the first time by a guide....from Valais, Matthias Zurbriggen. It was in 1897."

...Meanwhile

It's a happy man, albeit a four-kilogram [nine-pound] lighter man, whom I rediscover after an absence of several days.

For my part, I made the most of this period by completely changing my rhythm of life. I found myself feeling a little like at home. I slept in sheets that I found again each evening. How nice that was! That doesn't seem like much, but when you haven't relished that kind of comfort for such a long time, I assure you that it's appreciated. For the rest of the time, I got accustomed to a new routine. Every morning, at the same hour, I offered a croissant to the old familiar lady on the street; I chatted with the people of the neighborhood. And then, I rode a bicycle about 20 kilometers [12.4 miles] each day. This did me a lot of good by stretching my legs, because my joints suffer from being immobilized for such a long time on my motorcycle.

On the eve before taking back to the road again, I fear that I have become too "acclimated." I have the impression that I have recaptured my bearings to such a degree that it will be difficult to break away from them.

But in the end, the need to go on is always the strongest. Mendoza will remain in my heart as a haven of peace on this long road of the world. For Serge, this city will also represent something extremely powerful: the point of departure and the point of return for another great adventure, the ascent of a mythical summit that he was dreaming to conquer one day. Mission accomplished! So now, let's move forward!

...Sex on the forefront

The Argentineans loudly and strongly proclaim love everywhere: in the street, on the benches, at the red light, in the supermarkets. I am tempted to say that enough is enough. By constantly juggling great principles, they eventually end up upside down. On television, the ads are provocative, sexy, often vulgar. The machismo bursts forth in a way that is most demeaning for women. To say that Latin America is "hot" in the realm of sexuality is, without a doubt, not an exaggeration. It's really true.

Television today tackles sex and taboos without the fear of shocking; indeed, quite the contrary. You get the feeling that it was liberated in a single blow, and that it makes the most of its liberties. For a country where people wear their religion on their sleeves, it's as if you had passed from the *Catholic* religion to a *cathodic* fanaticism.

...Society living at two speeds

As soon as we're beyond the center of the cities, we are hit over the head with contrasting images of a society living at two different speeds. Parallel lives, two different worlds. There's a gigantic chasm between rich and poor. On one side, it's total modernity, technology, the wealth of the twenty-first century. On the other side, you find masses of people in perpetual survival mode. We pass by these fortunes and misfortunes at 12 km/h [7.4 mph]....

For several days now, monotonous horizons unfold before us. I have to cling to the poetry of the kilometers swallowed up under Serge's feet.... Sometimes, a secret desire is lurking: What if we just ditched this whole idea? In the time that the question takes, the answer is given: the space, the solitude, the pure nature are our "five-star" hotels!

...How immense Argentina is!

We had somewhat forgotten how immense Argentina really is! It is outlined in one endless stroke, and that's the pampa, as far as the eye can see. And beyond that, it's still the pampa! You could set it on fire, and it wouldn't change anything, that's how vast it is. We feel minuscule in the face of such nature. We have the feeling that a wave will carry us away. This dimension of total freedom ends up suffocating us, scaring us.

So as not to succumb to this vision, today we invent a game for ourselves. The type of game: whoever is the first to find some grass that's greener than the rest will have won.... In the deserts, the challenge would consist instead of finding a grain of sand redder or yellower than the rest.... It's a phony game, but it calms our tortured spirits, caught in the vise of monotony. Invent games ...kill time, occupy the mind. This is a way we manage to go to the depth of ourselves, a way of finding equilibrium in our daily existence.

The more we progress with our journey, the less mental fortitude we feel. One would believe that the adventure would toughen us, that having spent a breaking-in period "getting our feet wet," everything would become easy, that we would become like fish in the water. However, quite the opposite is true for us, in any case, for me. Yes, to be sure, one acquires a great experience of life, one rubs up against the most diverse "emotions," one shares the daily life of the human condition. However, it's crazy how the minutest detail becomes indispensable to our equilibrium. Something missing in the clockwork of our habits, and the whole edifice becomes fragile. In one stroke, one loses feeling, the desire to persist, to do battle. When we're engaging in physical effort, when it's very difficult like these days now, then from my motorcycle, I cry out to Serge: "What the heck are we doing here?" He answers me with a smile...which could mean: "Don't ask so many questions; keep going; this is our choice!"

"...we will finish this big world loop."

Take a map in your hands and observe the magical line that leads from Santiago, Chile, to Rio de Janeiro. It's nearly a straight line, but you can't imagine what that line means in terms of efforts expended, lasting for weeks, at a tempo that is our own. We progress like slugs. The flat landscape as far as the eye can see is our pain. I stop along the side of the road; I want to cry, but I am too proud to let myself go.

We have given a lot of ourselves during these four years. Just look, our lives are like the sudden rise or fall of the barometer. It's not necessary to hide behind words: it's hard, very hard! But what good would it do to complain? We know full well that tomorrow we will set out again! Because we are incapable of reasoning otherwise. Deep down, I am convinced of this: we will finish this big world loop. There's no question of giving up now. Afterward? Well, afterward, I will travel like everyone else. The word is out. Serge will make like the koalas of Australia: he will sleep eighteen out of twenty-four hours in his tree. He will only come down to be fed....

...Words that change life

The Argentineans dance with verbs, play with words, and ferry across their love songs. They know how to express tenderness and sweetness so well. They have the tango on their lips. It's a way of life that adds to the sympathy that we have for these courteous people, who do not wallow in self-pity about the difficult conditions under which they live.

The Argentineans don't look back to their past; they tame the future. Even if the future doesn't look rosy, their optimism shines through. In all circumstances, they have a clever remark on their lips. Ask them for directions, and they answer: "No problem, my sweetheart, my love!" And their manner of saying hello is delightful: "May your entire day be beautiful!" or "May God protect you on your voyage!" Daily life is embellished, without any cost. Each country gives us a lesson of life, a lesson of tolerance. In Argentina, we are in the best school in the world.

In spite of this report, today we resemble two bulls, heads lowered, with our noses in the fodder. It's as if we were pushing a wall. The wind is way too strong. We are taking refuge behind our fragility; our dynamism is dying bit by bit. Fortunately, once more, Serge's enormous potential helps us make it to the end of this leg of the journey, which is in a village that exudes serenity.

Tomorrow, we'll set out again....

...The smugglers on the Parana River

We are still as overwhelmed as ever by the suffocating heat in a flat, even landscape. It's a terrible monotony: enough to make you feel dizzy, even nauseous. Frankly, I'm fed up with it! Fortunately, to embellish our days a little, there are nights of camping in the shelter of some trees or the villages found along the Parana River. Up to 5 kilometers [3.1 miles] wide in some places, this river forms the border between Argentina and Paraguay. The stories of cigarette, alcohol, and drug trafficking fuel our discussions. In each of these localities, one can see dozens of boats, pirogues, and other vehicles confiscated by the local police! It's a sinister ambiance at times.... Therefore, we watch our luggage a little more carefully!

...The gauchos

The gaucho myth continues to imbue Argentine life. The gaucho is the symbol of the free man who flouts social conventions and prejudices. In its origin, gaucho meant a half-breed child, completely rejected by society. With his tight pants that have fabric pleated at the ankles, his wide belt decorated with pieces of silver, and his knife, which gave him a lordly image, the gaucho reigned on the vast stretches of the pampa. He recognized neither

More than 1,200 nights camping,
but only one cast-iron pot.

laws nor borders in this El Dorado of grass that grows throughout the entire year. The gaucho was, to some degree, a natural revolutionary.

The real gauchos have disappeared. Today, the guardians of the herds are *paisanos*, rather homebody individuals, who have no connection at all with their predecessors, those "magnificent brutes," who used to live on the edge of all legality until the end of the nineteenth century. The wire fences were the reason for the downfall of the gauchos. The horses are no less ubiquitous. We see a lot of children who go to school alone, riding their horses.

It's a day for a break, a rainy day, but our morale is back in good shape again...32,794 kilometers [20,377 miles].

...April 22, 2004: 33,000 kilometers at the Iguazu Falls

When we follow the contours of Argentina with our fingers on a world globe, we already feel all the magic of the adventure flooding over us. We have the good fortune of knowing pure happiness, a happiness that is, however, felt unequally by the Argentine population. The vast territories going from the Cordillera de los Andes to the pampa represent an almost theatrical scenery, which has its flip side. Even if democracy finally (since 1983) seems to make up part of the Argentine political landscape, the country still has problems inherent to Latin America, starting with the economic difficulties that render the social equilibrium very precarious. Things were functioning better and better, however, until the country was hit hard, in 2001, by a serious economic crisis, from which it has had great difficulty extricating itself.

By a sinuous road, very demanding for Serge's muscles, and with humid heat, we finally arrive at the Iguazu Falls! It's within this imposing scenery that we pass the 33,000-kilometer [20,505-mile] milestone. These falls are considered the third highest in the world. With their height of 72 meters [236 feet], they surpass the falls of Niagara by 25 meters [82 feet]. They are tiered, and flow from one into the other. Nearly three hundred cascades are squeezed into a frontal area of 2.5 kilometers [1.5 miles], surrounded by exuberant tropical vegetation.

The Iguazu Falls form a border for three countries: Argentina, Brazil, and Paraguay. We spend our last night on Argentine soil. Good-bye, Argentina, land of excessiveness, of endless, open spaces, of time that doesn't matter, of wind, and of the tango! Tomorrow we leave you in order to discover your great neighbor, Brazil. Your exceedingly beautiful pampa has left such an impression on us!

Braving our dreams
Roaring with laughter, shedding tears
Articulating the words with
Zero restrictions
Interpreting the innocence of
Language

...Border sieve

I don't know why, but as much as the world doesn't scare me, I'm now apprehensive on the eve of crossing the Brazilian border. Perhaps it's the result of pictures and media information that often portray Brazil, especially its cities, as a place of extreme violence.

At first glance, it's not at all like that. In fact, never before had we been able to cross a border so easily. And the reason—there's a general strike today! So, no milling crowds, no salesmen lost in the traffic jams. We're now in Brazil. Watch out for preconceived notions! And to start, luxury among luxuries...we go astray for a moment in the first McDonald's we come upon!

...The jungle in the city

We arrive in Foz do Iguaçu, the first Brazilian city on the road that should take us to Rio de Janeiro. The fact that we have not mastered Portuguese is a handicap. Under these conditions, it's difficult to get the information needed to follow the itinerary. This information is so much more necessary in this place, because here chaos reigns as though it were king. I scoot along as best as I can among the vehicles that choke the arteries of the city. Trucks, buses, cars, and motorbikes belch out thick blackish smoke. This infernal hide-and-seek makes me nervous. Everywhere the vegetation is married to the concrete, to the point that one truly doesn't know anymore which came first, the city or the jungle....

We find ourselves at a multiethnic intersection: More than 400,000 inhabitants represent how many different religions, cultures, cuisines, music, and smells? Downtown offers the image of a metropolis in full expansion, but as soon as you deviate a little, you notice that the city doesn't have any systems for sewage or for channeling drinkable water. The usual scenario of underprivileged, who are crammed together in unsanitary quarters, is repeated to infinity in South America, as in Africa and in Asia. With the shantytowns that encircle the city, you're on the verge of asphyxiation.

"Nicole, stopping is the only way of progressing."

...Superabundance as a driving force?

Serge, to whom I remark that we are stopping a lot, has these words of wisdom: "Nicole, stopping is the only way of progressing."

Giant of Latin America, Brazil maintains a formidable power of attraction. A new window opens up before us. Here, nature reaches the extremes of superabundance. Two figures as examples: the Amazon River, with a length of 6,300 kilometers [3,915 miles], is the longest river in the world, and 70 percent of Brazilian lands are covered by a forest that is completely self-renewing and that furnishes half of the oxygen on the planet. And what if, in the final analysis, it was this, this superabundance, that we sought in our adventure?

Each face has its history, its pain; each has a name, an identity. But opportunity doesn't belong to everyone. Often the only thing people have on their horizon is daily survival. I look at life, making its way through the maze of the narrow streets. I fall prey to alternating sentiments. Sometimes I feel irritated by all this poverty that surrounds us along this endless route. Since we've been in Brazil, the contrast has once again been shocking. We nearly constantly come into contact with poverty and luxury. The poorest make their rounds begging, and then return to their homes in the slums. What are their dreams?

...A room at a truck stop

We're sitting in the grass, at the back of a gas station, with the dull drone of a generator as a companion. About a dozen trucks are parked one behind another. Our motorcycle is camouflaged behind the refuse pile. In the evening of each leg of our journey, whatever the place may be, before supper, we like to have this moment of solitude, of total rapprochement with ourselves and with the natural environment that surrounds us.

The sun falls asleep peacefully; the temperature drops; the night is soon going to plunge into a concert of honking horns. This evening, we are sleeping in a "trucker's room," very simple, but clean. It's a little privacy for an inexpensive price. It's also the means of finding a little protection from the numerous aggressions in Brazil. I conjure up the aggressions; however, we haven't felt any violence for the time being. Everyone appears quite well-behaved and polite to us. My eyelids are closed to the curves that tomorrow may throw at us.

"Sometimes I feel irritated by all this poverty that surrounds us."

...I'm Luis, thirteen years old

Luis is originally from Argentina. He arrived in Brazil at the age of thirteen, with a guitar as his only luggage of life and hope: "I left my brother, my house, my family, because they were poor. I no longer wanted to know the shame and the rejection of society. I'm Luis, thirteen years old; I want to become great, to be proud. But for a year, I have spent my days at the intersections of large avenues. When the cars stop at the red lights, I play a melancholy tune, something that reflects how I feel. Sometimes, someone rolls down a window, and a hand offers me a few coins. The take is always meager. I am always disappointed, because it hardly allows me to survive."

We listen to him. This kid touches us. We ask him where he lives. He smiles at us: "Alongside the canal, full of refuse. My house is a heap of corrugated metal. It's necessary to fight to defend your territory. If another gang comes on my site, it's war."

Luis has a weary look, but his dream of fortune remains intact.

...May 24, 2004: Where to stop

Serge stops...why here and not elsewhere? He embraces me tenderly... his eyes looking into mine. It's a sublime sentiment, as with each time that we cross a new plateau of a thousand kilometers. Yes, how silly of me; have we just reached 33,000 kilometers? No, 34,000 [21,127 miles]! Frankly, I have doubts, because after so many years, so many kilometers, so many steps, so many strides, so many hours on the road, so many, so many... I really no longer know where we are with the count. Serge, he knows it better than I: "One can see that it's not you who's run them, these kilometers!"

A thousand kilometers more: for nothing in the world would we forget to thank each other on these occasions; to tell each other that we will continue on, we will go there; to tell each other that the road is still quite long....

...The Atlantic Ocean

We're back at the Atlantic Ocean! Phew, how happy that makes us! There's a little magic in the whole layout of the journey, like these anticipated points of reference to which we cling for weeks, months in advance. This evening, we are in a village named Peruibe. Tired of having to search for safe places to spend the night (having been strongly advised against open camping), tired of spending our evenings in back of gas stations, tired of not being able to dry our clothes, it's with enormous relief that we rediscover the coast of the Atlantic Ocean. Suddenly, everything seems to become easier again. We run from one village to another, and we find *pousadas* (simple but tidy lodgings) for the night.

We deliberately avoid Sao Paulo and its eighteen million inhabitants by passing to the south of it and crossing the more modestly sized cities of Itanhaem and Santos, pretty seaside resorts, where we find joggers along the beaches for the first time on the American continent.

After a mandatory passage by ferry, the run continues on through Bertioga, Juquia, and Sao Sebastian. Incredible: between each cove, the sinuous road climbs in an assault of the hill, only to go back down immediately into the following cove! Very beautiful, but very demanding!

Today, the sun sparkles like a diamond with a thousand fires. May this radiance also live in the hearts of the people—that is my wish!

...The place of Whites

And it's raining again.... The clouds don't want to dissipate. Serge runs once more in the midst of a throng of trucks. On the outskirts of the cities, the makeshift houses, covered with corrugated metal, cling to the flanks of the hills. What is most striking is that in all the countries crossed in more than four years, all the banished and rejected people, people devoid of a future, always have dark skin. No, never does a White live in these infamous places...why?

Everyone is a spectator of this human misery. What concrete action are we taking to remedy it? Quite little; it's disheartening.

Yet, we are in Brazil, known for its multiracial society. From the outset of colonization, contrary to the English, the Portuguese didn't suppress interracial relations. It should be mentioned that the lack of women favored unions between ethnicities.... For this reason, Brazil presents an impressive diversity of crossbreeding. More than forty adjectives designate the different nuances of skin color of the Brazilians.

But who is at the helm of Brazilian society? Well, the majority of male and female politicians are Whites.... The media, and notably advertising, primarily present the image of Whites. The immense majority of journalists are Whites, and the announcers most in view are blond dolls with blue eyes. We heard a local saying that states: "In Brazil, you get married to someone whiter than you, but you make love with someone darker than you." There is, alas, something like a shred of truth in this remark.

...The tramp from nowhere

We sleep again in a locale that has become familiar—in back of a gas station. We don't ever expect to find luxury in this type of place, but just the same! This evening, it's rather seedy. True-life experiences—you become accustomed to these places just as you do to the looks of the people with whom you cross paths. We occupy ourselves by guessing the future paths of the people who pass, without, however, making any judgments, because here it's a crossroad of anonymity, where you encounter "dropouts," unemployed people on the fringes of society. It's also a place for conversations and confessions.

Next to us is a poor fellow. Our first impulse would be to flee from him, but why wound him more, why give him one more affront? No. I greet him and hand him a bottle of Coke. He makes me understand that he would prefer cigarettes.... Dropping my anti-tobacco principles, I go to buy him a pack. A large smile takes shape on his lips, saturated with alcohol. Soon, he will sink into a dreamless night.

...My own home

Today, we are getting zapped by the heat, which is a good imitation of the heat of Africa and Asia. Serge is sweating all over. The sky is gray, but the humidity level is at maximum. Dehydration is obviously the greatest danger that haunts the runner. It's why we have always taken precautions to ensure that we have sufficient reserves of liquids.

This evening is our reward. Our lodging is a cabin filled with sweetness and tenderness. It's a little bit of home that crosses our path. I open the door. I'm hallucinating.... What? There's a stove, a big refrigerator, a bed with bedding? A true fairy tale, so I imagine myself as queen of the place, with a husband who spoils me, who sings to me of lovesickness, and who runs a hot bath filled with rose petals for me.... Come on now, all fantasies are permitted! These are such simple joys. Why not enjoy them fully!

Oh, how I would gladly stay one more day! What do you think of it, Serge? In more than four years of adventure, never had we granted ourselves a day of rest that hadn't been planned. So, Serge? His response drops like a guillotine: "No, my queen!" But a little later, there's some variation in his tone: "Perhaps we'll rest after all...."

...Rio de Janeiro, 34,539 kilometers

South America comes to a close for us by hitting the 34,539th kilometer [21,462nd mile] in Rio de Janeiro, after about 4,000 kilometers [2,485 miles] of running that enabled us to link Santiago, Chile, with Rio, a link from the Pacific to the Atlantic. A final leg of 40 kilometers [25 miles], and here we are with our feet back in the water, on the beach of Copacabana! Gabriel Torrent, a Swiss consul located in Rio and originally from Valais, gives us the pleasure of running the final kilometers with us. It's truly very kind! We had already met him during the "American Challenge" at the Swiss embassy in Lima nine years ago....

On the scale of difficulties, South America turned out to be a little less painful than expected, but as Serge says, "Running will always remain hard, no matter what country." The fact that we had already familiarized ourselves with this continent some years ago made the task easier for us.

We now have a week before us for dealing once again with the customs formalities. Then it's a new "detour" through Alaska....

...June 26, 2004: Extraordinary day of solidarity in Fairbanks

Running for the eyes of the poorest... After a week spent in Rio to obtain our U.S. visa and to ship the motorcycle and the trailer by boat to Miami, the next leg of our World Tour, we're here again in Alaska. This Saturday, June 26, a run is organized here in support of the cause championed by the surgeon, Ron Zamber. All the benefits are allocated to International Vision Quest, for the purpose of supporting the surgical missions carried out by the American ophthalmologist.

For once, Serge didn't run alone. A 5-kilometer [3.1-mile] run, a temperature of 30°C [86°F], with 120 people at the start, and a sum of 3,600 Swiss francs [about US$2,880] collected at the finish. It's a modest amount, but it will pay for operations on thirty patients with cataracts in underprivileged countries, or buy a few hundred eyeglasses, or even purchase medicines for suitable treatments. It's a first step; others will follow as opportunities arise.

The other day, Serge had a unique experience. Ron invited him to observe about a dozen cataract operations. He was impressed by the dexterity that the doctor and his five assistants demonstrated. What a tremendous gratification it is to be able to give back sight!

Operating on an eye—
giving back the gift of sight.

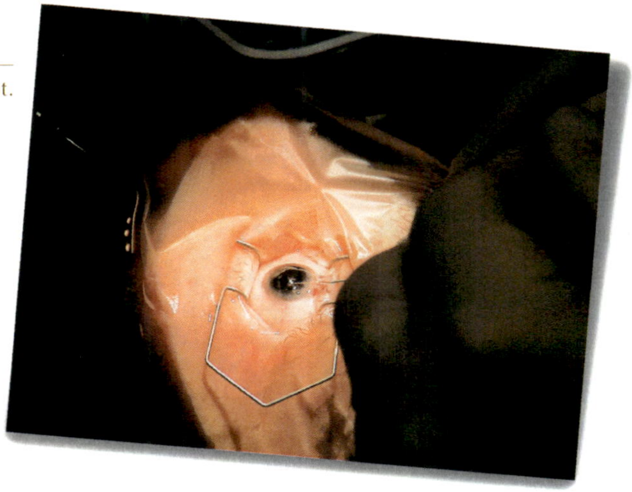

...Between fire and preparations

For four days, an opaque smoke has filled the sky. You can only distinguish an orange spot taking the place of the sun. The air becomes unbreathable. An acrid odor infiltrates the nostrils. By satellite telephone, we learn that it's necessary to evacuate, with the utmost urgency, the entire area ranging between the Chena River and the road linking Fairbanks to Circle. It is, moreover, highly recommended to wear a filter mask, not to play any type of sports, to stay inside "safe" houses, and above all else, not to panic! Nearly sixty forest fires are burning in Alaska, several of which are spread out over hundreds of acres. The lightning of the preceding days was probably the cause.

"Running will always remain hard, no matter what the country."

Anguished and miserable, we help as best we can to evacuate the house of our hosts. We carry out the essentials, beginning with the two children, the two dogs and cats, and a few precious belongings. Already we're fleeing southward to take refuge at the home of Ron's friends. It has been more than twenty years since Alaska has experienced such a situation. We spend the night listening to the news.

In spite of this hitch, Ron doesn't give up on his idea of a mission to Costa Rica. The scheduled departure is in two days. These events will prevent him from clearing all the surgical equipment through customs. What a shame that this time there won't be any operations but only ophthalmologic care, medical visits, eye examinations, and fittings for eyeglasses. Serge and I will be a part of this mission. I will be in charge of the patients.

The preparation for such a mission is stressful for Ron and his team. Numerous administrative formalities have to be carried out. As always, paradoxically, it's not easy to implement your desire to come to the aid of the most destitute. We can attest to this from personal experience. In Ron's case, he can't afford to make a mistake. With a single failed operation, his reputation would be at stake. This mission to Costa Rica is the fourth one that he has undertaken by taking time away from his work and committing his own funds, as well as those that he manages to collect through events such as the one that we set up the other day. The cost of a mission of this size runs up to $100,000.

...Costa Rica

Never would we have thought we'd return to Costa Rica after so few years. Sometimes, coincidences contradict us!

This week spent in San Jose has been insanely intense and full of emotions. Ron and his assistants have checked the eyes of 592 people, of whom 87 were orphaned children. Eyeglasses were distributed, medicines prescribed and distributed, and medical advice given. Ron, his wife, Suzan, Lucy, Mike, Emily, and Reily have worked miracles, laboring without interruption from

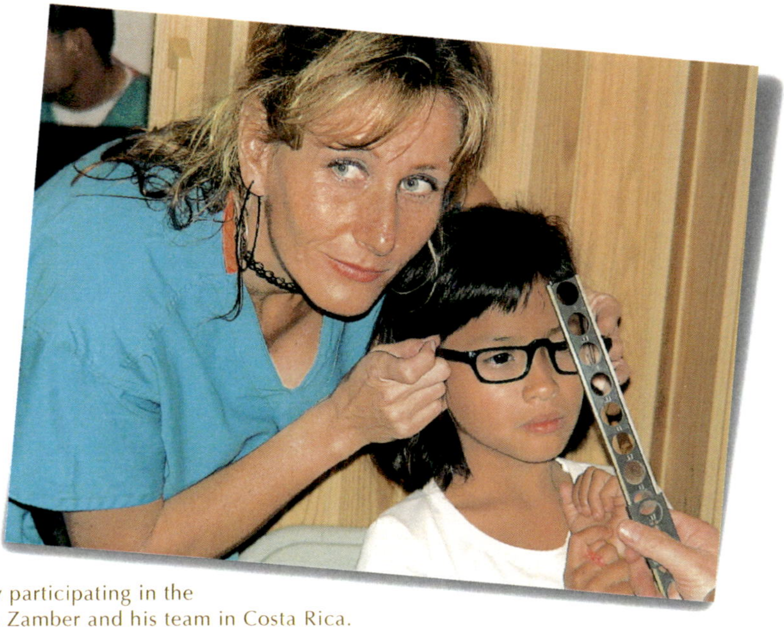

Nicole actively participating in the mission of Ron Zamber and his team in Costa Rica.

seven o'clock in the morning until eight o'clock—sometimes ten o'clock—at night. As planned, I fulfilled my mission of welcoming patients. I also had to administer drops, allowing for the dilation of pupils. For his part, Serge filmed the whole process, in order to immortalize on film a concrete effort that we have resolved to support through our modest means, but with conviction.

International Vision Quest also brought material aid to an orphanage: a supply of clothes dryers (it rains four months per year and the rest of the year ...it also rains, but a little less!), a supply of books for the library, clothes, etc.

Having experienced this other form of adventure, we're here anew on the route of our World Tour. Yesterday, we arrived in Miami. The air temperature: 34°C [93°F]! As soon as we take possession of our motorcycle and trailer, we will head in the direction of New York, a distance of around 3,000 kilometers [1,864 miles]. We're so close to the dream, but so far from the goal....

One more thing: according to the latest news, Ron and Suzan's house was fortunately not burned, but the blazes are still wreaking havoc.

Future
Lays in the steps within steps
Oriented toward the future
Rare privilege of being there
Illusion of being so
Distant from the goal
And yet so close to the dream

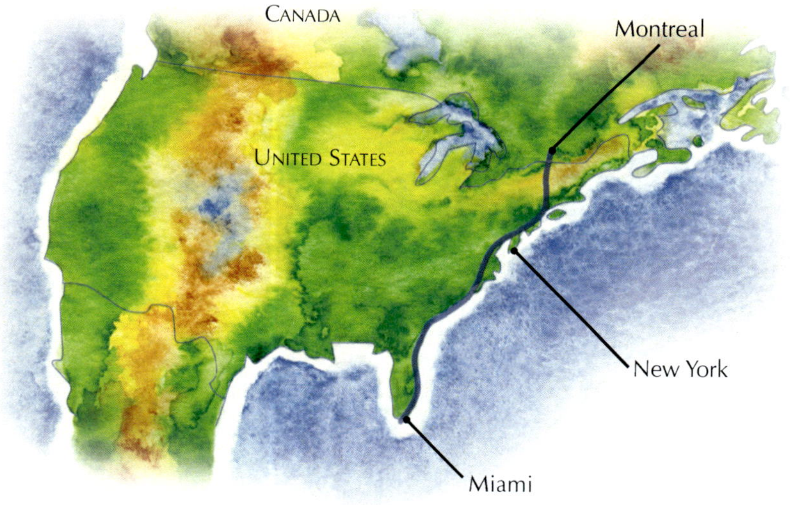

North America

...July, 2004, Miami: But where on earth is the motorcycle?

The motorcycle and the trailer still haven't arrived. They are "floating around" between Rio and... I don't know where! As always, the adventure has its mix-ups, but this one tops them all. The agency in Rio, commissioned with the transfer, committed only one mistake. They shipped our vehicle to...New York instead of Miami!

Nobody knows what to do, what to say. We have to figure out this mess on our own, and I really do mean on our own! We don't know at which end to start. We waste entire days running from one office to another, making telephone calls. With the latest news, things are moving.... So, it's not a lost cause after all! Who said that patience is the mother of all virtues? Easier said than done!

During this time, we remain in Miami, a typically American city. What immediately jumps to your eyes is the frenzy of the people. Everyone is running all over the place. Life is teeming everywhere; the ambient stress is palpable.

Miami is perhaps a city that indeed does allow for all dreams. But it is easier to dream when you're affluent than when you're on the fringes of society. At each turn of the street, the differences among social classes can be felt. The faces and the looks are hard. Courtesy doesn't seem to be part of the picture.

...Hurricane Charley

I'm at the pharmacy. A conversation between an old lady and the pharmacist startles me. "We'll have to get reserves of water and food." That's what I got out of it. But why reserves? With my elementary English, I ask what's going on. They explain to me that a hurricane is going to devastate Florida. I can hardly believe it, because when looking at the people, I have the feeling that they are not even stressed, that they're going about their business as normal. At the reception desk in the hotel, the information is confirmed. "This evening," the receptionist tells me, "you'll need to calmly stay in your room and not come out for twenty-four hours. Simply wait until it passes."

We turn on the television set. All the programs have been interrupted. Without a break, information is given concerning the nature of the hurricane, which has been named Charley. One of the journalists finishes his report with these words: "We wish you the best, but we fear the worst. Good luck!"

My first impulse is to fill up the bathtub with water, to unplug everything electrical, and to buy drinking water. I already imagine all the people who are going to lose something, even their life. I am very distressed. We fall asleep as best we can, but toward one o'clock in the morning, we are suddenly awakened. The storm is raging. It's incredibly violent, feeling like the end of the world. Through the window, we witness a spectacle, reminiscent of Dante's *Inferno*. Trees snap, roofs take flight, bridges collapse, cars are turned over.... It's not a movie, but rather a true disaster.

We look at the ceiling, hoping that it will hold. The windows seem to be withstanding the storm, but for how long? And afterward, what will happen? For an entire day, we live in anguish. Thank goodness, Charley finally calms down! Outside, what desolation! The final toll will be about twenty deaths, about ten thousand without shelter, a half million people deprived of electricity, and nearly a million people evacuated. Winds reaching 250 km/h [about 150 mph] were recorded! This hurricane will turn out to be the most deadly over the past fifty years in Florida.

...August 23, 2004: 35,000 kilometers

Dare to take the first step, without having to imagine the last. And yet, it will indeed take several months from here to there. We are no more than 5,000 kilometers [3,107 miles] from the goal. From here to there, how many more discoveries, how many more encounters, how many more bouts of the

"...the desire to go back home and be done with this World Tour has been quite real."

Miami, Florida.

blues, how many more campfires? Already at the handlebars of my motorcycle, while profiling the endless straight-line roads, I project before my eyes an avalanche of images with which we have been confronted since the beginning of our adventure—images that have been invariably unfolding at the rhythm of 12 km/h [7.4 mph] for four and a half years.

For some time now, the desire to go back home and be done with this World Tour has been quite real; I can't deny it. Therefore, the fewer kilometers we run per day, the longer the return road will be. *Palice* [French nobleman and military officer; 1470-1525] would not have said otherwise.... For the moment, it's difficult to acknowledge our feelings on this climb up the east coast of Florida. The heat is too oppressive; we are suffocating. Serge's head is like a cauliflower in a large pressure cooker. Every two kilometers [1.25 miles] he is forced to stop in order to drink, to sponge off his face, and to regain his composure. He is on his own; he must confront this challenge alone. His feelings are identical to those felt in other areas of the world, in the most trying moments.

Our daily runs scarcely exceed 30 kilometers [19 miles]. It's impossible to do more. Our morale is taking a blow. But Serge is his best coach: "When doubt overcomes you, chase it away, blow it in another direction." So, we set out again, one more day, and then yet another... 35,281 kilometers [21,923 miles].

Georgia, state prisoners

At the end of a long, straight-line road, letters in bold print on a fluorescent-colored sign attract my attention: "Caution: State prisoners at work." Ah, yes, it does exist. Is it quite necessary to post such a humiliating inscription? We are as free as the wind; they're there, watched twenty-four hours per day, every day. I wave to them. Serge does the same. What strange destinies!

...Chasing kamikazes

Nothing stops us; our mindset is focused on the exercise of this folly, our run; every man for himself. The heat is overwhelming; it plunges us into the extravagance of an endless solitude. I can't wait for the next break in the shade! It's best not to miss the tiniest nook, the tiniest shaded spot. Having just found happiness, it quickly turns into a nightmare. An invasion of kamikaze mosquitoes attacks us mercilessly. Our dripping, sticky skin surfaces are first-class bait. Then the chase, the battle is on. We spray, we squash, we slap relentlessly. There's no pity for these bugs that make our lives hell. They are traitors who prefer to attack from behind. Oh, these mosquitoes, they're putting us through the mill! Nasty beasts!

...Silence is golden

Initially, it was just two minuscule points on the horizon. Then it became clearer: two people along the side of the road, for whom we are apparently not strangers. When we get close to one another, there's nothing but big demonstrative gestures, jumps of joy, head shaking, swinging of arms that dance in the flames of the sun, spontaneous embraces. These two youngsters are deaf and dumb. As best we can, but obviously in an awkward fashion, we try to make ourselves understood. We would really like not to disappoint them.

We grasp that they are also Swiss. On the other hand, upon leaving them, we still do not know the reason for their presence in this place. A strong feeling, once more, will linger. And one certainty: the most beautiful form of speech is still silence.

...Good-bye, Aunt Arlette!

Sitting in front of the fire, looking down, gazing at the embers, I feel the flames crying my pain. I'm mad at myself, I'm angry, I'm sad. We just received a telephone call. Mama tells me of the death of my beloved Aunt Arlette. I listen while crying. In the span of a minute, a life stopped. In the span of a minute, a deep emotion takes hold of me. Serge consoles me; I sink into the memories of my childhood.

It's quite difficult to learn about such bad news at the other end of the world, but that doesn't change anything. Not being present at my family's side perhaps amplifies my pain. A life has gone away, but the memory of Aunt Arlette will remain etched in my heart. Our journey continues; hers moves on into an unknown world. "One must recall moments from the past, since life continues its inescapable course."

...Durham, 36,000 kilometers

Thirty-six thousand kilometers [22,369 miles] of running and thirty-three countries traversed. Each meter, each kilometer is a conquest of the unknown. North Carolina. Let's hurry up! After Charley, Hurricane Jeanne is announced, the fourth to hit the East Coast in the span of a few weeks.

...In front of the White House

The approaching run that leads us to Washington is endless. Drowned in the vastness, my thoughts are adrift. Serge confines his steps to the shoulder of the road. His strides echo. It's been more than a year that he's felt that his left leg is shorter than his right. Since his sciatica set in, he has always run in an unnatural way. But there's no question of giving up! Serge continues to clench his teeth. What his legs can hardly do, his *mindset* accomplishes! Today, we planned a short stage of 32 kilometers [20 miles]. But now, having passed the village scheduled as our stop, he decides to add an extra "stretch...."

This evening, I jealously keep my wish to myself.... Our camping place will be here and nowhere else. No noise comes to disturb the serenity of this privileged place where magic settles in under a hazy light. The sun disappears into the eternity of silence to make way for an intimate evening. The water boils on the embers. It's almost the time for enjoying ourselves, for savoring a nice hot coffee. It begins to get cold. My fingers grow numb; my eyelids become heavy from fatigue. Serge relaxes, his legs crossed, alone with himself, like an old solitary tree. It's in the silence of a night without commotion that we let ourselves be guided by the best sentiments. Tomorrow, we will make a stop in front of the White House.

Making a fire in order to find a bit of warmth from those who miss us.

...November 3, 2004: Good-bye, dear mama of Serge!

What should we make of intuition? At first glance, the day begins similar to the preceding ones. But it's as much Serge as I who admits to a certain listlessness. No, we're not up to it.

We pull up to a red light. A lady begins speaking to us in French: "Are you believers?" she asks us. Perplexed, we don't know how to respond. Green light, and we go a few hundred meters more, and lo and behold, she addresses us a second time. She hands us a brochure entitled "When Death Strikes a Loved One." Usually, it's the kind of document that winds up in the first trash can we pass by. This time, it's not. I keep it on my person.

We stop our day after a leg of 36 kilometers [22 miles]. The title of this brochure intrigues me. I broach the subject of death with Serge: "Serge, how would you react if you should lose me, or lose your mama, or one of your children?" His response is succinct: "Like everyone..."

We temporarily set aside our reflections. I'm on my way to take a shower. It's then that the cell phone rings. Serge answers. On the other end of the line is his brother, Yves... Serge comes closer to me. He is pale. He asks me to lie down. I understood: "Mama Nora has left us!"

Nora left for her longest stroll, a journey without a return. She died peacefully in her home in Sion. We were going to call her in two days for her seventy-fifth birthday.

At the other end of the world, it's the shock of words, the shock of distance. At the very moment that Serge was running, his mama left this world without saying a word. We did not suspect that a drama was unfolding thousands of kilometers from here.

The pain is intense. We listen; emotion stifles us into silence; we don't understand. No, it's not possible! Why her? She was in great shape; death struck her down. She took her leave as she had lived, peacefully, disturbing no one. It's best not to regret the beautiful days that have passed, but to give thanks that they existed. We must not forget. Nothing can be changed now.

Serge's mama was a woman endowed with boundless energy. Her entire life had been enlivened by the mountains. Moreover, I would affectionately call her the "little goat of the mountains." It's from her that Serge got his passion for life. Nature and the summits were her refuge. No, it's not possible; we won't see her ever again....

All night long, we try to make arrangements for a flight to Europe. We obviously want to find the fastest possible way to be with Nora. It's a very long day, when you find yourself in such a situation!

Serge will spend many hours next to his mama. He will talk to her at length. It's a way of starting the process of mourning. Nora has left us something great, strong, and beautiful. She would always tell us, no matter what happens, one must always persevere to the end. There is no doubt: our run must continue. From now on, her words and her memory will live on in the continuation of the journey.

A few days later, we find ourselves at the gates of New York. It's for certain: Serge's mama makes her entry into Manhattan at our sides....

Nora, we love you. An eternal bon voyage!

...Manhattan in sight

I can't explain to you the emotion we felt upon our arrival on Fifth Avenue in New York! For a long time, I dreaded this moment. The more we progressed, the more immense it seemed to me. Even more immense than anything that I had imagined. No city in the world produces such an effect. New York is a megalopolis beyond the norms, which plunges us into the unknown. There's electricity in the air; everything is melodramatic.

With our luggage of misfortune, we have the look of people who come from far away. Numerous are the passersby who gratify us with a spontaneous hello. The police officers here also extend their gestures of welcome. My heart is filled with pride. We could believe, for a moment, that we have become the royalty of Manhattan. My fears fade away. I zigzag in the dense traffic; I make my way among innumerable yellow taxis. The display windows are richly decorated; lights sparkle everywhere. Christmas is near.

We move along a clogged traffic artery. Seeing the heads of the people in the cars, I try to imagine what they think of us, while watching us as we move along on this avenue in our own manner. Running in the middle of traffic jams—what an absurd idea! We understand...that they can't possibly understand it. We are not really adapted to this milieu. Our strange appearance is even a subject for caution. But in a certain way, I'm having fun with these hypothetical questions: Why are they running? Are they poor? Are they doing it for a set purpose? We raise questions, that's obvious.

Suddenly, Serge stops running. There's no question of dodging the ritual that marks the passage of a thousand additional kilometers. Our 37,000th kilometer [22,990th mile] right on Fifth Avenue! What does a number of this magnitude really mean? For the average person, quite simply: nothing. For us, this means a new stretch of a thousand kilometers completed, encounters evermore, unproductive periods, moments of pure bliss. It also means that we are getting ever closer to Switzerland, and that we are in a hurry to arrive there. But let's make sure that we don't let down our guard! We still have around 3,500 kilometers [2,175 miles] to run, and the challenge is not yet over. A lot of things can unexpectedly occur during the last months.

This leg of the journey is completed a half hour later in front of what were, until the attacks of September 11, 2001, the twin towers of the World Trade Center. A kind welcome committee awaits us there—our Swiss friend, Henri Rappaz, a cameraman, and his son Dorian, Ron and Suzan Zamber, who have come directly from Alaska, and Joe Roetheli from Kansas City, a distant relative who follows our trek via our Internet site. Everyone is here for us; this truly warms our hearts!

...Astonishing, unnerving, fascinating New York

New York is the city of all superlatives: astonishing, unnerving, fascinating, so many adjectives that seem to fit it to a tee. The center of Manhattan exhibits an incredible character of internationality. More than half of its population is of foreign origin. It's as if a mania for greatness prevailed here: the highest, the most beautiful, the biggest. Urbanism blends the old with the modern to the point of excessiveness. The architectural feats are phenomenal. New York also wears a cloak of multicolored lights.

The bad reputation of Manhattan doesn't fly. Anyway, we feel like fish in the water, fully confident. We walk up and down the streets and alleyways lined with bars, trendy nightclubs, and restaurants of all nationalities. It isn't just a lively ambiance, it's euphoria. Here, everything is excessive! Manhattan tenders us an enticing declaration of love. A little bit more, and we would fall for it; we would be ready to admit our infidelity to so many other cities traversed and loved!

...Her favorite scarf

Who isn't in search of the extraordinary, the grand, the beautiful, the best? For us, the best is spontaneity, the language of the heart. With Virginie, we found it. She is the sister of Alexandre Poussin, the adventurer we met in South Africa in the company of his wife, Sonia. Mother of four adorable children, she lives in the United States. She gives of her time to organize a conference for us at a French-American school. It's a resounding success!

When we're about to leave, several people present at the conference are at our sides. A lady spontaneously offers me her favorite scarf, which she tells me she's been wearing for years. She wishes for me to carry it with me: "It will be a way of traveling for me." Another gives me winter shoes, still another leather boots and a large cape to withstand the rain....

... *The first snowflakes*

The first winter warning. While heading north this morning, we find our feet in the snow again. Oh well, snow always exists! It's been ages since we've been in contact with nature. On my motorcycle, I must adopt new habits, avoiding any skidding. It's a new source of pressure. Vigilance is essential. With the "mortal fear gauge" at maximum, I steer my motorcycle, feet dragging on the ground.

Although happy as children confronted by the spectacle of snowflakes that fall in abundance, we're suffering. Frozen through and through, we decide to make a stop. Serge lights a fire at the edge of a street, in a gutter. We have no time to appreciate the warmth, because, with all their sirens screaming, the police arrive at the scene of the "crime." Although kind, the officers demand that we end our "little game." A little later, we stop at a service station, the only means offered along the side of the road to get warm for a few moments.

We take off again into the cold. The day is endless. Concentration is called for. This long climb toward Canada bodes to be a lot more trying than planned.

... *Are they really free?*

I don't claim the competence to boast about understanding the subtleties of how the economy works. Nevertheless, certain situations perplex me. The American economy is based on the principle of a very broad liberalism, a creed often debated but never disavowed. It consists of a few very simple principles: to see the big picture, not to interfere with the laws of supply and demand, to never thwart the financial free reign of industrialists and businessmen, to let the investors work relentlessly, to be at the forefront of progress, to pay the least possible in taxes, and to let the public sector cope with social problems.

But then, if this formula is so miraculous, why is it that the official unemployment count in the United States is constantly increasing? And why is it that the household consumption is at a constant slowdown? There is something that escapes me in this ambiguity. Sometimes in this regard, I ask myself if the poor countries are truly so far behind the times. In the final analysis, it could indeed be they who live in the true wisdom of life.

...At -29°C [-20°F]

I am bundled up like a fortress. The temperatures don't stop dropping. Today it's registering -29°C [-20°F]. We had better be dressed very warmly! We are surprised by the suddenness of this arctic cold. To the cold, one must add the humidity level that oscillates between 50 and 84 percent, which is considerable. This humid, arctic air pierces us through and through. We are totally focused. We don't have the privilege of error. Our equipment is not adapted to such conditions. I take refuge, as best I can, in the silence of my ski mask and my scarf. I can hardly make out the road.

Is our tenacity open to criticism? In our analysis, each kilometer traveled is a kilometer gained. I'm having a hard time maintaining my mental equilibrium. A few kilometers farther down the road, we take a short break, make feeble attempts to get warm, and already we're setting out again. This same scenario repeats itself numerous times during the day.

Serge is frozen through and through. Small, unsightly yellow balls are forming on his face. His perspiration transforms nearly instantly into tiny icicles. As soon as he stops, he has to protect himself, which he has a tendency to neglect, since he is so preoccupied with a tendonitis problem that is beginning to throb. His performance is affected; we progress at a very slow pace.

This evening, we don't have it in our hearts to sleep in a tent. We decide to go knock on the first door that we come to. It's the first time that we are proceeding in this manner, but we can't take much more of this!

We spend a comfortable night sheltered from the astral cold. But tomorrow will be another day....

Storm between New York and Montreal.

...Trailer theft

The days are currently short.... At 4:30 p.m., it's already dark. This evening, we choose to sleep under a bridge on the I-87 freeway, to the south of the city of Albany. This is no great luxury, but at least we are sheltered from the icy rain that accompanied us the whole day. The advantage is not having to pitch the tent.

At the end of an unromantic and almost comfortable night, there's an unpleasant surprise: the luggage stored in the trailer has disappeared! We didn't hear anything.... We get up hurriedly. The bags are scattered all around. The majority are empty. Fortunately, upon looking a little more closely, we note that only the camera and a lens have been stolen. We deduce that the crooks were only interested in money. Fortunately, we always have the reflex of camouflaging money and official documents in the bags we use as pillows. Notified, the police fill out a police report, and then they're on their way.... We put away all our things and... the run continues! It's a little hard on the morale!

...*Periostitis, enemy of the runner*

Switzerland is still far away; however, we think of it a little more each day. Snow, rain, cold, and arctic wind are our daily companions, all of which are not making Serge's task easy. For some time now, a persistent pain on the right side of his left tibia has been causing him pain. It may well be a sign of periostitis, the runner's sworn enemy. The long stretches of the journey before New York and the battle against the wind and the cold are undoubtedly the cause of it.... Serge treats himself with the means at hand: ice compresses many times per day, anti-inflammatory drugs, and gulping down liters and liters of water. Glen Falls, New York: 37,422 kilometers [23,253 miles], -14°C [7°F].

...*Merry Christmas!*

I decorated a little fir tree...with love and happiness. In this way, we are in communion with the people we love. This makes the fifth Christmas that we are spending on the roads of the world. Nora, we think of you while looking at the sky; and you, too, Louisa, while looking at the stars; and you, Arlette, while looking at the moon. Finally, for all of you, our departed acquaintances, men and women suffering all over the world, homeless people, friends of the "Run for Kids," Merry Christmas!

Crossing the world on foot
An adventure for us, a discovery of others
No doubt
Afterward it's the great return to our final
Destination, our old continent
Afterward, for sure, it's finished

...On the Jacques Cartier Bridge

Today we're experiencing our final stretch on American soil: a year and nearly 8,000 kilometers [4,971 miles] farther along from Santiago, Chile. In Montreal, our Quebeçois friends, the Beaudry "clan," are expecting us. When we're about ready to cross the Jacques Cartier Bridge, which spans the Saint Lawrence River, our emotions are at their peak. It's hardly believable. So many images cross our minds, like cascades falling one upon the other! It should be said that our friends have something to do with it. They have put all their energy and their enthusiasm into making the reception a grand celebration.

For a distance of 3 kilometers [1.85 miles], a lane has been closed down specifically for us. And to open the road, if you'll pardon the expression, the police cars lead the dance! Radio-Canada and Television-Canada are also on hand. They film us live. It's a concert of congratulatory honking horns. We completely forget that the temperature is -7°C [19°F], and Serge clenches his teeth in order not to show to what degree his tendonitis is making him suffer. Carried away by the intoxication of the moment, we feel as if the world belongs to us. We are like light, carefree snowflakes that dance about. A day unlike any other, a day of celebration, a day of recognition!

The renown of the Swiss cuckoo is not overestimated. We arrive on the dot at the agreed-upon hour at the door of our hosts. They are also globe-trotters. They have crisscrossed the world with their three children and have thus brought back eternal dreams in their backpacks.

For Serge, it has become urgent to find some peace and quiet in order to be able to take care of his tendonitis, which is on the verge of taking a nasty turn. For several days, he has been continually pressing ice packs on his hurt leg. He knows from experience that there is no better remedy than this. It's certainly necessary to add a lot of patience, as well. No point in trying to take shortcuts; this would only mean pushing back the expected recovery date.

...To remember them

Our stay in Montreal coincides with the announcement of the tsunami that's just shaken Southeast Asia. We are stuck to the television and to the radio; we read the papers. The subject is indeed on everyone's lips. The expression is certainly trite, but never will it lend itself better to the circumstances: you feel quite small, but then truly minuscule, when faced with a disaster of this magnitude. The death count is tens of thousands, perhaps hundreds of thousands. How horrific!

We visualize several areas struck by this tragedy. We passed by several identified places. To think that the people with whom we crossed paths in these countries are today perhaps dead adds to the emotion that overwhelms us. And then, I can't help but think that one day, in the not-so-distant future, this catastrophe, among so many others, will be forgotten; a page will be turned over as with all catastrophes and wars.

We will try not to let you fade in our memory, dear anonymous, departed souls.

Parting in order to return
Opening your heart
Roaring laughter or tears
Together as one
Upon a day
Grandiose
Amid the conviction of not having changed...and yet
Looking back...

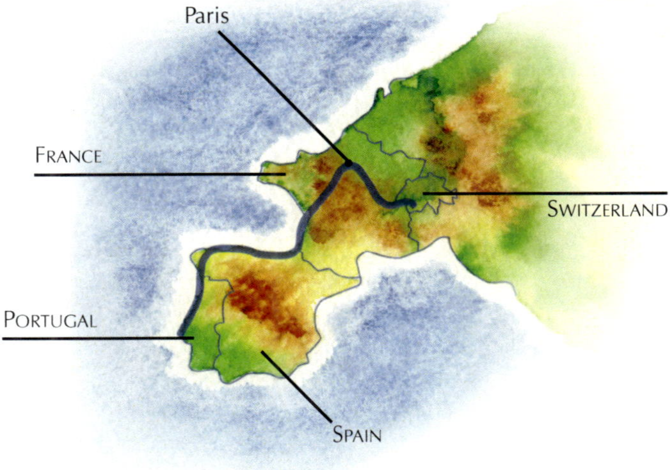

Europe

...January 2, 2005: We fly over Madrid

We fly over the ocean, we fly over Madrid. There's nothing as far as the eye can see, as if the world were disappearing beyond the horizon. A landscape resembling a head that has been shaved. Patches of land, scraps of love, of mapped-out routes, of scattered roads. In the middle of a vertiginous fissure, a village in the shape of a circus tent pushes up, as if it were an enormous mushroom, nourishing itself on its own flesh. It's a peaceful countryside, a peaceful solitude. Already we imagine ourselves running—everything is approaching, everything is coming closer. Our considerations, our judgments are always tied to the logistics of the run. But initially, it's going to be necessary to head toward Lisbon, our starting point for our return to Switzerland. Portugal, Spain, France, and finally Switzerland. If everything goes well, we will rejoin our close relatives at the beginning of May, at the beginning of May of this year!

Lisbon, a roguish air

It's 7:00 p.m. in Lisbon. Life passes before me; no, it's I who pass into this life. The images mingle with one another, contradict one another, sometimes impertinent, sometimes moving. There's no need to travel for so many years: here travel comes to you. Lisbon is a compendium of nomadic life.

No need to go to Africa: there are only Africans there. No need to go to India: there are only Indians there. No need to go to the Middle East: there are only Arabs there. Here there are only Gypsies, beggars, alcoholics, derelicts, the "Sunday folks." A concentration of life under the microscope parades down its sidewalks—a pulsing life in all its length, its width, and its height.

Lisbon is an unassailable fortress, a true seaport, an opening to the Atlantic, and yet it has a wholly Mediterranean soul. Lisbon has a roguish air. The Lady of Fatima has reasons to cry. Sunday prostitutes entice the passersby; drug addicts lay their need bare in frenzied spasms. There's an accident here, there's an ambulance there, and over there, lovers on a public bench. An old lady soaps her staircase; another tosses a can from her balcony. Lisbon and its seven hills are like so many wise men. The city comes alive; the city falls asleep amid its vestiges.

…Casting off

The sun has risen like a theater curtain. The colors explode in an azure sky; the colors recede into the horizon. It's time to start, it's time to leave, to tread the land of our ancestors, this European land. The people are talking; the people are looking. Each one does his own thing. After a prolonged break, I have the feeling of no longer knowing how to drive. But very quickly, the desire to cast off takes hold again. I rediscover my natural "instincts."

…Nazaré

Serge's steps pound the paving stones of the harbor city of Nazaré. On the narrow, sloping alleyways of "old town" Praia, perpendicular to the beach, I don't act haughty at the handlebars of my motorcycle, which slips on the large sandstones. Old ladies dressed in black animate the auction at the fresh-fish market. They raise the bids, a century-old custom. The seafood restaurants abound; others limit themselves to offering succulent corn, accompanied by a good vegetable soup.

…Tendonitis and grimaces

This morning, our morale is not at its finest. We hardly greet each other, which is not in keeping with our habits. The mood is morose. Serge doesn't have a pleasant countenance. He is preoccupied. I avoid asking him how his tendonitis is coming along. "My heart just isn't in it," he tells me a little later. "I have a very bad feeling." In spite of two weeks of care, of ice, of appropriate meals, and after four legs of the journey on Portuguese soil, his malady still persists and settles in. A poorly treated case of tendonitis can cause us to fail, but what is the meaning of failure after 37,938 kilometers [23,574 miles]?

I know Serge's performance as if I were taking care of a Formula One car. Each grimace, each look, each step taken is such a telling sign for me. I know exactly what his body or his morale is undergoing.

With no question of abdicating, Serge sets out again. He adopts a slower tempo than his usual average. And just look, another 34 kilometers [21 miles] on the meter. Tomorrow will be a mandatory day of care. On the bill of fare: drinks, ice, anti-inflammatory drugs, and... patience!

...Hunger pang

In the manner of all European countries, but in a truly incredible proportion, Portugal is aging. There's no need to examine the statistics to perceive it, for it leaps to your eyes. The main part of its population is concentrated along the coasts. While crossing the villages and the fishing ports, you see hardly any young people. On the other hand, the older women, the majority clad in black, with heavy woolen stockings, a scarf or a shawl, and old shoes, are legion. One would think they were all in mourning.

Ten forty-five in the morning: 38,000 kilometers [23,612 miles]. Am I feeling okay? There's no feeling of joy—why? I don't have an explanation. A kiss to say thanks and we take off again, but not for long. A hundred meters farther, Serge comes to a dead stop. It's a hunger pang. He stuffs himself with bread and chocolate, and I join him....

...Nothing is simple

Heavy traffic, crazy traffic. After three hours of intense concentration, I'm at the end of my rope. The road is so narrow. Everyone uses it: trucks, pedestrians, bicycles, tractors. It's a little game of "the most aggressive wins." What a grind! I feel like I'm at the intersection of death. Without a doubt, the trucks, loaded beyond the maximum permitted, "borrow" the secondary roads in order not to have to pay the highway taxes. So many people! So much of everything!

In Argentina, I was depressed by the straight-line roads as far as the eye could see; today I wish I had them.... The part of Portugal that we're crossing resembles an ant colony; there's activity everywhere. At this moment, I dream of space and solitude without noise. It just goes to show you that nothing is ever simple!

...*Continual rendezvous with ourselves*

Porto. I look outside. The sky is hazy, drowned in sorrow. My mind jumps back and forth between the endless line of cars that clogs the avenue. It's like a long ribbon without end...nonstop. The people apathetically cross the sidewalks. Their glances are expressionless, distant, each one doing what needs to be done, silent in the noise of the city. An old lady tries to cross the lane of traffic. In vain, for nobody helps her...not even I. A windowpane, a step separates us. Everything is going too quickly. Life goes by like a melody that stifles its notes.

In these moments, the memory of Nora, this mother so dear, is even more vivid. Nora, already so far from us! Our sole comfort is the journey; it's the long road that still must be run to its final end. A day doesn't pass without our thinking of her, each in our own way. Each in our silence. It's as if we were hiding behind our own fragility. The sadness of her "disappearance" doesn't leave us in peace.

...*What rain!*

There is always something that causes the progress of the run to be rendered more difficult than what we would wish. It's either too cold, or too hot, or too humid. The road is either too straight, or too steep, or too dangerous. But what would the adventure be, if the conditions were always ideal? And what is the ideal?

Here, in the north of Portugal, it's indeed the rain that overwhelms us. It's our worst enemy. (Well, I'm not so sure of that. In retrospect, that is not what I was telling myself during the crossing of the Sahara or the Sinai Desert....) In any case, the rain is truly something detestable for those who spend their days on the road.

On my motorcycle, I am dressed like a warrior, ready for combat. With a fixed stare, I don't say anything; I just endure. Serge runs, head lowered. The road is slippery. He must be careful not to sprain his ankles. The closer we draw to the goal, the more we come to fear this kind of incident.

Two hours, three hours, four hours of running, and continual rain! Why does it hound us so much?

...Our campaign is continuing

Our campaign for the benefit of causes championed by Doctor Ron Zamber and his team is continuing with small steps. By mutual agreement, a sum of a thousand dollars has been contributed to orphans of the catastrophe that took place in Southeast Asia. An equivalent amount has been placed in an account for the benefit of a program for children affected by AIDS in Africa and in Malawi. We reiterate: through our run, we are not going to change the world, but we are simply trying to set it up so that the "Run for Kids" can alleviate the plight of some human beings in need. It's one more step, one step added to the millions completed by Serge all around the planet.

...The end of Portugal

One of the oldest countries in Europe, Portugal conveyed the flavors of the south to us. This country, which represents a sixth of France in surface area, has established its history and its myths, which it jealously protects. It knew how to charm us. The run along the coast of the Atlantic has not been without risk—all the more so because Serge is always playing with fire. His tendonitis has subsided, but it is always latent. Let's hope that it stays that way!

Saying to be or not to be; on the tracks of someone
Parting is perhaps returning
Again, having the courage to say thanks; to nibble on life
Is not to say that it's over
Needing to forever advance on our own tracks

...Santiago de Compostela

It's taken more than 38,000 kilometers [23,612 miles] of running and motorcycling to reach Santiago de Compostela, like so many pilgrims! The streets, flanked by beautiful houses with archways, are teeming with shops. The scenery is nearly theatrical. On the plaza of the basilica, pilgrims collapse with relief and joy. You feel an immense ardor growing in them. Some have walked hundreds, even thousands of kilometers to achieve this goal. I can just imagine the power of the emotion that grips them.

We climb a few steps of the basilica. The proportions of the building take your breath away: 97 meters [318 feet] long by 65 meters [213 feet] wide. The vaults reach a height of 22 meters [72 feet]. A man-made construction fit for the world. In the silence, we meditate.

...February 2005: Leidera

For several days now, the cold wind has been slapping our faces; the rain has been accompanying us. We arrive in Leidera, a village nestled around a small port. Reaching a height of about 600 meters [1,968 feet] straight up above the waves, the cliffs of Vixia pride themselves on being the highest on the coast. In any case, they are impressive.

The souls of the inhabitants seem to be sleeping. It's winter siesta time. Nobody is in the streets. From the store across the street, a pleasant aroma of hot bread reaches us. It stirs the hunger pangs! Serge is hungry, his stomach heavy with solitude. We haven't had a varied and balanced diet for the past four days.

And then life resumes, slowly. Some women clothed in black slip through the door of a church. At the same time, glasses of white wine are clinked on the counter of a bar.... We set out again. We feel the glances at our back. Everything is done in discretion; the curtains are only drawn halfway.

...*The rain*

The rain...it's boredom, it's oblivion. Step by step, we follow our road. We are actors in roles that stick to our skin, just like our wet clothes...our drenched morale; there's no way to shelter ourselves. It's quite often what we experience on a daily basis. How can we resist the temptation of this inn that opens its arms to us? The easy thing would be to stop here. But, no! The distance traveled isn't sufficient! Continue on your way! This will be for another time....

...*Faithful companions*

Everything is on the floor, in disarray, filthy. These bags could say a lot. Ah, if they did start to talk! I wash them, I brush them, I repair all that is still repairable. As already stated, the trailer has sheltered our "house" for five years: our tent, our sleeping bags, our clothes, our utensils, our toiletries. This odd house is our equilibrium. Sometimes solitude slips in through openings in the tent. We ask ourselves how we've made it living in this manner for such a long time. Am I a vagabond, unconventional, ambiguous, or quite simply free? How can we love these old, filthy, undecorated bags, full of stale odors? Maybe we just like to get lost in our doubts and our fears. These bags are like an old teddy bear that we've loved since our childhood. They are our idiosyncrasy. They will take us back to the spot where we departed. They are faithful companions.

...The blind man at the ATM

Sitting in a smoky café, I am on the verge of asphyxiation. Serge isn't faring any better either. We crunch on some bread; we're hungry, we're thirsty. That's nothing new. Yet, in spite of this confounded smoke, we're enjoying the good fortune of a well-deserved break. In the preceding hours, the wind didn't stop harassing us, punching us full force in the face.

Suddenly, my glance is focused on a man who enters with some difficulty. His white cane indicates that he is visually impaired. He moves in the midst of the brouhaha. His gestures are calculated, studied. This man knows the place to its smallest details. He approaches the ATM, inserts his credit card, punches in his personal code, his eyes gazing off into space, withdraws from it a few bills, and goes away as he arrived—in silence. Impressive! What a beautiful lesson in tenacity! This goes to show that man is an exceptionally gifted being, who doesn't always utilize his gifts to their best advantage.

...February 24, 2005: 39,000 kilometers

I stop the motorcycle. It's always the same ritual. We smile at each other; we embrace each other: the 39,000th kilometer [24,233rd mile] has been attained!

...The Spanish shantytowns

I don't believe my eyes. I must be hallucinating: the so-called rich Europe hasn't replaced all its shantytowns through social legislation. Here in Spain, this is the third precarious dwelling place that we've crossed. And this one has nothing to "cause envy" in those of Africa, Asia, or South America. The houses are made of reused boards and plastic, their roofs composed of whatever's available, with rocks superimposed to retain these odds and ends. We are perplexed. The people live in the mud, along the side of the road. But who are they?

A skinny dog with an apprehensive look barks and approaches us; we feel sorry for him, too. Children live here and drag broken toys on the ground. Sooner or later, these miserable people will be expelled from this territory. It always ends that way with the disinherited, with the exiled.... It's an insult to the human condition, these images of shame!

...At the foot of the Pyrenees

The Pyrenees appear as a mountain chain that separates Spain and France. In fact, it's a little more subtle than that. Through the interplay of tectonic plates and earth movements, the Pyrenees don't plunge directly into the Atlantic. At the level of Roncevaux, they curve downward toward the southwest, and the crest line separates Navarre from the Basque Country. There they bulge anew, with summits that culminate at more than 2,600 meters [8,530 feet].

Finishing a new leg; nothing
Restricts us
And it will
Never change our objective
Continuing to run, to cry, to laugh
Evermore between him and me

...Between the 18th and 26th kilometer

Having arrived at this stage of our World Tour, I imagine that certain readers would like to know some more about themes touching on the athletic aspect of our epic journey. At the risk of disappointing them, I must indeed acknowledge that Serge didn't ask himself a thousand questions. He launched out onto this adventure with the experience that he had acquired over so many years. We haven't ever quit or given up, but every day between the 18th and 26th kilometer [11th and 16th mile], there was a bout of the blues, a bout of hunger pangs, a bout of sudden fatigue.

...Questions among athletes!

Serge, how many hours do you run per day?

Just enough to go up to the next kilometer, the next village! The effective average of a day-to-day run is 3.5 to 4 hours, which represents between 5 and 8 hours on the road.

How many pairs of shoes do you use?

I change my "tires" once per month, that is, every 800 to 1,000 kilometers [497 to 621 miles].

At what pulse rate do you run?

I know that I have one.

What is your weight?

Between 61 and 62 kilograms [134 and 136 pounds], but next to my wife, I don't measure up! (She outweighs me in many other ways!)

What food do you eat?

I eat everything. I vary it as much as possible. I can't follow a particular diet, because I must adapt to the countries that we cross. What is consistent: the plates of pasta, tuna, and tomato sauce.

What do you do to avoid a salt deficiency after so much effort?

I drink a lot of hot bouillon—effective and inexpensive.

How many hours do you sleep?

Just the time to rest well, that is, nine to ten hours per night.

What are your criteria for success?

I've trained my whole life! Besides that, a lot of sleep, a lot of stretching, a lot of liquids, not worrying too much about my health, accepting being sore, and having a strong discipline.

What is the best moment of the day?

When I stop!

...Between Bordeaux and Angoulême

The road calls us. It chokes us like the Amazon rain forest did. The sky is low and heavy; a storm is threatening. This strange day numbs me in the mystery of an intuition that provokes fear. Yes, the road scares me: truck after truck, car after car. I'm afraid; I cry. Serge brings me back to reality. I feel my stomach knotted; that's not the norm. Damned steps, damned run, damned kilometers! I want to shout: "Serge, stop running; we're taking too many risks. What purpose does this serve?" I retreat into this day of dizziness—dizziness or delirium? I dream of calmness. I dream of monastic life. I dream of the desert, of heights. I dream of milestones....

...March 28, 2005: Easter Monday

Easter Monday, March 28, 2005, 1:05 p.m.: At this moment, our World Tour reaches the milestone of 40,000 kilometers [24,855 miles]. Forty thousand kilometers is the symbolic distance that we've dreamed of for more than five years. Five years, six continents, thirty-five countries crossed at the speed of 12 km/h [7.4 mph]. We've made it! Forty thousand kilometers, or the culmination of a common challenge, shared in all its excessiveness. And yet, "constantly, we dream of doing just the opposite of what we're doing." Serge, who makes these remarks, is disarming....

...Paris, we're here!

It's under a cloak of friendship that Sonia and Alexandre Poussin guide us through the narrow streets of Paris. In our heads and our hearts, there's nothing but emotion.

After having run in front of the pyramids in Egypt, the Taj Mahal in India, the Sydney Opera House in Australia, and the Statue of Liberty in New York, we've arrived here at the foot of the Eiffel Tower, where a formidable welcome committee awaits us. Serge's children, my parents, members of our family, close relatives, journalists, and numerous children from the bilingual school of Paris are present. Even if we must still reach Saillon by Saturday, May 7, the eve of Serge's fiftieth birthday, we truly have the feeling that nothing much can stop us from the conclusive fulfillment of our World Tour. 40,130 kilometers [24,936 miles].

...A friend on the road

Jean-Bernard is a longtime friend and a skilled runner. He is also our editor. It's been more than five years since we've seen him! Today, he has come to rejoin us on the roads of Burgundy, to run a lovely leg of 46 kilometers [28.6 miles] with us. They're delectable moments!

Returning
Ever knowing
Turning the page of a tale
Unfolding another chapter
Ready to close another door
Nothing will ever change

...Nothing exceptional

A dream is built at a slow pace from an illusion, then from a plan, and finally, from the realization of that plan. Each of us possesses within himself this secret weapon. On the other hand, what everyone doesn't have is the courage to move to action, the courage of flexibility, the grit to believe in it. It's true: Serge and I have this chutzpah. We have had to learn to accept physical effort and difficulties of all sorts.

We don't have a great universal message or philosophy to pass on. Our school of thought is instead based on a present reality that each of us can accomplish. What we're doing, each person can do, can undertake. Yes, indeed! It's simply necessary to run, to drive the motorcycle at 12 km/h [7.4 mph], to accept being hungry, being thirsty, being cold or hot, being sick, and feeling a form of insecurity on the other side of the world. It's necessary to learn new languages, tame daily life, love the unknown, and accept discomfort. How many times have we heard: "You are fortunate?" Previously, I would have given endless explanations. Today, I respond: "It's true; you're right, because fortune belongs to the daring and not to the lucky." To dream, you must learn to leave. To dream, you must learn to love, to love each other.

"To thrust yourself into the world of adventure, you have to have a determination beyond the norms."

The good moments are always too short.

...Concept of adventure

To thrust yourself into the world of adventure, you have to have a determination beyond the norms. To be an adventurer is, above all, to accept rules of discipline. It's applying them to yourself. It's constantly being on the margins of time, on the fringes of a comfortably settled society. It's finding your own rules to advance your own universal causes. The most difficult thing is making the right choice at the right moment. Adventure is continually questioning your instincts.

You must have a natural ability to make a rapid decision about what is good or what isn't. Being an adventurer is a part of everyone's dream. The price to pay is daring to leave and daring to take risks, not always calculated, until you become a prisoner of your own freedom.

Our adventure is a chosen way of life that carries a message of friendship, encounters, happy moments, and bitter moments. This nonconformist approach to life leaves us free in our mode of thought, our manner of behaving.

Adventure, voyage, world trek, achievements: what is hidden behind these words encountered in the detour of a phrase? It's difficult to say. Their significance evolves according to the kilometers traveled, the places, the encounters, the states of mind. They are evoked from a mouth that is thirsty ... for life!

...Each day from point zero

But how does he do it, to run so many kilometers, so many marathons, to spend so much time on the road? You can naturally guess that this question arises. To tell the truth, I don't have a set answer. When I met Serge, he was already dedicating himself to slightly crazy endurance runs. By linking this with the idea of adventure, I've found my place at his side. But it is indeed he who is the driving force of this epic journey. Every morning, it's he who laces his tennis shoes, does lengthy stretching exercises, and sets out again at point zero. Each day he suffers, each day he toils mentally, and each day he reaches his objective.

...Return to the unknown

Five years of demanding adventure in search of ourselves and of others. What will the future hold for us? The unknown, which we will get accustomed to like a name given to a newborn. Each day, we had to learn to appreciate each moment. Returning home is losing a bit of control over your own life, your own anxieties. At home, everything will return to order, to comfort, to mandatory restraints. But going back home is also learning to live with your own true-life experiences. It's keeping your dreams alive.

I followed my instinct by traveling the roads of the world. It hasn't always absolutely meant happiness, but something else more precious: I've acquired the certainty of existing, really existing.

After all these years, what remains for me to see, to get to know, to learn, to say? It simply remains for me to start all over again, to see everything all over again, to learn everything all over again, because the world is infinitely large, infinitely small, infinitely interesting.

...The malady

Returning to my homeland is also to imagine what my life will be like health-wise. Since my first big crisis erupted in Madagascar and then my repatriation from Nepal, I remain very vulnerable, even in spite of all the treatments put in place. How many times have my crises caused disequilibrium of the entire day? I am infinitely grateful to Serge for agreeing to continue the journey in conditions that were sometimes at the limit of acceptability. It's not he who forced me into this choice. For nothing in the world would I have thrown in the towel. I have sometimes been exhausted, been at the end of my strength, but giving up has never been a part of my vocabulary. What will happen when everything comes to an end? I don't have an answer. The future will tell.

...Feminine gestures

Those who know me, know it. Every morning, for five years, I have dedicated a few precious moments to grooming myself. I attach the greatest importance to these simple feminine gestures at the onset of the day. In this way, I relate to my daily routine. Each day is a new departure. I love to tell myself that today will not be tomorrow. Being feminine and showing it without provocation, whatever the conditions may be, is for me a way of identifying myself totally with the women I encounter. I love the elegance of something natural. And then, while living twenty-four hours per day with the same person, it also involves principles of attraction and charm. With next to nothing, I transform my personal universe.

I don't like ruts, so I change myself into a "turquoise sea, into a starry sky." I change clothes, as if I were rummaging in my clothes closet... I change hair color, while thinking about finding new friends... I change makeup, because I simply find it beautiful... I remain a woman; I remain faithful to my persona. Anyway, in the span of five years, the wheels of time have continued to turn. This can be confirmed through several wrinkles that are beginning to modify my countenance....

...*Fear*

I have never feared lacking anything whatsoever. Liar! Even so, there's the anxiety of not succeeding, of lacking financial means, the fear of nothing, the fear of everything. But my only real apprehension (I live it on a daily basis): the anxiety of facing death. Why should we die, when we dream of being eternal? Fear generates nothing but anger and doubts.

I think that anxiety must make up an integral part of such an adventure. Besides, it does not ask our opinion; it comes and sows trouble, discord. It allows us to stay alive, to get closer to the truth. The day when I no longer have this feeling in me, it will only be a lie. Adventure brings answers to us. But it doesn't always bring solutions!

... *The plight of people calls out to me*

I look at the world; I listen to the world. This world fills space. Each human being has his own history, his own experiences, his own unhappiness. This old woman, is she happy? Is this person a civil servant? Is that one condemned? Is this one rich or poor? Has he made mistakes? Does he have children, cats? What mysteries there are in all of us! I love to lose myself in my own language. Am I right or wrong?

...Simply to continue

In several days of rediscovering our next of kin and our corner of our homeland, we indeed feel that we are in the process of leaving a destiny, a past, on the road. No, we are not going to look back. We are simply going to continue: he, running toward a better goal; I, driving toward a better world. Two lives, two beings, two destinies are prisoners of one destination for success, for a shared thanksgiving. Yes, we think of it, and we hope to cross that invisible line that we invented five years ago. How long it is; how short it is! It's been five years of complicity, of simplicity.

Beyond a run, we took on a personal crusade. We have created friendships; we have encountered so many people. In spite of the difficulties, we have succeeded in funding our humanitarian project, "Run for Kids." During the course of the journey, our objectives have been modified, but funds have been collected with the intention of supporting various causes, notably in Costa Rica, in Colombia, and in Africa.

...The world

The world is a hand; it's five continents. They are the five fingers of the hand.

Africa, full of laughter, full of tears.

Asia, full of warmth, full of smells.

Australia, full of colors, full of vast spaces.

America, full of superlatives, full of uncertainties.

Europe, full of beauty, full of closed-mindedness.

The world is also as beautiful as a palette of makeup. It can also be as ugly as makeup removal. The world is so vast when you travel it by running. It is so small when you stay at home. The world of the beautiful, of the competitive, and of the rich is omnipresent. For the little people of this world, there's little room. I plead guilty.

...Nearly the end

Only four days remain until the end of our adventure. Everything is drawing to a close at a fast pace. For us, it's time to turn the page, to say good-bye for good to our run. We'll have to take another kind of stride, perhaps more rapid. Certainly, nothing will be easy. Each morning, we will have to set out again from point zero. But in essence, we don't hide it: we're happy to be returning to normality.

We are melancholy but not sad.

The time for sharing has arrived....

40,912 kilometers [25,422 miles].
Thank goodness, we're alive!

International Vision Quest

Run For Kids
World Tour

Dear Serge and Nicole,

It's a great pleasure and privilege to work together for the Run for Kids/ International Vision Quest World Tour. Through your heroic efforts, people all over the world will be made conscious of the tragedy that blindness represents for a great number of underprivileged children.

Thanks to International Vision Quest, thousands of men, women, and children have today regained their sight. The funds collected have also allowed us to give the most necessary goods to several orphanages and villages for children.

Our hope is that by means of our collaboration a lot of people will be made conscious of the cause that we champion.

Thank you for your tremendous efforts.

Sincerely,

Ronald W. Zamber, M.D.
Founder and President of IVQ

You can support this cause by sending a gift to:
International Vision Quest (IVQ)
P.O. Box 10159
Fairbanks, AK 99710
USA

IVQ is an Alaska-based, non-profit organization, with 501 (c)(3) tax-exempt status as a charitable organization.

Epilogue

To run the world as I've done with Nicole is a way of living and of encountering emotions—those of others and our own. We aren't setting ourselves up as examples. Each one makes use of his own destiny as seems best to him. Our choice is only a little bit more unique than that of the majority of people.

"What is it that can prevent somebody from realizing a dream or an adventure?" The fear of failing! Yes, having the courage to dare, that's what's important. As for the rest, I don't pretend to be able to offer a miracle formula. I can only speak of my experience and draw some lessons from it.

When we decided one day to change the course of our life, to leave, to run the world as we have done, we made the decision to leave behind our families, our friends, our homeland, our certainties, and our comfort. Leaving is one thing; succeeding is another. As my boxing trainer way back when taught me: in order to win, you have to learn how to lose. During this World Tour, we would have had numerous reasons to give up:

- illnesses (malaria in Africa, cerebral-malaria-related coma and dental problems, etc.)
- accidents (car accident in India)
- injuries (three cases of tendonitis, a muscle tear, an eye bitten by a snake)
- weather (temperatures oscillating between 48ºC and -29ºC [118°F and -20°F], enormous variations in the humidity rate
- countries at war, discouragements, insecurity, Mama's death

There is one factor that could have incited us to give up: the abdication of our humanitarian partner after two years of collaboration. We felt this situation was an injustice. We found ourselves with a loss of equilibrium: moral, emotional, and physical. Humility and tolerance permitted us to overcome this obstacle. The real-life experiences in the field helped us surmount the difficulties—to believe in our tour, when nobody else believed in it.

In South America, we were rich with a scooter and a pair of shoes. With the same equipment, we were poor in North America! However, possessing more or less doesn't ensure happiness. The real-life experiences force us to question ourselves, and they stir our hearts. They lead us to modify our vision of others, to broaden our minds, and thus force us to change our habits.

You don't succeed at the big things; you can only try to do the little things well....

–*Serge*

Saillon, August 2005

About the Authors

Two years after having linked Ushuaia, Argentina, to Fairbanks, Alaska, while covering more than 24,000 kilometers [14,984 miles], he running and she at the handlebars of a motorcycle, Serge and Nicole Roetheli of Valais, Switzerland, took to the road again in February 2000, for a world tour of more than five years. At the end of their crazy tour, they had chalked up some figures to make you dizzy: 40,912 kilometers [25,422 miles] run, which is the equivalent of nearly a thousand marathons, sixty-three months of running, six continents traversed.

During this "adventure à deux," Nicole recorded her impressions—her outrage when confronted with injustices and inequalities, her joys of sharing, her times of sadness, and her happiness of living a different way.

"In South America, we were rich with a scooter and a pair of shoes. With the same equipment, we were poor in North America! However, possessing more or less doesn't assure happiness. The real-life experiences force us to question ourselves and they stir our hearts. They cause us to modify our way of looking at others, to broaden our minds, and thus force us to change our habits.... Our goal has been, above all, to make progress in the search for the humanity in all of mankind. A run conveying feelings, a run of pitfalls, a run at 12 km/h [7.4 mph]."

25,422 MILES

5 YEARS

6 CONTINENTS

About the Translators

Josiane Karlsson is a native speaker of French who was born and raised on the island of Guadeloupe in the French Antilles. She studied English and Spanish at the University of Bordeaux where she received her BA and Maîtrise (advanced degree) in English. In 1969 she came to the University of California in Riverside as a Fullbright Exchange student, where she served as a cultural assistant at the Maison Française (one of the foreign language resident halls) and later earned her master's degree in French Language and Literature. She taught French and Spanish for 34 years in Southern California.

Agnes Roetheli Gaertner, pursuing her Swiss heritage, studied German and French at the University of Missouri, where she received a BA in German and a BS in Secondary Education. She later earned her master's degree in German Language and Literature at California State University, Fullerton. She taught German and French for 34 years in Southern California and was a Fullbright Exchange Teacher, teaching English at a German Gymnasium (college-prep high school). She has traveled extensively and has organized and led family trips to Switzerland, where she enjoys using her language skills.